EX LIBRIS

VINTAGE **CLASSICS**

NIK COHN

Nik Cohn was brought up in Derry, Northern Ireland. His books include *I Am Still the Greatest Says Johnny Angelo*, *Ball the Wall*, *The Heart of the World* and *Need*. He also wrote the story that gave rise to *Saturday Night Fever* and collaborated on *Rock Dreams* with the artist Guy Peellaert. He lives in New York.

ALSO BY NIK COHN

I Am Still the Greatest Says Johnny Angelo
Market
Today There are No Gentlemen
Arfur
King Death
Rock Dreams (with Guy Peellaert)
Ball the Wall: Nik Cohn in the Age of Rock
The Heart of the World
Need
Yes We Have No: Adventures in the Other England
Twentieth Century Dreams (with Guy Peellaert)
Triksta: Life and Death and New Orleans Rap

NIK COHN

Awopbopaloobop Alopbamboom

Pop From The Beginning

VINTAGE BOOKS
London

5 7 9 10 8 6 4

Vintage
20 Vauxhall Bridge Road,
London SW1V 2SA

Vintage Classics is part of the Penguin Random House
group of companies whose addresses can be found at
global.penguinrandomhouse.com

 Penguin
Random House
UK

First published in Great Britain by Weidenfeld & Nicolson
Ltd in 1969
Published by Pimlico in 2004

www.vintage-books.co.uk

A CIP catalogue record for this book is available
from the British Library

ISBN 9781784870485

Typeset in India by Thomson Digital Pvt Ltd, Noida, Delhi

Printed and bound by Clays Ltd, St Ives plc

Penguin Random House is committed to a sustainable future
for our business, our readers and our planet. This book is made
from Forest Stewardship Council® certified paper.

To Jet Powers,
Dean Angel and
Johnny Ace

NB: Since I have set out to write a critical history of pop, I write about artists, managers and other people concerned, mainly in the past tense. This is simple because I'm putting them where they appear in the context of the general historical development of pop as I see it. It doesn't mean that many of those people aren't still very much part of the scene and doing well – just that in this book I have only tried to show where, to me, they made their original contribution or changed what existed before.

CONTENTS

PREFACE TO THE VINTAGE CLASSICS EDITION

Matt Broughton set me off. Before seeing his cover design for this new edition of *Awopbop*, I hadn't read the text start to finish in over forty years. At best I'd manage a page or two here, a paragraph there, come across something that made me squirm and slam the book shut double-quick, like the character in a Hammer movie who opens an old trunk in the cellar and finds a mummified corpse inside.

It took Matt's dancing letters to lure me back in. Enthralled by their tumbled-dice effect, I started to dance along in my head, trying to recall where each one came from. 'That B is from The Byrds, right? The wobbly O is *Rubber Soul*, I think the L comes off an early Elvis album, that's a Warner Bros. W,' and so forth. I managed to guess less than half, but each opened its own door. Gradually, I found myself checking out the corresponding passage in the book, which would lead me to another, and then another. It became addictive, as when you walk past a half-done jigsaw, stop to fill in a piece or two, and the next thing you know it's five hours later. Soon I'd gone through the whole book.

I won't pretend I enjoyed it much. Any man, at seventy, who claims he relishes being confronted by his raw self at twenty-two is crazy or lying or both. Hard to believe that this speed-freak gunslinger, so pushy and cocksure, one moment obnoxious, the next devout, could ever have been me. I struggled to find connections. In the end, I came up with only one: young or old, I've always been hooked on lost causes.

Beneath the book's roiling surface, I now saw what had always escaped me, even though Kit Lambert, in his brilliant intro to the first edition, spelled it out clear enough.

Awopbop, at root, is a jilted love letter – the headlong, unfiltered outpouring of someone whose girl has done him wrong. Page after page, I keep trying to joke it off, pretend I'm not hurting. The bitch is worthless; I'm better off without her. But who am I fooling? Certainly not Kit. 'Half-martyr to his own myth, he sprints across the gilded landscape, although his feet are bleeding inside the carefully dirtied-down sneakers,' he wrote of me. At the time, I felt outraged that he would accuse me of footwear abuse. In fact, he'd got me dead to rights. *Awopbop* was born of thwarted passion. From the first blast of *Tutti Frutti*, rock 'n' roll had possessed me, body and soul. It didn't occur to me that my love might not be requited or that it could die some day. I was prepared for bumps along the way, some wrong turnings, yes, but my basic faith was absolute. And then, quite suddenly, all was over between us. Rock 'n' roll and its jailbait sister Superpop were obsolete. My lust had been geared to quickies; the cheap and perfect thrills of the three-minute single. Instead, here came the concept album, the ten-minute guitar solo, the hour-long jam, all sweat and wallow. The quicksilver flygirl I fell for had morphed into a flatulent, acid-addled hag who never shut up.

Awopbop has often been cited as the birth of rock criticism. Strictly in terms of date, this may be true. But I wasn't much of a critic; reasoned argument was not my strength. My writing, when it was good, lived off characters, sounds, atmospheres and snapshot impressions. Questions of good or bad were afterthoughts. Often, as with *Wooly Bully* or the Monotones' *Book Of Love*, the absence of musical quality was exactly what I treasured. Did Dion's *Ruby Baby*, let's say, have any aesthetic value? Who cared? What it had was dirty magic – the slurred, sex-drunk vocal, those shambolic handclaps, the whole glorious unmade bed. And the magic hasn't died; not for me. In that, the young pup survives in the old dog. My tail has been docked, I'm a bit gimpy in the hind legs, and my fur's coming out, but I still chase after pick-up trucks with their radios on, blasting out the lines that could stand as shorthand for the whole of *Awopbop* and the helpless yearning that drove it:

Said I love a girl and Ruby is her name.
This girl don't love me, but I love her just the same.[*]

Nik Cohn, 2016

PREFACE TO THE 2004 PIMLICO EDITION

This edition of *Awopbopaloobop Alopbamboom*, the first to be published in England in the new century, seems a good moment for taking stock. The book is now thirty-five years old, or roughly three times the age of rock itself at the time I wrote it. The obvious question is, does it still have any relevance? Or has rock changed and developed so much that *Awopbop* is now no more than a period curiosity, the literary equivalent of the hula hoop?

I am hardly unbiased, of course, but my own feeling is that it still has roughly the same value, for better or worse, that it had when it was originally published. Rock has evolved enormously as an industry, but remarkably little as music. Whenever I'm approached to update this book, and I try to focus on what might conceivably be new and challenging for me to write about, I think immediately of early punk, and after that I'm stumped. I would enjoy praising Prince, and, to a lesser extent, Sly Stone, Björk, George Clinton, Al Green, Tricky, PJ Harvey, a few others; I would certainly enjoy rubbishing Bruce Springsteen and Sting. But only hip-hop, in the last four decades, has marked a radical change from what went before, and that change has been so far-reaching, it would need a whole second volume to encompass.

Everything else – disco, metal, grunge, glam, funk, techno, and all their innumerable sub-genres – has been in some way a rehash or, at most, a reconfiguration. The basic playing field was already marked out in that first mad rush between 1956 and 1968, the year I signed off. The rest has been nine-tenths marketing.

I wrote *Awopbop* in spring of 1968, shortly after my twenty-second birthday. I'd been in love with rock 'n' roll for a dozen years and had written about it, in English and American publications, for the last four. I had met most of the people who interested me, and the edge of my passion was starting to dull. Time, I thought, to gather my thoughts into one final package, and move on.

If this sounds off-hand, it was. Rock in the late Sixties was still a spontaneous combustion. Nobody bothered with long-term strategies; hanging on once the thrill was gone was unthinkable. If anyone had told me then that the Stones or the Who would still be treading the boards in thirty-plus years, I'd have thought they were out of their minds. 'Hope I die before I get old' – that was the stuff. All I was doing in *Awopbop* was trying to get a jump on the mortician.

To that end, my publisher packed me off for seven weeks in a rented house in Connemara and told me not to come back without the completed MS. So I sat down and wrote, ten hours a day, sometimes halfway through the night as well.

In a sense it was a homecoming; a completing of the circle. Ireland was where I had grown up, and rock the main reason I'd wanted to leave.

I was raised in a staunch Protestant area of Derry, where Bill Haley and Elvis were never mentioned. Then one evening, at the age of eleven, I went astray. I wandered into the fringes of the Bogside, the heart of the Catholic city, and heard Little Richard's *Tutti Frutti* on a coffee-bar jukebox. From across the street, I watched a bunch of Teddy boys, with drainpipe jeans and winkle pickers, grease-loaded duckarse haircuts. It was my first glimpse of danger, and sex, and secret magic. I never got over it.

What was it about the Teds? Swagger, and wildness, yes, and something else, which stirred me even more deeply – the force of self-invention. By every rule of birth – religion, politics, economics – these boys were losers. Papist scum, with no future or hope. But that wasn't the way they carried themselves. To me, they looked like stars, transformed and made heroic by the power of Little Richard: rock &' roll.

For an undersized weakling, mamma's boy, and all-round fuck-up like myself, the image was irresistible. Suddenly, I seemed to have another chance; the possibility of creating a whole new self. I took Elvis as my personal saviour. Squandered my pocket money on 78s. Snuck into *Loving You* and *Jailhouse Rock*, both strictly off limits, and cultivated a kiss curl, and lost what was left of my innocence in the seedy pages of *Tidbits*. Rock was my religion, nothing less.

At fifteen I was out of Ireland, at sixteen out of school, and by seventeen down to London. It was 1963, the year the Beatles broke through, and the climate seemed to change by the day. Only months before, most of England had still been locked in the post-war chill. No glamour, no spare cash; not a chance. Snotty youths like myself, drop-outs with bad posture and worse attitudes, didn't have a prayer. But *She Loves You* had changed everything. Suddenly, potential employers were gripped by a recurring nightmare – the dreadful fate of Dick Rowe, the A&R man who'd turned down the Beatles at Decca Records, leaving them for E.M.I. to snap up. Better to get landed with a hundred no-talent tossers, whole armies of degenerates, than risk becoming a second Rowe.

The feeding frenzy wasn't confined to rock. Newspaper editors, book publishers, fashion mags and film financiers were all caught up in the same fever. Almost overnight, being a teen degenerate was the hottest ticket around. One day I was your British Rail representative in a travel agency, on five guineas a week before tax and lucky to have it; the next, I had a job at the *Observer* pontificating on yoof. From there, it was fast forward to lunch at the Trat with Terence Stamp, dinner with Andrew Loog Oldham, and breakfast in bed with . . . never mind who. Taxis everywhere, free records and comped invites, a brand-new outfit every Saturday, and never, but never, wear the same shirt twice.

The week after I turned nineteen, a publicist slipped me an envelope stuffed with crisp fivers. Though I lacked the balls to take it, I was profoundly flattered. Nineteen, and someone thought I was worth bribing. It felt like a knighthood of sorts.

None of this had come my way by design. I'd simply jumped in at the deep end and started thrashing at random. My timing was immaculate, though. The London scene was already crammed to bursting with musicians, photographers, designers, hairdressers, models, but virtually no young writers. Most pop columnists were middle-aged hacks, whose true loves were Sinatra and Ella Fitzgerald. They didn't go in for shades and skintight velvet strides; they certainly didn't type their columns on the buttocks of a Lebanese snake-charmer. Or even pretend they did.

Heady days. But not, by their nature, made to last. Even as I was pigging out on the moment, rock and pop were already changing. The world I knew and savoured was basically an outlaw trade, peopled with adventurers, snake-oil salesmen, inspired lunatics. But their time was almost over. With each passing season, the scene was becoming more industrial. Accountants and corporate fatcats were fast driving out the wild men. The new buzzword was 'product'. It wouldn't be more than a few years, at most a decade, before rock became just another branch of commerce, no more or less exotic than autos or detergents.

My options seemed clear. Either I could keep the faith as laid down by the Teds in the Bogside, stay true to rock as a doomed romance, a passionate beating against the tides, or I would shortly be bored. Rich, no doubt, and pampered. But a traitor at heart.

That's how it felt when I was twenty-two and came to the house in Connemara, with the March rains lashing at the windows and wild waves pounding the rocks below, the perfect melodramatic setting, as I sat down to write my farewells.

My purpose was simple: to catch the feel, the *pulse* of rock, as I had lived through it. Nobody, to my knowledge, had ever written a serious book on the subject, so I had no exemplars to inhibit me. Nor did I have any reference books or research to hand. I simply wrote off the top of my head, whatever and however the spirit moved me. Accuracy didn't seem of prime importance (and the book, as a result, is rife with factual errors). What I was after was guts, and flash, and energy, and speed. Those were the things I'd treasured in the rock I'd loved. They were the things I tried to reflect as I left.

Nik Cohn, 2004

INTRODUCTION

Nik Cohn has chosen a grim and appropriate moment to make this brilliantly clear, aerial survey of the pop world. Out in the audience, too many British teenagers are listening dutifully to their Government-approved diet of ballads and recipes: on stage, the scene is a little brighter. Key musicians are playing for other key musicians. The Beatles and the Stones, seemingly, have become too vast and trunkless ever to play at all. I hope this book will not be thought of in five years' time as the definitive history of a forgotten age. Fortunately, Nik is no obituarist: anyway, if he did write your obituary you'd be better off dead.

He showed up about 1965. The Beatles were into their first million, the disgruntled Rolling Stones were touring USA circuses, billed virtually as a freak show, and a nervous Carnaby Street tailor had just refused to put his scissors into a large Union Jack, which was meant to wind up as stage-clothes for the Who, when a thin young man – he looked about fourteen – wearing carefully dirtied-down sneakers, grabbed me in Wardour Street and informed me that he was writing an article for the *Sunday Times*. I believed him a lot. He landed up in a Chinese restaurant, interviewing the Merseybeats.

But a major article *did* appear quite soon in the *Sunday Times*. It revealed a knowledge of pop (and a rudeness about it) which was fairly frightening. Then came a series of tough and highly partisan record reviews in *Queen*. He mastered the art of the loving *clinch* which turned into the killing punch, making enemies along the line. There were accusations of intellectual – even cash – payola. But Nik just got forgiven without getting cynical.

He has been described as the speed-writer of pop. Half-martyr to his own myth, he sprints across the gilded landscape, although his feet *are* bleeding inside the carefully dirtied-down sneakers. At least, I hope they are: you see he is very bright, he knows too much and he *still* doesn't shave.

KIT LAMBERT
Co-manager of the Who
Co-director of Track Records
1969

1

ROOTS

Modern pop began with rock 'n' roll in the middle fifties and, basically, it was a mixture of two traditions – Negro rhythm 'n' blues and white romantic crooning, coloured beat and white sentiment.

What was new about it was its aggression, its sexuality, its sheer noise and most of this came from its beat. This was bigger and louder than any beat before it, simply because it was amplified. Mostly, pop boiled down to electric guitars.

Of course, electric guitars were nothing new in themselves – they had been around for years in jazz and R&B and had even been featured on some white hits, notably those by Les Paul, but they had never been used as bedrock, as the basis of a whole music. Crude, powerful, infinitely loud, they came on like space-age musical monsters and, immediately, they wiped out all of the politeness that had gone before.

Pre-pop, from the thirties on, dance music had got bogged down in the palais age – the golden era of the big bands, when everything was soft, warm, sentimental, when everything was make-believe.

It's one of the clichéd laws of showbiz that entertainment gets sloppy when times get tough and, what with the depression, the war and its aftermath, times had gotten very tough indeed. Hemmed in by their lives, people needed to cling tight

1

in the dark of dancehalls, to be reassured, to feel safe again. Reality they could very well do without.

Always, that's the kind of situation that Tin Pan Alley thrives on and songs about moonlight, stardust, roses and bleeding hearts were duly churned out by the truckload. The big bands lined up strict and formal in penguin suits, the crooners slicked their hair back heavy with grease, the close harmony groups went oo-wah oo-wah in the background and everybody danced. It was warm and snug like a blanket.

Sometimes, the palais age caught an odd freshness, an innocence, an atmosphere a bit like a Fred Astaire film. But when it was bad, which was almost always, it was only dire.

The worst thing was that it all dragged on so long without changing. Most dance eras last a few years, a decade at most, but the war froze everything as it was, gave the big bands a second life and, by the early fifties, the scene had come to a standstill.

All this time, the music industry was controlled by middle-aged businessmen, uninterested in change of any kind, and they were making money as things were, so they made no effort to find anything very new. They'd switch a few details, dream up some small novelty gimmick and leave it at that. And the only reason they got away with it was that nobody offered any alternatives. Mostly, showbiz survived on habit.

There was no such thing as teenage music then, nothing that kids could possibly identify with. The business was structured in such a way that singers were generally well into their thirties by the time they made it. There'd be occasional novelties, cute comedies, but basically teenagers had to put up with the same songs that their parents liked.

The nearest thing to an exception was Frank Sinatra.

In the early forties, when he first happened, Sinatra was still in his middle twenties, a novice by the standards of that time, and he was the first heart-throb.

2

He was hardly a teen idol – he was a conventional balladeer, he was backed by an ordinary big band, he sang the same songs as everyone else. But he was also good-looking, he had soulful eyes, and almost all of his fans were women. They swooned for him, rioted for him, even screamed for him, and this was something new. Of course, film stars had always been treated like that. Sinatra was the first singer to join them, that's all.

As a prototype for pop, though, Johnnie Ray was much closer, the Nabob of Sob, the Million Dollar Teardrop himself. If Elvis Presley was the great pop messiah, Ray played John the Baptist.

Born in Oregon, 1927, he was tossed high in a blanket at the age of ten, landing on his head which affected his hearing. According to his hand-outs, he also changed from a happy, well-adjusted child into a full-time introvert, solitary and sad. At any rate, by the time he became a singer, he was wearing his neuroses like a badge. The gimmick was that, when he got towards the climax of his stage act, he would collapse into helpless sobs. Not just once or twice but every time he performed. It was a ritual.

1952 was his big breakthrough year and the record that did the trick was a double-sider, *The Little White Cloud That Cried* on one side and just plain *Cry* on the other, titles that more or less summed him up.

Anyhow, he caused riots, real live ones – he had his clothes ripped off, his flesh torn, his hair rumpled, and the police kept having to rescue him. He sang the same trash as anyone else, but he contorted himself, buckled and gulped, and that released an intensity of aggression that nobody else had stirred.

Johnnie Ray himself upped his earnings to four thousand dollars a week and sold records by the million. All this time, he did nothing but cry. 'I've no talent, still sing as flat as a table,' he said, 'I'm a sort of human spaniel: people come to see what I'm like. I make them feel, I exhaust them, I destroy them.'

He was underrating himself. He couldn't sing, true enough, but he generated more intensity than any performer I ever saw in my life, Judy Garland excepted, and it was impossible not to feel involved with him.

He was a very skinny man and, when he moved, his limbs jerked out sideways as clumsily as a puppet's. He'd start his act slowly, out of tune, and he'd be almost laughable, whining and amateurish, gangling around the stage like some fevered crab. But then, just when you'd dismissed him, he'd launch himself into one of his major agonized ballads and suddenly everything would come alive.

He'd hunch up tight into himself, choke on his words, gasp, stagger, beat his fist against his breast, squirm, fall forward on to his knees and, finally, burst into tears. He'd gag, tremble, half strangle himself. He'd pull out every last outrageous ham trick in the book and he would be comic, embarrassing, painful, but still he worked because, under the crap, he was in real agony, he was burning, and it was traumatic to watch him. He'd spew himself up in front of you and you'd freeze, you'd sweat, you'd be hurt yourself. You'd want to look away and you couldn't.

Frail as he was, thin and deaf and sickly, his fans would be twisted into paroxysms of maternal hysteria by him and they'd half kill him. All round, it was the kind of orgiastic exhibition that simply hadn't happened before and it was entirely pop. The music wasn't, the atmosphere was.

Ironically, considering that he'd helped pave the way for pop, he was destroyed by it. As soon as rock came in, he sounded hopelessly back-dated and melodramatic. Soon he stopped having hits. He kept on touring but he sagged.

Still, he keeps going and, when he turns it on, he's as fierce and agonized as he ever was.

All the time that moonglow ballads were dominating the white market, coloured music, as always, was bossed by the blues. The old country blues, raw and ragged and often wildly emotional, had been increasingly replaced by rowdy big city blues, by electric guitars and saxes and, right through the forties and early fifties, the movements had been towards more noise, more excitement. Beat came in, passion went out and, somewhere along the line, the new style became known as rhythm 'n' blues, R&B.

What this actually involved was a small band, five or six pieces, maybe more, belting out a succession of fast twelve bars. Styles varied, of course, but generally the trend was towards the jump blues, loose-limbed stuff played by people like Louis Jordan, Lloyd Price, Wynonie 'Mr Blues' Harris and Fats Domino.

It was good-time music, danceable and unpretentious and, by comparison with the mushiness of white music in the same period, it was like a window opened to let some bad air out.

In particular, it was straight about sex, it used no euphemisms about hearts and roses. A lot of the time, in fact, it was downright filthy – Hank Ballard's *Work With Me Annie*, Billy Ward's *Sixty Minute Man* and the Penguins' *Baby Let Me Bang Your Box* were typical. All of them were big hits in the R&B charts and, predictably, all of them got banned by the white radio stations.

Just the same, R&B somehow began to filter through to white kids and they liked it. In 1951, a DJ called Alan Freed launched a series of rhythm reviews at the Cleveland Arena and immediately drew crowds three times as big as the venue capacity.

These shows featured coloured acts but were aimed at predominantly white audiences and, to avoid what he called 'the racial stigma of the old classification', Freed dropped the term R&B and invented the phrase Rock 'n' Roll instead.

Right through the early fifties, however, white stations persisted in blocking the R&B off their airways and the biggest names were still people like Doris Day, Perry Como and Frankie Laine.

Black hit songs were usually covered and castrated for the white market – Pat Boone did Fats Domino's *Ain't That A Shame*, for instance, and Dorothy Collins assassinated Clyde McPhatter's *Seven Days* – and even multi-million R&B sellers like Joe Turner, Ruth Brown and Bo Diddley never made the pop charts.

Pop and R&B apart, there was also, throughout the South, a massive market in Country 'n' Western, jogalong stuff to be sung through the nose. In England, this was thought of as cowboy music and it didn't sell much. But in the States, people like Hank Williams, Slim Whitman, Eddy Arnold and Tennessee's Ernie Ford rated as big as anyone.

Each of these musics – country and R&B and Tin Pan Alley – had its own hit parade. Sometimes, of course, these would intertwine – LaVern Baker's *Tweedly Dee* was a hit in both pop and R&B markets – but mostly they ran independently and it was quite possible for someone like Eddy Arnold, say, to sell fifty million records and still mean hardly anything on the national charts.

So these were the musical ingredients that made pop happen – the white ballad tradition, the exhibitionism introduced by Johnnie Ray, the elaborate sentimentality of C&W, the amplified gut-beat of R&B. Between them, they would have been enough to produce a major craze and what made rock 'n' roll more than a craze, what turned it into a small social revolution, was nothing to do with music.

Basically, it all came down to the fact that with fuller employment, teenagers now had money to waste. If they were white, if they came out of anything but the worst slums, they weren't going to be hungry. More likely, they were going to get solid jobs and make money. They were even going to get time to spend it in.

Even more important than any factual economic changes was the shift in atmosphere. For thirty years back, in both America and Britain, most working-class kids had come out of schools with a built-in sense of defeat. They might be headed for some dead-end job, they might be sent off to win wars, they might wind up in dole queues. Whatever happened, they weren't going to have much fun.

By comparison, the fifties were lush. Of course, there was always the chance that everyone would get blown sky-high by an H-bomb but that was too huge a concept to be really frightening and, at least, there was no depression now, no blitz, no rationing. It wasn't just a matter of keeping afloat any more – teenagers could begin to call cards.

The only snag was that, when they went looking for things to spend their new-found bread on, they found absolutely nothing. They had no music of their own, no clothes or clubs, no tribal identity. Everything had to be shared with adults.

It was tough. After all this time, teenagers had finally made it through to the promised land and they'd found it barren. Definitely, it was frustrating. They had all this money, nothing to do with it and they went spare.

Always, the moment of maximum revolt comes just when things are beginning to get better, when the first liberalization sets in. When kids had had nothing at all, they had somehow accepted it. Now that life was easier, they began to riot.

Juvenile delinquency became all the rage. In Britain, Teddy boys came in and they dressed like Edwardians, drainpipe jeans and pointed shoes and three-quarter coats, and they wore their hair heavy with grease.

They weren't quite like any movement that had happened in earlier decades. There were so many of them and they were so aimless – they'd roam around in packs, brawling and smashing at random. A bit later, they dressed up in black leather and rode motorbikes. And all they did was to break things, windows and locks and bones. There was nothing else to do and, right through the fifties, the Teds held command, they were the only action going. If you didn't want to join them, you had to sit indoors and vegetate.

There was something else: businessmen had never before seen teenagers as independent commercial units, as having entirely separate needs and tastes from the rest of the community. Now the possibilities hit them like a prophetic vision and they moved in fast, fawning like mad.

Predictably, kids bought just about anything that was put in front of them – motorbikes, blue jeans, hair oils, ponytails, milkshakes and, most of all, music. All you had to do was label something Teen and they had to have it.

In music, the one snag was that the record companies had no idea what teenagers really wanted. All they could do was to release noise by the ton and see what caught on best. In this way, it would only take time before they struck gold.

This was solid thinking: in April 1954, an ageing Country 'n' Western singer called Bill Haley made a record called *Rock Around The Clock*. By 1955 it was a hit in America and then it was a hit in Britain and then it was a hit all over the world. And it just kept on selling, it wouldn't quit. It stayed in the charts for one year solid.

By the time it was finished, it had sold fifteen million copies. It had also started pop.

2

BILL HALEY

Bill Haley was large and chubby and baby-faced. He had a kiss curl like a big C slapped down on his forehead with grease and water, and he was paunchy. When he sang, he grinned hugely and endlessly, but his eyes didn't focus on anything. Then he was almost thirty, married, father of five children. Definitely, he was unlikely hero food.

Just the same, he was the first boss of rock. At his peak, he made a film called *Rock Around The Clock* and, when it was shown here in the summer of 1956, audiences danced in the aisles, ripped up cinema seats, hit each other and destroyed anything they could lay their hands on. In one shot, it crystallized the entire rock rebellion.

The main plot of the film was that Bill Haley grinned. He picked his guitar and his kiss curl wobbled. He sang the title song and the beat stoked up and Teds everywhere went berserk.

Teds wore drainpipe jeans, three-quarter length jackets, winkle pickers, Mississippi string ties and, mostly, they were small, skinny, spotty. They'd been nourished on rationing and tended to be underfed, rat-faced. At any rate, as teenage movements go, they were the least attractive, most malicious ever and, when roused, they took out their flick knives and

9

stabbed each other. Because of this, *Rock Around The Clock* was banned in some towns.

Up to now, the Teds had been very much a minority but, once they'd rioted, the press discovered them as copy, decided that they spelled full-scale revolution. For the first time, the concept of Teenager was used as news, as a major selling point and, in no time, everyone else was up on the bandwagon. Churchmen offered spiritual comfort, psychologists explained, magistrates got tough, parents panicked, businessmen became rich and rock exploded into a central issue.

Of course, teenagers weren't slow to respond. There were more riots, more knives, even a few killings. And the papers hollered harder, the panic got greater, the circle kept spinning and suddenly the generation war was open fact. It wasn't an undertone, it wasn't just a novelty any more. It really mattered. Above all, it meant money.

As for Bill Haley, he was a trouper and kept right on grinning. Born in the suburbs of Detroit, 1927, he'd been playing guitar for a dollar a night from the age of thirteen up. Later, he fronted a Country 'n' Western group and buzzed around the Midwest, busily getting nowhere. Then he put in six years playing on a small-time radio station until finally, around 1951, he got wise, abandoned country music for good and swung across to commercial R&B.

First, he listened hard to the biggest-selling coloured blues of the time, Louis Jordan and Wynonie Harris, and copied the beat. Second, he watered down the lyrics, the sexuality of the original and made it acceptable to white audiences. Third, he changed his group's name to the Comets ('It sounded kind of far-out, wild') and worked out some acrobatic stage routines. Then he got moving.

In 1951, under his new format, he had a minor success with *Rock The Joint*. The next year he did even better with *Crazy, Man, Crazy* and, in 1954, he finally made it big with *Shake, Rattle And Roll*. Later that same year he made *Rock*

Around The Clock, which was a cover of Ivory Joe Hunter's big hit in the R&B charts.

Musically, it was all pretty dire. Haley was a fair country guitarist but he wasn't remotely a singer and his Comets sounded like they all had concrete boots. The beat was lumpish, dull. Alone of all the early rockers, Haley has no charm now, not even nostalgia value – *Rock Around The Clock* became a minor hit again in 1968 but, to me, it just sounded period bad.

Rock Around The Clock was no better and no worse than most of his work. The song was laughable, the arrangement non-existent but the beat was there and Haley shouted quite loud. In honesty, it was a dog but it was also a first and that's where it won. It had no competition.

Originally, it sold as a novelty, as a joke almost. Then the press took it up, hammered it, called it anti-music and suddenly it became a big generation symbol, a social phenomenon on its own. By the end, it was the source of an entire new music and Haley was automatically leader. He'd been lucky, of course, but he'd been around a long time and no one could reasonably begrudge him his break.

Soon, he was featured in a film called *Blackboard Jungle*, a corny old soapbox about juvenile delinquency and generalized teen hang-up. The opening sequence showed schoolkids jiving debauchedly in the playground and Haley was singing *Rock Around The Clock* on soundtrack. It all helped – the film was successful, caused fuss, helped sell records. Above all, it cemented the fiction of a uniquely teenage way of life with Bill Haley as its leader.

Through 1955 and on into 1956, he held complete control. He racked up another million seller with *See You Later Alligator*, had another monster film in *Don't Knock The Rock*. And he was everything – singer, face, prophet, explorer – and no one else counted. But all the time he was on a rain-check, he was doomed. He'd jumped the gun and

11

he was ahead only as long as it took the rest of the field, younger, tougher, sexier, to catch him and swamp him.

Don't Knock The Rock was the signal. It was Bill Haley's film but he lost it, he had it torn right out of his hands by Little Richard, a guaranteed genuine rock howler out of Macon, Georgia. Little Richard was the real thing. Bill Haley wasn't. Haley kept grinning but he sounded limp by comparison, looked downright foolish.

But what really did him in was the coming of Elvis Presley. The moment that Elvis had cut *Heartbreak Hotel*, Haley was lost. Suddenly his audience saw him as he was – ageing, married, corny, square, deeply boring – and that was that. Within a year, he couldn't get a hit to save his life. It was cruel, of course. It was also inevitable.

In early 1957, he toured England. By this time, he was already sagging on the ropes in America but Britain hadn't yet caught on and his arrival spelled bonanza time. He rode from Southampton to London in state on the Bill Haley Special, laid on for him by the *Daily Mirror* and, at Waterloo, he was met by three thousand fans, many of whom had waited all day for him. He grinned. 'It's wonderful to be here,' he said. 'I'm going to like England just fine. I only hope it likes me back.' The only stroke he missed was the bit about our English policemen being wonderful.

On 12 February he played the Dominion, Tottenham Court Road. It was the prototype of all pop concerts since. The music was drowned out by screaming, whistling, stamping, roaring and the gallery shook so much that people below could see the floor buckling above their heads. All you could hear was the beat, the amplification, the non-stop thump. The big beat, the monster. That was all there was.

The only trouble was Haley himself. Instead of a space-age rocker, all arrogant and mean and huge, he turned out to be a back-dated vaudeville act. The saxophonist squealed, honked and leaned over backwards until his body was parallel with the floor, his head almost touching the stage, him blowing madly all the time. The bass player lay on his instrument, climbed up it, used it like a trampoline. Haley grinned. It was slapstick, knockabout. It was pure embarrassment. And the audience was too pre-hyped to turn against it at the time; but when it was over, when the shouting and stamping had all died down, everyone finally had to face facts and Haley was through.

It was really quite bitter. After all, he was everyone's first try at pop and having him turn out like this was very much like getting drunk, losing one's virginity and then waking up in an empty bed the next morning.

As for Bill Haley himself, you couldn't help feeling sorry for him. He was an amiable man and he couldn't figure what had happened to him. Admittedly, he had made a fortune and he was assured of well-paid work for the rest of his life but it must still have been a cruel turn-around for him.

He took it philosophically. He kept plugging away, made new singles, toured, plastered his kiss curl down with grease and water, picked guitar and grinned at all times. In 1964, he was back in England, almost unchanged. This time nothing much was expected of him, he was seen as a historical curiosity and was received with some affection. At thirty-seven, he was attractive in his resignation. 'I'm old now,' he said. 'But I've been around. I sure have been around.' And he shook his head slowly as if he had truly seen everything there was to see.

3

ELVIS PRESLEY

What rock needed to get it off the ground now was a universal hero, a symbol, a rallying point. Someone very young, private, unshareable – exclusive teenage property. Someone who could crystallize the whole movement, give it size and direction. Obviously, Bill Haley didn't measure up. Equally obviously, Elvis Presley did.

Elvis is where pop begins and ends. He's the great original and, even now, he's the image that makes all others seem shoddy, the boss. For once, the fan club spiel is justified: Elvis is King.

His big contribution was that he brought it home just how economically powerful teenagers really could be. Before Elvis, rock had been a gesture of vague rebellion. Once he'd happened, it immediately became solid, self-contained, and then it spawned its own style in clothes and language and sex, a total independence in almost everything – all the things that are now taken for granted.

This was the major teen breakthrough and Elvis triggered it. In this way, without even trying, he became one of the people who have radically affected the way that people think and live.

In the beginning, he was a country boy out of Tupelo, Mississippi. He was born 8 January 1935. His twin, Jesse, died at birth. His father was a farmer, not a successful one, and, when Elvis was fourteen, the family moved to Memphis. There was no work around. The Presleys lived in one room and survived. By the time he was sixteen, Elvis was a professional lawn-mower. At nineteen, he did better – he became a truck-driver and brought home thirty-five dollars each week.

There was nothing special about him – he was stolid, respectable, unambitious. He liked trucks. ('I used to see them drivers with their shirts off, handkerchiefs around their neck, a little cap on their head. They looked daring to me. I always dreamed of being a real wild truck-driver.') He was country, naïve, very religious. Beyond that, he played a bit of guitar, sang some.

Definitely, he was young for his age – collected teddy bears, ate ritual peanut butter and mashed bananas sandwiches last thing before he went to sleep each night and loved his mother to the point of ickiness. In fact, he was cutting an amateur record of *My Happiness* as a birthday present for her when he first got discovered.

Later, he was signed to Sun Records, a local label, and went out on the small-time Southern circuit, playing school dances, country fairs and so forth.

And his first record, *That's All Right*, was quite marvellous. Elvis had been exposed to a lot of different musics – coloured R&B, fundamentalist preachers, country ballads – and his singing was a mixture of all of them, an improbable stew to which he added sex. His voice sounded edgy, nervous, and it cut like a scythe, it exploded all over the place. It was anguished, immature, raw. But, above all, it was the sexiest thing that anyone had ever heard.

By May 1955, he had a manager, Colonel Tom Parker (the title was honorary). If nothing else, Parker was a man of experience. At forty-nine, he'd been through peepshows, carnivals, patent medicine, the Great Parker Pony Circus and just about anything else before Elvis came along. Canny but

15

unsophisticated, he hadn't been unsuccessful and he managed some successful country stars but, then again, he'd hardly struck gold either. On all known form, he was an unlikely revolution-maker.

Under Parker, Presley was moving up. His records were selling quietly but well round Memphis and the girls had just begun to scream at him. His singing was as good now as it was ever going to get and he kept moving his hips, wriggling and, every time he did that, there was some kind of riot.

Early in 1956, Elvis was signed by R.C.A.-Victor and made a record called *Heartbreak Hotel*. It sold a million and a half straight off. By the end of six months, he'd sold eight million records, worked up to ten thousand fan letters a week and raised the shrillest, most prolonged teen hysteria ever. It really was as fast, as simple and complete as that. By the next year, he had grown into an annual twenty-million-dollar industry.

He would come out on stage standing on a golden Cadillac. He wore a golden suit and, on his feet, he had golden slippers. His sideboards reached down to his earlobes and his hair, heavy with grease, came up in a great ducktail plume off his forehead. He had a lopsided grin and he used it all the time.

When the music started, he'd begin wriggling and he wriggled so hard that quite a few cities banned him for obscenity. 'Elvis Presley is morally insane,' shrieked a Baptist pastor in Des Moines and that just about summed it up.

He was flash – he had four Cadillacs, a three-wheeled Messerschmidt, two monkeys, much jewellery. He built himself a house for one hundred thousand dollars and it glowed blue and gold in the dark.

On stage, he sang hymns in between his hits. With strangers, he was invariably charming, boyish, immensely courteous. He'd smile shyly and mumble. He'd call men 'sir' and women 'ma'am', drop his eyes, look around frequently for approval. And, of course, this was all tremendously flattering.

16

In these ways, he had real talent for handling people, for making himself liked.

At the centre of everything was his mother. But, shy and deferential as he was, whenever he got pushed into fights by passing madmen, he'd invariably take them apart. No question, he was a very Southern boy.

Always, he came back to sex. In earlier generations, singers might carry great sex appeal but they'd have to cloak it under the trappings of romanticism, they'd never spell anything out. By contrast, Elvis was blatant. When those axis hips got moving, there was no more pretence about moonlight and hand-holding; it was hard physical fact.

With crooners, with people like Sinatra and Eddie Fisher, girls had suffered crushes and they'd sigh, swoon and sob gently inside their handkerchiefs. Always, they'd been romantic and quite innocent.

With pop, though, it's all been down to mainline sexual fantasy. Sitting in concert halls, schoolgirls have screamed, rioted, bawled and fainted. They've wet themselves and they've masturbated. According to P.J. Proby, they've even ripped the legs off their chairs and mauled themselves. They've done all kinds of outrageous stuff that they'd never do anywhere else and they've been so uninhibited because there has always been a safety belt, because the pop singer himself has been unreachable, unreal, and nothing could actually happen.

In this way, it's all been sex in a vacuum – the girls have freaked themselves out, emptied themselves, and then they've gone back home with their boy-friends and played virgin again. As rituals go, it's not been beautiful but it's been healthy, it's acted as a safety valve. Screaming at Elvis or the Beatles or the Rolling Stones has been as good as saying confession or going to an analyst.

At the same time, offstage, Elvis read the Bible, loved his mother. 'He's just like a paperback book,' one of his girl fans explained. 'Real sexy pictures on the cover. Only when you get inside, it's just a good story.' He looked dangerous but ultimately was safe and clean. This is what young girls have always wanted from their idols, an illusion of danger, and Elvis brought a new thrill of semi-reality to the game.

With all his peacockery, his implied narcissism, he was also a major pose-maker for boys. A lot of the time he sang conventional romantic lyrics but some of his biggest hits were breakaways – the harshness and contempt for women in *Hound Dog* was typical.

Blue Suede Shoes was even more to the point. This had been a hit for Carl Perkins in 1956 but Elvis took it over the following year and gave it wholly new dimensions. It was important – the idea that clothes could dominate your life. Girls and cars and money didn't count. All that mattered were shoes, beautiful brand-new blue suede shoes. It was the first hint at an obsession with objects – motorbikes, clothes and so on – that was going to become central.

By 1958, Elvis had ruled for two years solid and the hysteria showed no signs at all of dying down. He'd gone into movies – *Love Me Tender*, *Loving You*, *Jailhouse Rock*. He had racked up twenty worldwide million sellers. Still, he had some long-term problems. He was already twenty-three, he couldn't go on being a teen idol for ever. The difficulty was how to turn him from an adolescent rebel into a respectable establishment figure without his fans feeling cheated.

At this point, a godsend: Presley's army draft came through and he went on ice for two years. It meant losing a lot of money but Elvis took it philosophically. As for Colonel Parker, he was delighted.

From here on in, Elvis got more and more saintly. On army training, he was a paragon of diligence, cheerfulness, humility. His officers praised him warmly, the press swung behind him. Adult America was much reassured – the monster had shown that it was only kidding.

18

In August 1958, his mother took sick, had a heart attack and died. At the funeral, Elvis was hemmed in tight by reporters, jotting down every word he said, noting every last sob and whimper. 'She was the sunshine of our home,' Elvis moaned. 'Good-bye darling. We loved you. I love you. I love you so much. I lived my whole life just for you.' Next morning, his ramblings were splashed syllable by syllable across the papers. It was diseased, ghoulish, but it finally cemented the new Presley image. The boy was all right.

There was even a record about it all, *New Angel Tonight* by a certain Dave McEnery. The first verse went:

> There's a new angel tonight
> Up in heaven so bright,
> The mother of our Rock 'n' Roll King –
> And I know she's watching down
> On her boy in Army brown,
> In her angel mother's heart remembering.*

By the time he was shipped out to Germany, Elvis was everything that an all-American boy ought to be, working and playing hard, dating but not too much, visiting spastics, drawing emotional tributes from rugged G.I. buddies. He wound up a Specialist Fourth Class, a rank equivalent to corporal and worth $122 a month. The whole operation was a triumph.

By the time that he came back to civilian life again, he was almost as respectable as an Andy Williams or a Perry Como. Predictably, his first new record was a ballad. *It's Now Or Never*, an inflated updating of *O Sole Mio*. Also predictably, it was his biggest seller yet, doing more than nine million worldwide.

*Words of *New Angel Tonight* by permission of Southern Music Publishing Co. Ltd, London.

He never again went back on the road. Instead, he hid himself away in vast mansions in Hollywood or Memphis and there he has stayed ever since. He hasn't toured in years. He lives a life of almost total privacy, kept company only by his wife, his small daughter and twelve ex-G.I.s, who amuse him and fetch him drinks and play touch football with him. Whatever he does, whatever fires him, he's discreet about it – nobody knows for sure what he thinks or wants to do. He gets slightly lonely, we're told. That's all.

Most of his time is spent in churning out an endless series of safe and boring musicals – *Kissin' Cousins, Clambake, Frankie and Johnnie, Harem Scarum, Girl Happy* – and each one seems worse than the one before. Elvis himself is thirty-four, paunchy, slow and his voice has lost its edge, until he now sounds a bit like Dean Martin. His songs are drab, his scripts are formula-fed and his sets look as if they've been knocked together with two nails and a hammer. He still makes a fortune but his singles sell patchily and his films break no box office records.

To be fair, he's shown recent signs of getting back into business. He issued three strong singles running – *Big Boss Man, Guitar, U.S. Male* – and did a much-publicized TV spectacular on which he sounded tougher, more rocker than he'd done in years. Whether this will grow into any major revival remains to be seen.

As far as his fans are concerned, he could just as well be on another planet. From time to time his gold Cadillac is sent out on tour across America and they come to see it, touch it. His annual earnings are around ten million dollars. He has sold the best part of a hundred and fifty million records. And somehow his fans accept his absence and have come almost to like it.

The point is that he has passed beyond the edge of criticism, that he's somewhere out of reach on a plateau of showbiz untouchability. The obvious parallel is with Frank

Sinatra – both of them have changed so much, have earned such astronomical money, have so dominated the entertainment worlds of their time that what they do for the rest of their lives has become largely immaterial. They have run out of challenges.

All that's left now is the image, the vision of him as he was when he was twenty-one, twenty-two, strutting and swivelling and swaggering, hanging his grin out, putting on the agony, riding on the top of his Cadillac, gold on gold, and freewheeling through everything. He was magnificent then, he really was. And his whole story has been an ultimate perfection of the Hollywood romance, an all-time saga of what happens to sexy little boys when they get fed into the sausage machine.

So Elvis now is a godhead – unseen, untouchable, more than human. The demon lover has turned into a father, an all-powerful figure who can rule a fan's life without actually having to be there. His remoteness is a positive advantage, his present badness is irrelevant, and there's no reason why it should ever end. Worship is a habit that's hard to break.

4

CLASSIC ROCK

Rock 'n' roll was very simple music. All that mattered was the noise it made, its drive, its aggression, its newness. All that was taboo was boredom.

The lyrics were mostly non-existent, simple slogans one step away from gibberish. This wasn't just stupidity, simple inability to write anything better. It was a kind of teen code, almost a sign language, that would make rock entirely incomprehensible to adults.

In other words, if you weren't sure about rock, you couldn't cling to its lyrics. You either had to accept its noise at face value or you had to drop out completely.

Under these rules, rock turned up a sudden flood of maniacs, wildmen with pianos and guitars who would have been laughing stocks in any earlier generations but who were just right for the fifties. They were energetic, basic, outrageous. They were huge personalities and they used music like a battering ram. Above all, they were loud.

It was a great time – every month would produce someone new, someone wilder than anything that had gone before. Pop was barren territory and everything was simple, every tiny gimmick was some kind of progression. Around 1960, things evened out and much of the excitement died out. Pop had become more sophisticated, more creative, more everything.

But the fifties were the time when pop was just pop, when it was really something to switch on the radio and hear what was new right that minute. Things could never be so good and simple again.

For instance, the first record I ever bought was by Little Richard and, at one throw, it taught me everything I ever need to know about pop.

The message went: 'Tutti frutti all rootie, tutti frutti all rootie, tutti frutti all rootie, awopbopaloobop alopbamboom!'* As a summing up of what rock 'n' roll was really all about, this was nothing but masterly.

Very likely these early years are the best that pop has yet been through. Anarchy moved in. For thirty years you couldn't possibly make it unless you were white, sleek, nicely-spoken and phoney to your toenails – suddenly now you could be black, purple, moronic, delinquent, diseased or almost anything on earth and you could still clean up. Just so long as you were new, just so long as you carried excitement.

In a way, we were moving towards some kind of democracy. Under the new system, all you needed was dollar potential: earn, baby, earn. So that's what Little Richard was celebrating in *Tutti Frutti* and he was very right.

Most of the best early rockers came out of the South – Elvis from Mississippi, Little Richard from Georgia, Buddy Holly from Texas, Jerry Lee Lewis from Louisiana, Gene Vincent from Virginia. These were the states where the living had always been meanest, where teenagers had been least catered for and, where, therefore, the pop kickback was now most frantic.

Anyhow, the South was by far the most music-conscious section in America. It always had been. It had huge traditions

*Words of *Tutti Frutti* printed by kind permission of Burlington Music Company Ltd.

23

in R&B, country, trad and gospel, and its music was in every way more direct, less pretentious than up North. Mostly, it had a sledgehammer beat and pulled no punches. Down here, rock was an obvious natural.

The only innovation was that the rockers made use of all the sources around them. Up to this, whites had used country, Negroes had used R&B and the two had never remotely over-lapped. Now everyone incorporated anything they could lay their hands on and it was this mix-up of black and white musics that gave Southern rock its flavour.

(Needless to say, this racial interaction had nothing much to do with tolerance. Black stole from white, white from black – that didn't mean that they liked each other, it just meant that they accepted each other's uses. And then white kids liked playing black-sounding music because it shocked their parents and black kids liked playing white-sounding music because it made them money. From any angle, it was strictly a fair deal all round.)

Out of all the great Southern rockers, just about the most splendid was the before-mentioned Little Richard Penniman out of Macon, Georgia, who was and still is the most exciting live performer I ever saw in my life.

The background on him was that he'd been born on Christmas Day, 1935, one of thirteen children, and had an archetypally harsh childhood. At fourteen, he was singing solos with the local gospel choir. At fifteen, he was blues shouting, dancing and selling herb tonic in a medicine show. From there, he got into a variety of groups, made a sequence of nothing records and finally, in 1955, when he was twenty, sold a million copies of *Tutti Frutti*.

He looked beautiful – he wore a baggy suit with elephant trousers, twenty-six inches at the bottoms, and he had his hair back-combed in a monstrous plume like a fountain. Then he had a little toothbrush moustache and a round, totally ecstatic face.

He played piano and he'd stand knock-kneed at the keyboard, hammering away with two hands as if he wanted to bust the thing apart. At climactic moments, he'd lift one leg and rest it on the keys, banging away with his heel, and his trouser rims would billow like kites.

He'd scream and scream and scream. He had a freak voice, tireless, hysterical, completely indestructible, and he never in his life sang at anything lower than an enraged bull-like roar. On every phrase, he'd embroider with squeals, rasps, siren whoops. His stamina, his drive were limitless. And his songs were mostly total non-songs, nothing but bedrock twelve bars with playroom lyrics, but still he'd put them across as if every last syllable was liquid gold. He sang with desperate belief, real religious fervour: 'Good golly, Miss Molly, you sure like a ball – when you're rockin' and rollin', you can't hear your momma call.'*

As a person, he was brash, fast, bombastic, a sort of prototype Muhammad Ali ('I'm just the same as ever – loud, electrifying and full of personal magnetism') and right through the middle fifties he was second only to Elvis. Most of his records sold a million each – *Long Tall Sally*, *Lucille*, *The Girl Can't Help It*, *Keep A Knockin'*, *Baby Face*. They all sounded roughly the same: tuneless, lyricless, pre-Neanderthal. There was a tenor saxo solo in the middle somewhere and a constant smashed-up piano and Little Richard himself screaming his head off. Individually, the records didn't mean much. They were small episodes in one unending scream and only made sense when you put them all together.

But in 1957 he suddenly upped and quit. No warning – he just stopped touring, stopped making records and went off to play piano in a Seventh Day Adventist church off Times Square.

*Words of *Good Golly Miss Molly* by permission of Southern Music Publishing Co. Ltd, London.

Apparently, he'd been in a plane and a fire had broken out. Richard got down on his knees and promised that, if he was spared, he'd give up the devil's music for ever and devote himself to the gospel instead. 'And God answered my prayers and stopped the fire.'

So he announced that he was giving up but his entourage thought he was mad and laughed at him. Then Richard, in a typically flash performance, took his many rings from his fingers and flung them into the sea. Eight thousand pounds' worth: 'I wish I'd seen the face of the man that caught those fish. A King's ransom, all courtesy of Little Richard.' And he quit on the spot. At least, that's the story he tells.

Five years he kept it up, made no records, gave no interviews. But in the early sixties he began to cut gospel records and from there it was inevitable that he'd go back to rock again. He didn't get any further hits but he was still a name. Several times he toured Britain and each time he went down a storm.

The first time I saw him was in 1963, sharing a bill with the Rolling Stones, Bo Diddley and the Everly Brothers, and he cut them all to shreds. He didn't look sane. He screamed and his eyes bulged, the veins jutted in his skull. He came down front and stripped – his jacket, tie, cufflinks, his golden shirt, his huge diamond watch, right down to the flesh. Then he hid inside a silk dressing-gown and all the time he roared and everyone jumped about in the aisles like it was the beginning of rock all over again.

Objectively, he didn't even do much. Anyone else that has a great stage act, they always have an obvious selling point – James Brown has speed, Johnnie Ray has pain, Elvis has sex. Little Richard had none of that. All he had was energy.

He howled and hammered endlessly. On *Hound Dog*, he dropped down on his knees, grovelled and still he howled. It was all gospel – 'that healing music, makes the blind to see, the lame to walk, the dead rise up.' He kept it up so long, so

26

loud it made your head whirl. Good hard rock, he murdered it and murdered us. When he was through, he smiled sweetly. 'That Little Richard,' he said. 'Such a nice boy.'

Fats Domino came from further back. In fact, he was almost pre-pop. As early as 1948, he cut a big hit called *Fat Man* and he'd already tucked about ten smashes under his belt by the time that Bill Haley came along.

At this period, he sold mostly around his home town of New Orleans and worked for a strictly Negro market. The music he peddled was a nicely relaxed line in R&B, backed by tightly-knit small bands, and everything he did was casual. Fats himself wrote the songs, played piano and sang.

When rock came in and R&B was acceptable, the fat man very quickly cashed in. He had whole strings of American hits and, by 1960, he'd sold upwards of fifty million records. Fifty million is a lot of records. Officially, he's also credited with twenty-two individual million sellers, which puts him ahead of everyone outside of Elvis and the Beatles.

Mind you, it has to be said that these figures make him sound a lot bigger than he ever was. Most of his alleged million sellers were only regional hits and he never made much sustained impression on British charts. All the same, he was a figure. More important, he made good records.

The way he was so lazy and good-humoured, he was a bit like an updated Fats Waller. Most of his best songs – *Blue Monday*, *I'm Walkin'*, *Blueberry Hill* – were dead simple, straight ahead, and Fats sang them as if he was having himself a time. When he was at his best, he conjured up small-time coloured dancehalls on Saturday night – he played a bit, sang a bit and everyone got lushed. Good-time music, that's all it was and it hit the spot just right.

In his unpretentious way, he also had quite an influence on what came after him. The British jazz/blues bands in the early sixties used his understatement, his idle beat, his tight backing sound. Georgie Fame especially was a big Domino man.

In 1967 he did a Sunday night show at the Saville in London and the audience was made up of rockers from way back – all greased hair, drainpipes and three-quarter coats. Fats weighed in at sixteen stone and smiled all the time. He ran through hits and diamonds glittered on his fingers and he wore bright orange socks.

When he came to his finale, he went into an endless and very corny workout on *When The Saints Go Marching In*. It went on and on and on. Fats glistened and gleamed all over, his band cavorted like circus clowns and it was all a bit embarrassing. At the end, Fats got up and started to push his piano across the stage with hard thumps of his thigh. He was past forty and not fit and it was a very wide stage. By the time he was halfway across, he was flagging. The music rambled on and Fats was bent almost double with effort. It was a very ludicrous situation – the rockers stormed forwards at the stage, willing him on, and he kept on heaving, he wouldn't give up. And it took him maybe five minutes but finally he did make it and everyone cheered like mad.

Two of the rockers jumped up on stage and lifted his hands holding them aloft like he was a winning fighter. They were big kids and Fats, for all his weight, is quite squat. He stood shaking between them and he looked vulnerable, almost old. Everyone was rioting. Fats streamed sweat and kept smiling but he also looked a bit confused. Very likely, no one had gone quite that wild for him in ten years.*

Like Fats Domino, Larry Williams came out of New Orleans. He started out playing piano with Lloyd Price, who was one of the biggest Negro R&B stars of the fifties and had world bestsellers with things like *I'm Gonna Get Married*, *Personality* and, biggest of all, *Stagger Lee*. But in 1957, Larry went solo, started writing songs and became the first

*During 1969 Domino was brought out of Las Vegas semi-obscurity by Reprise Records and has cut an excellent new album.

rock 'n' roll whistler. Straight away he turned out some of the best rock records ever made.

He specialized – almost the only songs he wrote were about girls' names – *Dizzy Miss Lizzy*, *Short Fat Fanny*, *Bony Moronie*. This obsession with names was quite a central part of rock, one manifestation of the massive swing towards gibberish, and Larry didn't introduce it but he did give it new dimensions and turned it into a whole tiny anti-art form on its own. In *Bony Moronie*, which was his best, he touched true inspiration:

> I've got a girl called Bony Moronie,
> She's as skinny as a stick of macaroni.*

As a contribution to pop history, this was all very righteous stuff but maybe less than earth-shattering and I wouldn't give him this much space for his music alone. What gets him in is that his personality epitomized everything flash and catching about Mister Rock 'n' Roll.

Like most of the classic rockers, he didn't tour Britain until the sixties and by this time things had very much run down for him. He'd moved on from rock to soul but still he didn't get hits. He was almost thirty and said he felt like an old man.

Most of the time he sat in his small hotel room and played cards with his wife and, even in decline, he was a smooth man. He wore rings on all his fingers and brushed his hair far forward like the Beatles. He had shiny silk suits and ever-present shades. And he talked a lot, with a turn of phrase that was truly elegant. In this style, he made my all-time favourite remark about rock. 'I'm truth,' he said. 'It has no beginning and no end for it is the very pulse of life itself.'

Bony Moronie by Larry Williams © 1957 and 1966 Venice Music, Inc., Hollywood.

29

Another noble rocker was Screamin' Jay Hawkins, who had been around ever since the middle forties. He wore a zebra-striped tailcoat, a turban, polkadot shoes. He began his act by emerging flaming from a coffin and he carried a smoking skull called Henry, he shot flame from his fingertips, he screamed and bloodcurdled. At the end, he flooded the stage with thick white smoke and, when it cleared, he was gone.

'I used to lose half my audience right at the start, when I came up screaming out of my coffin,' he said. 'They used to run screaming down the aisles and half kill themselves scrambling out of the exits. I couldn't stop them. In the end, I had to hire some boys to sit up in the gallery with a supply of shrivelled-up elastic bands and, when the audience started running, my boys would drop the elastic bands on to their heads and whisper "Worms".'

Jay's biggest hit was the original version of *I Put A Spell On You* and he had other things like *The Whammy* and *Feast Of The Mau Mau*. Actually, he had quite a pleasant baritone but, on stage, he'd only scream and ghoul. 'I just torment a song,' he said. 'Frighten it half to death.'

Then there were the Coasters, who had the most sly-sounding lead singer in the whole business, not to mention the most lugubrious bass. The lead, Carl Gardner, played the school bad boy. He sang like he had some bubblegum permanently stashed away inside his cheek and everything he did was sneaky, pretty hip. Then he was a loudmouth, a natural-born hustler and all the time the bass groaned and grumbled below him, the voice of his conscience speaking. The lead took no blind notice.

Mind you, they could hardly miss. For a kickoff, they had the most prolific song-writers in rock going for them, Jerry Lieber and Mike Stoller, a partnership that shifted upwards of thirty million records in five years. Lieber and Stoller also wrote some of the best early Elvis hits, notably *Hound Dog* and

Jailhouse Rock, but they were natural humorists and Presley was just a bit straight for them. The Coasters were ideal.

Lieber and Stoller churned out stuff that was inventive, wry and sometimes very shrewd – a running commentary on the manifold miseries of being teenage – and the delinquent talents of Carl Gardner did the rest with no sweat. Between them, they came up with some very funny records.

The format was simple: they got a fast shuffle going, reeled off the assembled lyrics and then stuck a frantic yakety sax chorus into the middle. It was a comforting scheme of things. You always knew what was coming and could relax. So the lead snickered, the bass moaned and everyone was happy.

Probably their most classic effort was *Yackety Yak*, a knock-down and drag-down row between a bullied teen-ager and his monstrous parents. The teenager, of course, is seen as martyr. He spends his whole time tidying his room, doing homework, washing, generally flogging himself. And when he complains, he's frozen stiff by the ultimate deterrent threat – no more rock and roll.

From there, they went on to further explorations of teenage hell – *Charlie Brown, Poison Ivy* and *Bad Blood*. Each one was perfect in its own way but the whole style was completely geared to rock attitudes and, when times changed, they were among the first to slip.

They're still around, though, and occasionally a new single filters through. Nothing vital is changed. The lead still sounds maybe fifteen years old and carries himself as if he's just seen his geometry coach slip on a shrewdly-planted banana skin. The bass still groans. They live in a cut-off private world and everyone is sweet sixteen for ever.

While I'm talking about Lieber and Stoller, I'd better stick in a short bit about the Drifters, who were hardly rock but who don't fit too well any place else. Really, they were just commercialized R&B and their most major contribution was that they introduced the violin into modern pop.

31

Lieber and Stoller, who produced them, wrote natural hit songs for them and then used string sections to play what would normally have been the lead guitar part. It was good stuff, too – stylish, relaxed, always melodic. Over the years, they came up with some beautiful things – *Under the Boardwalk*, *Save The Last Dance For Me*, *I'll Take You Where the Music's Playing*, *Up On The Roof* and quite a few more.

The only comic thing about them was that their personnel changed completely every time they turned around. They ran through themselves like fire, the turnover was amazing. What's more, other groups all over America turned up under the same name, so that you wound up with umpteen different outfits, all called the Drifters, all swearing blind that they were the original and only genuine article.

The Lieber and Stoller Drifters recorded for Atlantic and ran through such good lead singers as Clyde McPhatter and Ben E. King, both of whom later made it as soloists. No matter how many individuals came or went, they always kept the same basic sound, tight and immensely commercial. Good-time music, they were unusually polished for their time and, like everything else that Lieber and Stoller handled, they were fun.

Chuck Berry was possibly the finest of all rockers and he's easily my own favourite pop writer ever. He wrote endless Teen Romance lyrics but sang them with vicious, sly cynicism and this is the clash that makes him so funny, so attractive.

His most perfect song was *You Never Can Tell*, an effort that gets a lot of its flavour from the knowledge that it was made soon after Chuck had served a hefty jail sentence for transporting a minor across a state boundary without her parents' consent. Its full lyrics went:

It was a teenage wedding and the old folks wished 'em well,
You could see that Pierre did truly love the mademoiselle,

And now the young monsieur and madame have rung
    the chapel bell –
C'est la vie, say the old folks, it goes to show you never
    can tell.

They furnished off an apartment with two rooms, they
    were all by themselves,
The coolerator was crammed with TV dinner and
    ginger ale,
But when Pierre found work, the little money coming
    worked out well –
C'est la vie, say the old folks, it goes to show you never
    can tell.

They had a hi-fi phono, boy did they let it blast,
Seven hundred little records, all rockin', rhythm and
    jazz,
But when the sun went down, the record tempo of the
    music fell –
C'est la vie, say the old folks, it goes to show you never
    can tell.

They bought a souped-up Jidney, was a cherry-red '53,
They drove it down to New Orleans to celebrate their
    anniversary.
It was there where Pierre was wedded to the lovely
    mademoiselle –
C'est la vie, say the old folks, it goes to show you never
    can tell.*

A jangle piano rambled away legato in the background and
there were great swirling sax riffs and Chuck himself more

*Words of *You Never Can Tell* by permission of Jewel Music Publishing Co. Ltd, London.

intoned than sang, sly and smooth as always, the eternal sixteen-year-old hustler. That was it – the Teendream myth that's right at the heart of all pop and *You Never Can Tell* expressed it more exactly, more evocatively than any of the other fifty thousand attempts at the same theme.

Of course, this is all very naïve and undeveloped by comparison with what has come since, but then Bogart proved thirty years ago that, in mass media, you don't need to be a monster intellectual to be great. In fact, it's a definite disadvantage if you are. What you do need is style, command, specific image and these are the exact things that Chuck Berry has always been overflowing with.

Basically, what it boils down to is detail. Most pop writers would have written *You Never Can Tell* as a series of generalities and it would have been nothing. But Chuck was obsessive, he was hooked on cars, rock, ginger ale and he had to drag them all in. That's what makes it – the little touches like the cherry-red Jidney '53 or the coolerator.

Chuck was born in California in 1931, but grew up in St Louis and, when he was older, got to be a hairdresser. By nature, he was an operator and he was always going to be successful. The only question was how. So he tried singing, he wrote, he made progress. In 1955, he had his first national smash with *Maybellene* and from then on he was a natural Mister Big.

As a writer, he was something like poet laureate to the whole rock movement. He charted its habits, hobbies, hang-ups or celebrated its triumphs or mourned its limitations and he missed nothing out. *School Days* pinned down exactly that schoolkid sense of spending one's whole life listening for bells and *Johnny B. Goode*, guitarslinger, created a genuine new folk hero and *Roll Over Beethoven* should have been adopted as the universal slogan of rock. But almost best of all was *Sweet Little Sixteen*. Nothing summed up better the twined excitement and frustration of the time:

34

Sweet little sixteen, she's just got to have
About half a million famed autographs.
Her wallet's filled with pictures, she gets 'em one by
  one,
Becomes so excited, watch her, look at her run.

Sweet Little Sixteen, she's got the grown-up blues
Tight dresses and lipstick, she's sportin' high-heeled
  shoes
Oh but tomorrow morning she'll have to change her
  trend
And be sweet sixteen and back in class again.

They're really rocking in Boston, in Pittsburg, PA,
Deep in the heart of Texas and 'round the Frisco Bay,
All over St Louis, way down in New Orleans,
All the cats want to dance with Sweet Little Sixteen.[*]

Beyond his writing, he played a very fair blues guitar,
Chicago-style, and sang in a voice as waved and oily as
his hair. On stage, his speciality was the duck walk, which
involved bounding across the stage on his heels, knees bent,
body jackknifed and guitar clamped firmly to his gut. Then
he would peep coyly over his shoulders and look like sweet
little sixteen herself, all big eyes and fluttering lids. He had
a pencil moustache and had the smoothness, the cool of a
steamboat gambler. A brown-eyed handsome man, in fact.

Just when things were going so well for him, he made his
mistake with the minor and was put away. By the time he got
out again, in 1963, rock was finished but the British R&B
boom was just getting under way and he was made blues hero
number one by the Rolling Stones, who started out playing

*Words of *Sweet Little Sixteen* by permission of Jewel Music Publishing
Co. Ltd, London.

almost nothing but Chuck Berry songs. Almost as a matter of course, he'd landed on his feet.

He was brought over and made much of but turned out to be hard to deal with. He was arrogant, rude. When he liked to turn it on, he could be most charming but often he couldn't be bothered. First and last, he was amazingly mean.

There's an authenticated story about him that, on his first British tour, he used to study the evening paper nightly and check to see if there had been any fluctuation in rates of exchange. If there was any deviation in his favour, no matter how small, he'd demand payment in cash before he went on. On one night, this supplement came to 2s. 3½d.

Still, all of that is irrelevant when you hear his records again. In any case, his hardness, his greasiness is all part of his double-edged appeal. And when he does his duck walk, when he flirts over his shoulder and unfolds one of his best flowerpot teen epics, you know that he's one of those few people in pop that really count.

By and large, white rockers were a lot less impressive than their coloured counterparts. After the wildness of Little Richard, the lyricism of Chuck Berry, they sounded samey and half-hearted. As personalities, too, they were less colourful, less articulate. Mostly, they were plain boring.

The major exception was Jerry Lee Lewis, a pianist and shouter from Louisiana. He used R&B and country in about equal doses and attacked the keys in very much the same style as Little Richard, bopping them with fists, feet, elbows and anything else that was handy. Towards the end of his act, he'd climb on top of the piano, hold the mike like a lance and stay up there until the audience got hot enough to dash forward and drag him down.

His great gift was that, no matter how frantic he got, his voice remained controlled and drawling country. He seemed to have a lot of time to spare, an unshakeable ease, and this gave him class.

He had long yellow crinkly hair that fell forward over his eyes when he worked and a thin, slightly furtive face. He always reminded me of a weasel. And when he got steamed up, he'd sweat like mad and his face would collapse into nothing but a formless mass of heaving, contorting flesh. Still, his voice would be strong, easy. As stage acts go, it was hardly pretty but, definitely, it was compelling.

After he'd rampaged through his earliest hits (the apocalyptic *Whole Lotta Shakin' Goin' On* and *Great Balls of Fire*), he did a 1958 tour of Britain and immediately plunged neck deep into trouble. He had brought his young wife with him. His very young wife, as it turned out. Her name was Myra and Jerry Lee said she was fifteen. Later, he admitted that she was only thirteen. He also said that, at twenty-two, this was his second marriage. His first had been at fourteen ('Hell, I was too young').

The British press duly disgraced itself. It howled blue murder, screamed babysnatcher, and finally got the tour cancelled. Jerry Lee flew out in disgrace. 'Hell, I'm only country,' he pleaded, but no one took any notice.

Before the cancellation, he'd had time to do two concerts and, doomed by so much bad publicity, they were disasters. In the first, Jerry Lee dashed out in a pillar-box red suit and smashed straight through two numbers without let-up. He was brilliant, by far the best rocker Britain had then witnessed and he half won his audience round. Then, before going into the third he took out a golden comb and very delicately swept his hair back out of his eyes. It was a fatal move. Someone yelled 'Cissy!' at him and from there on in it was solid murder. Finally, Jerry Lee just upped and walked off stage. The curtain came down. Pandemonium.

All of which goes to show how superficial the rock revolt had really been. On paper, Jerry Lee's marital junketings were exactly calculated to improve his prestige, make him into an even better symbol of rebellion. In practice, it only took a fast burst of pomposity in the papers and the kids were just as appalled as their parents. And when Jerry Lee left his hotel, he was hissed and insulted and spat upon.

Jerry Lee wasn't downcast. Arriving back in New York, he announced that his concerts had been 'Great, just great' and that, as he'd left, 'three thousand stood and cheered'.

The final irony was that the marriage worked out idyllically well. They settled down, had children. They were both intensely religious and Myra carried a bible with her everywhere.

In any case, he was forgiven. Through the sixties he toured here often and always went down a storm, which isn't surprising because he has huge command and plays his audiences exactly as he likes. Recently, he's been peddling C&W rather than straight rock and his *What Made Milwaukee Famous* made number two on the American country charts.

There are people around who'll tell you that he's the greatest pop figure ever. I wouldn't agree but he certainly rates. I also like his attitude. 'You are either hot or cold,' he says. 'If you are lukewarm, the Lord will spew you out of his mouth.'

Buddy Holly was really called Charles Hardin Holley and first came out of Lubbock, Texas, with broken teeth, wire glasses, halitosis, plus every last possible kind of country Southernness. He wasn't appetizing. In fact, he was an obvious no-hoper.

On the other hand, he had a voice, he wrote natural hit songs and, what's more, he was by no means prepared to sit tight in the background and churn out smashes for other artists. He said he wanted to sit in his front room and watch his face singing to him out of the television screen. He was very firm about this. So a man called Lloyd Greenfield, a toughened Northern agent, took him up and changed him into another person. Buddy had his teeth capped, his breath cleansed, his hair styled, his wire glasses exchanged for big impressive black ones, his voice toned. Then he was put into high-school sweaters and taught how to smile. Suddenly, he was all-America.

Holly sang lead with a group called the Crickets and promptly cut a succession of monster hits with them – *That'll Be The Day, Oh Boy, Maybe Baby*. By 1958, growing big-time, he had dumped the Crickets and gone solo, clocking up a further sequence of million sellers on his own – *Peggy Sue, Rave On, It Doesn't Matter Any More*. He was smooth, he was clean. He had a smile straight off a toothpaste ad and his new black glasses were major trendsetters. In every detail, his career was perfect and in February 1959, just to round it off, he got killed in an air crash at Fargo, North Dakota. He was then twenty years old.

Long-time rock fans have always been bitterly divided about him. He wasn't a hardcore rocker, being too gentle and melodic, and this eccentricity can be construed either as back-sliding or as progression. Even ten years after his death, it isn't an academic question. I have seen rock preservation meetings reduced to brawling knuckle-dusted anarchy. On the wall of a pub lavatory in Gateshead, there is a scrawled legend: 'Buddy Holly lives and rocks in Tijuana, Mexico.'

He was all adenoids – twanged them like a catapult, propelled each phrase up and out on a whole tidal wave of hiccoughs and burps. As sound, it was ugly but at least it was new. It was also much copied: Adam Faith, for one, built his early career largely around his variations on it. For that matter, so did Bobby Vee and Tommy Roe.

Holly's breakthrough, in fact, was that he opened up alternatives to all-out hysteria. Not many white kids had the lungs or sheer hunger to copy Little Richard but Holly was easy. All you needed was tonsils. The beat was lukewarm, the range minimal – no acrobatics or rage or effort required. You just stood up straight and mumbled. Even the obvious rockers, things like *Rave On* or *Oh Boy*, were Neapolitan flowerpots after *Tutti Frutti*.

In this way, Buddy Holly was the patron saint of all the thousands of no-talent kids who ever tried to make a million dollars. He was founder of a noble tradition.

Also killed in the same air crash that did for Holly were Ritchie Valens and the Big Bopper. Valens, at seventeen, had already made some of the direst records in pop. The Bopper, on the other hand, had made one of the very best: *Chantilly Lace*.

His real name was J.P. Richardson, he was a Texan disc jockey and *Chantilly Lace* was his only hit. A fat man in his late twenties, he wore vast baggy striped suits, the jackets halfway down to his knees and the trouser seats big enough to hide an army in, and he owned a grin of purest lip-smacking lechery, a monster. *Chantilly Lace* is his testament.

He's in a phone booth, ringing some girl, and he's having to hassle like mad to get a date out of her. He sweats, he giggles. He drools, overflows himself . . .

You can feel him wriggling his fat shoulders in delirium, his joke suit draped around him like a tent, his eyes bugging and his bottom lip hanging slack: 'Chantilly lace and a pretty face, ponytail hanging down, wiggle in her walk, giggle in her talk, Lord, makes the world go round round round . . . Makes him feel real loose like a long-necked goose.'* And all this time he's melting.

He's getting nowhere, of course, but he doesn't give up, he campaign shouts like a Southern democrat. The result doesn't matter anyhow, it's the performance that counts. *'Ooh baby,'* he howls. *'You know what I like. You KNOW.'* And when he says that, he bursts, he just disintegrates.

*Words of *Chantilly Lace* by permission of Southern Music Publishing Co. Ltd, London.

40

Apart from being so funny and good, *Chantilly Lace* was a big step – it was the first time ever that white popular music owned up to lust.

Also, in classic rock, there were instrumentalists but they came a bit later. Duane Eddy played guitar man. He twanged. He was from Arizona and he was a big country man, who just stood still on stage and laid down sound like someone playing at the bottom of the Cheddar Gorge. He didn't use the top of his guitar at all – it was all solid bass, big and booming. Sensitivity wasn't the name of the game but he made nice noise.

Apart from his own hits, he set the standard of all instrumental groups for almost five years. The Shadows copied him. So did the Ventures and just about everyone else.

Eddy had his first major smash in 1958, *Rebel Rouser*, and Johnny and the Hurricanes made it the following year. Johnny himself blew anguished sax and the Hurricanes featured a shrill little organ. Their records were strictly novelty, small musical jokes. My favourite was *Rockin' Goose* with Johnny pretending to be a wild goose on sax. It was one of the most ludicrous records ever made.

Gene Vincent had a bad leg. It had been first mangled when he was a child and later it was made worse in a motorbike smash. Because of it, he couldn't fling himself around the stage like other rockers. He could hardly move at all.

Instead, he went through his whole act in one fixed pose. He'd dress himself entirely in black leather, right down to gauntlets and high-heeled boots, and he'd stand with one leg thrown back, the other forward and his body twisted aggressively sideways, a bit as if he was just about to start a punch-up. There'd be a single spotlight on him and he'd look agonized. He had unruly greased hair hanging in rat's-tails across his forehead and a very painful mouth. The way he stood, so still, his body simultaneously thrust forward and dragged back, he looked like he was chained.

The image wasn't so very phoney – he had two fast hits in 1957 (*Be Bop A Lula* and *Bluejean Bop*) and things had looked good for a time but from then on it was all struggle. Simply, he couldn't cope. He had a constant pain from his leg and, in any case, he was naturally depressive. He went through repeated breakdowns and treatments and failed comebacks.

For a time he lived in Britain and he was always popular here but he couldn't cash in. He was in the 1960 car crash that killed Eddie Cochran, his closest friend. That was virtually the end.

He's still remembered with a lot of affection. He wasn't much of a singer but, in his calmer moments, he had great gentleness, built-in innocence, and he roused up protective instincts in some most unlikely people. Above all, it's not possible to forget the melodramatic picture of him in his black leather, gauntlets clutching the mike, his body twisted.

He has been back in Britain several times in the last years, made sporadic comebacks without ever getting very far but right now he has disappeared and nobody is sure where he is or what he's doing.

Next, the Everly Brothers. There were two of them, Don and Phil, and they sang in high nasal voices like dentists' drills. They sounded delinquent and when you saw them on stage, they had bony faces and sharp eyes, they looked like classic drop-outs and you might think that they were really mean.

They were Kentucky boys and troupers. Their parents were long-time country singers and straightaway dragged their sons in on their act. Through to their late teens, Don and Phil toured by summer, schooled by winter and kept travelling. When they got out of high school, they turned into rockers and very soon their parents were able to retire in comfort. In many ways, it was the classic showbiz story, the genuine Judy Garland article, but, as childhoods go, it must have been toughening and the Everlys were always the sharpest, most professional rockers of the lot.

Musically, they were pure country, only brought up to date a bit and given a rock bias. They'd use a fast shuffle beat, light and nervous, and throw their voices up high over the top in perfect and agonizing harmony, wild and clear and piercing. They even recorded their hits back home in Nashville, Tennessee, heart of all things country, and had publicity pictures taken of themselves eating ham and black-eyed peas. They're not easy to write about because they had no outrageousness, no major image, but, from 1957 to 1961, they turned out roughly the most consistently good records around – *Wake Up Little Susie*, *Bird Dog*, *Bye Bye Love*, *Walk Right Back*, *Cathy's Clown* and so on. They were melodic, tricksy, entirely original. They introduced the idea that sound was all-important, the words and voices and backing and production all fitting to make one great booming noise. And as they went along, they lost that look of awkward delinquency, that dirty squeal in their voices, and turned into nice boys again, smooth young millionaires. They sold almost twenty million records.

But just like most of the other rockers, things began to go wrong for them at the beginning of the sixties. They had to do a service stint in the Marines, which didn't help much, and then they started to fall out with each other. Whenever they toured here, there'd be an atmosphere of solid bitch. The music was still as good as ever but the background disturbance came across even on stage and mostly their records weren't hits any more. In 1964, they did a single called *The Ferris Wheel* and I thought that it was their best ever, a marvellous careering melody line above a deepdown throb beat, a kind of Spanish-Moorish chant turned into pop terms. In England, it struggled to the edge of the top twenty and then quietly died its death.

Ultimately, there was Charlie Rich.

Rich was an ex-Georgia cotton farmer and he was into his thirties, he had grey hair and a paunch. He looked most square, he was one natural-born ticket collector. Still, he wrote songs, played piano and sang. And he was beautiful, he was the most mellow sound in the world. He didn't have many hits, admittedly, but he kept going right through into the sixties and, always, he was classic.

His finest efforts of all were collaborations with Dallas Frazier, a song-writer. Best ever was *Mohair Sam*, made in the middle sixties, a work of genius.

And that's about where it ends, that was rock, those were the great rockers.

Looking back through what I've written, I'm struck hardest by two things – just how good the best of rock really was and just how sadly most of its practitioners have ended up.

I suppose the trouble was only that rock was such committed music, such a very specific attitude, so tied to its time, that it wasn't possible for real rockers to ever move on. Of course, this is a stock problem in any field – revolution so quickly becomes boring – but the thing about pop is that its generation cycles last five years at the very most.

Never mind: the best rock records stand up still as the most complete music that pop has yet produced. Everything about it was so defined – all you had to do was mix in the right ingredients, stir well, and you had a little rock masterwork on your hands. It was that simple, that straightahead and, finally, that satisfying.

Of course, rock wasn't ever anything like as complex, as creative as pop is now. Does that matter? It was Superpop. On its own terms, it was quite perfect.

5

HIGHSCHOOL

Southern rock was hard rock, Northern rock was highschool.

Stan Freberg made a record that summed up Northern rock exactly. In it, he's a record producer-cum-manager and he discovers a totally talentless kid who wants to be a rock 'n' roller. So he takes this kid and records him, standing behind him with a sharp stick to help him hit the high notes. And all that the boy has to do is sing the word highschool over and over again. His record is an instant hit.

Highschool wasn't a musical form. It was an attitude and that attitude read: 'We go to highschool. We dig rock 'n' roll. We date and go to parties and yes, we sometimes neck but no, we never pet. We also fall in love and that really burns us up. Then we pass notes in class and don't eat and even cry at night. We also think coke and hamburgers are really neat. We wear sneakers, short shorts, highschool sweaters. The girls have ponytails and the boys are crew cut. Our parents can be kinda draggy at times but, gee whiz, they were young themselves once and they're only trying to do their best for us. Finally, we dig America. We think it's really peachy-keen.'

There's a pop film that has been made maybe a hundred times over and it is the absolute epitome of everything highschool. A girl from a nice home falls for a singer in a rock 'n' roll group. He had a mean childhood, therefore he's a bit surly and sad but really he's a nice kid. The girl's father hears about this and orders them to break up. There is much tragedy and heartburn all round. Finally, the rock singer finds some way of convincing the father that he's all right. Everyone is happy. In the last scene, all the kids jive while the father gently foxtrots. Everybody laughs.

Where Southern rock introduced something new to popular music – noise, violence, the mixing of R&B and country, gibberish, semi-anarchy – highschool was basically a continuation of existing white traditions. The solo singers were pretty boys, very much in the tradition of Sinatra, Eddie Fisher or Vic Damone, and the groups sang harmony roughly in the style of the Ink Spots, the Four Preps, the Hi-Los or the Four Freshmen. All that was changed was that highschool catered solely for a teenage market and that it had no conception of quality whatsoever. Its very badness, in fact, is what made it attractive.

Another big difference was that Southern rockers, by and large, had been their own bosses. They had business managers but they conceived their records, worked out their stage acts, built their image all by themselves. Highschool rockers were almost always puppets.

Highschool is where the middle-aged businessman happened. He was a manager, agent, producer, disc jockey or general hustler. He found the act he wanted and also made a record. This record was then released and it either sold or it was hyped.

Hype is a crucial word. In theory, it is simply short for hyperbole. In practice, though, it means to promote by hustle, pressure, even honest effort if necessary, and the idea is that you leave nothing to chance. Simply, you do everything possible.

Hype has become such an integral part of pop that one hardly notices it any more. From certain angles, it's justifiable – you believe in your product and you spend money promoting it in every possible way. You have faith.

46

At any rate, the fifties were the golden age of hype. There was a huge scandal about in 1959, the payola fuss, and a lot of people came crashing down. Things have never been quite the same since. In the four years before the fall, however, everyone had themselves a carnival.

At the core of highschool was an unlimited assortment of faceless spotty groups. Mostly they made one big smash right off and then disappeared without trace. Sometimes they hung on for maybe a year. They hardly ever lasted longer.

The names and songs were virtually interchangeable: *Short Shorts* by the Royal Teens ('Who wears short shorts? We wear short shorts''), *At The Hop* by Danny and the Juniors, *Little Darlin'* by the Diamonds, *When* by the Kalin Twins, and so on *ad nauseam*. Almost all of them used a bass voice like a foghorn at the bottom, an anguished falsetto over the top and much mumbling in the middle. They cavorted and bounded and frolicked. They smiled constantly.

The true masters of the form, the originators and still champions, were the Platters, who derived from the Ink Spots. They had a good song-writer going for them, a man called Buck Ram, and they made a whole streak of hits – *Only You*, *The Great Pretender*, *Twilight Time*. Their strength was that they took banality to the point where it nudged real inspiration. 'Only you,' they sang, 'could make this change in me. For it's true – you are my destiny.'' And the high tenor wailed and choked, half strangled himself in his own chords, and the bass grumbled like a volcano. They rolled soulful eyes, hammed it like mad. It got you right there. And they were all coloured but the lead sang exactly like an Irish tenor. That's how confused they were.

Besides the groups, there were umpteen boys on their own and they were interchangeable, too. Frankie Avalon, Tommy Sands,

*Words of *Short Shorts* by permission of Essex Music Ltd, London.
*Words of *Only You* by kind permission of Sherwin Music Co., London. Copyright 1954.

Jimmy Clanton, Jerry Keller, even Ricky Nelson – they had neat hair, they had neat voices. Sometimes they made good records and more often they made bad. Whichever, it was irrelevant.

The most successful of them all was Paul Anka, a Canadian boy from Ottawa, who wrote a song called *Diana* when he was just past fourteen years of age and then sold nine million copies of it.

In his early teens, he'd been fat and a bit isolated. So he'd written songs and flogged them around, not with much success. Then he coughed up *Diana*. He didn't stop at that either: he sold thirty million records in five years. He was number one cute teenager.

He was a showbiz natural. He had a flashy grin and much confidence. He found no difficulty in posing with night-club managers, kissing starlets, winking at cameras and, therefore, he expanded easily from being just a singer into playing tycoon. Very fast, he was making an average half million pounds a year and was reputedly America's youngest self-made millionaire.

In 1959, to celebrate, he wrote a song called *Lonely Boy*:

I'm just a lonely boy,
Lonely and blue,
I'm all alone
With nothin' to do.
I've got everything
You could think of
But all I want
Is someone to love.[*]

Too bad, too tough, but he managed to keep going. Admittedly, he stopped having such big hits but he bossed a

[*]Words of *Lonely Boy* © Sparta Music Ltd, and reprinted by permission of Hal Shaper.

48

whole empire of music and production companies and, in a situation like that, who needs hits? Now he sits in Manhattan in splendour, an institution by his middle twenties, a perfection of all American dreams. He has it made. And all because inspiration hit him at fourteen and he wrote the lines: 'I'm young and you're so old – this, my darling, I've been told.'*Diana: it's the archetypal pop record.

Highschool was very much a family charade. Father was played by Dick Clark, a disc jockey who looked like an all-American choirboy and who, in the late fifties, got to be about the most powerful man in the whole industry. He was around thirty, married, and he was clean-cut as hell. He had a TV show called American Bandstand and, on it, he preached God, America, Mother, True Love and Washing Behind Your Ears. He turned into the voice of teen conscience.

Apart from his TV showcases, he promoted nationwide pop tours, giant ninety-day caravans which were notoriously rough on the artists.

Now his TV shows have gone down a bit but his tours still make fortunes and you'd be making no wild guesses to imagine that he was one of the very richest men in pop. Godly or not, he surely had his head screwed on.

Big brother was Pat Boone from Florida, great-great-great grandson of Daniel Boone. He started out in 1955 watering down other people's rock hits and then progressed to ballads and on to films. He was married with very many children and, like Dick Clark, he was a preacher. Interviewed, he suggested that his own moral strength was due to being regularly bent over the side of the bath and beaten when he was a child.

Musically, he was an updating of Perry Como, an ultimate in blandness, and he had thirteen million sellers. Through the

*Words of Diana by kind permission of Robert Mellin Ltd, London. Copyright 1957.

fifties, he sold more records than anyone but Elvis. 'It isn't me,' he explained. 'It is the will of God.'

Big sister was Connie Francis, a large lady from Newark, New Jersey, with a taste for sentimental ballads and a dirty great vibrato. She was ideal because she inspired no sinful thoughts in anyone. Sometimes she was given good rock songs to do – *Stupid Cupid*, *Lipstick On Your Collar* – but she always managed to make them sound as if they'd just been sprayed with insecticide. As a sideline, she studied psychology.

And that's just about all on highschool. Musically, it was a dog, but, as myth and noise and comedy food, it did have its perverse attractions and sold in quite phenomenal quantities – Connie Francis, Pat Boone, Ricky Nelson, Paul Anka, these were the real superstars of the fifties. Most of all, it was an exact reflection of what white American middle-class teenagers really liked and dreamed of. Probably it was the most POP pop ever.

6

EDDIE COCHRAN

Eddie Cochran was pure rock.

Other people were other kinds of rock, country or high-school, hard, soft, good or bad or indifferent. Eddie Cochran was just rock. Nothing else. That's it and that's all.

There's not much fact on him: he was born in Oklahoma City, October 1938, youngest out of five children. His family moved to Minnesota, then to California. He grew up to be one sweet little rock 'n' roller, a nice looker, and he made records and had hits. He played good guitar and worked on sessions in Los Angeles. He wrote songs, got to be quite big. He even toured England. And on 17 April 1960, he was killed in a car crash on the A1. He was then twenty-one years old.

As a person, there's even less on him. He looked like another sub-Elvis, smooth flesh and duck-ass hair and a fast tricksy grin, the full uniform. He was quiet, a bit inarticulate, a bit aggressive, and he cared mostly about his music. He was polite to journalists, helpful even, but had nothing much to tell them. I was once told that he had a deep interest in toads but I have no evidence on it. He was nothing special. He just came and went.

What made him such pure rock? In a way, it was his very facelessness, his lack of any detailed identity. With so little for anyone to go on, he seemed less a specific person than an identikit of the essential rocker, a generalized fifties blur, a bit pretty and a bit surly and a bit talented. Composite of a generation.

But he was something more than that, his songs were perfect reflections of everything that rock ever meant. They were good songs, hard and meaty, but that wasn't it. In every detail, they were so right. So finally rocker.

Summertime Blues, *My Way*, *C'mon Everybody*, a few more – there were only maybe half a dozen things that did him full justice but, between them, they added up to something really heavy.

There is almost a continuous storyline running through them. Eddie is still at school and hates it. Lives at home and hates it. Works in his holidays and hates that worst of all. Still, he's a pretty ready kid, can handle himself. And he runs in some kind of gang, he's a leader of the pack. Eddie Cochran, no punk or palooka of '59.

When he gets very lucky, his father gives him the car for the night and then things are wild. Of course, after he gets back home, four in the morning, bushed and busted, he is kept in for a fortnight but that's the name of the game: he can't win. The world rides him. When he works, he's paid chickenfeed. When he enjoys himself, he is automatically punished. Tough.

Still, when he walks down the street so nice and slow, his thumbs hooked into the belt-loops of his blue jeans, his hair all plumed and whirled, the girls look up from their chewy mags, sip coke through a straw and they think he's cute, real cute. Sure good-looking, he's something else. So, after all, he gets by.

You can see him: hanging around on the kerb outside the billiard hall. Slouching always last into class and who calls the English teacher daddy-o? Mooching along with his transistor radio held up tight against his ear, mouthing all the words but not making a sound. Real romantic visions. It's only some new version of the old American dream.

It's not as easy as it sounds. Anyone who can compress the atmosphere of a whole period into six songs, who can crystallize the way that any generation worked, must have something very unusual going for him. Pete Townshend of the Who is the only person who has caught the sixties in the same way and he has had to work his ass off to do it. Cochran did it almost instinctively. For that alone, I'd rate him very high indeed.

He was the first major American rocker to do a full, unaborted tour here and his impact was tremendous. He was the starting point from which British pop really began to get better.

He was a mover and writer and voice. He played his own things on guitar, he was really a musician. He sang songs that weren't just crap but did somehow get across a real basic attitude. All of that was new. No poncing about, no dressing-up or one-shot gimmicking: he was something solid happening. So Billy Fury saw him and woke up. Or the Beatles saw him, or the Stones, or the Who, or the Move. That's how things got started. And at the point, after the style of James Dean, Cochran got killed.

7

ENGLISH ROCK

British pop in the fifties was pure farce.

Nobody could sing and nobody could write and, in any case, nobody gave a damn. The industry survived in a state of perpetual self-hyped hysteria, screaming itself hoarse about nothing in particular. There was much assorted greed, schnidery and lunacy. Trousers dropped like ninepins. Sammy Glick would have had the time of his life.

Before this, in the early fifties, the biggest stars were people like Dickie Valentine and Anne Shelton and Joan Regan. Mostly they had come up through dance bands and, once they had established themselves, they were safe for life. Nothing changed from year to year. The stuff they sang was just as maudlin and meaningless as its American counterpart. Worse, they didn't even have that certain flair and style that made Sinatra or Como or Tony Bennett halfway bearable. They didn't have anything.

At this time, records weren't too important. The really big money was in stage performances and sheet music sales and, accordingly, the business was controlled by agents and publishers.

Especially publishers. They had a long-term agreement with the BBC by which they paid fixed rates to get songs plugged. In return, the BBC ensured that at least half of every popular music programme was made up of songs that had been paid for.

What it meant was that nothing got hard-sell plugging unless Tin Pan Alley willed it. Effectively, this was monopoly and, until the system was abolished in the middle fifties, it wasn't possible to have a hit song without falling meekly in line.

In these years, the industry was structured around the massed publishing offices of Tin Pan Alley. The men in control were mostly middle-aged and they ran very cautious businesses. If they had to be ruthless, they were always sentimental with it and many of them did truly believe that they were turning out quality. They tended to be married with children. They had great sense of tradition. If you asked them, they'd probably tell you that there was no biz like showbiz.

Rock knocked all of that on the head. Tin Pan Alley still thrives, of course. Publishers get a cut every time their records are played on the radio and they make deals, get rich as they have always done. But they don't hold control any more, they have no monopoly. No one interviews them on TV, no one fawns. They buy their new Rolls and no one is even interested.

Rock brought in operators who were younger, faster, tougher, cleverer. More complicated and more neurotic. In every way, more interesting. They were young hustlers who had probably been hanging around in some other trade, films or journalism maybe, and immediately saw rock as a gold-mine dream come true. Sometimes they genuinely liked pop and sometimes they didn't. Either way, they cleaned up.

Most of them were homosexual. They'd see some pretty young boy singing in a pub and fancy him and sign him up. They'd bed him and then they'd probably very quickly get bored with him.

The boy would fade and disappear again. Or, every now and then, he would turn out to be a stayer after all and he'd somehow keep himself afloat. It was this scrabbling, this desperate jockeying for favour that made the fifties such black comedy.

The first attempt at a major British rocker was Tommy Steele. Launched in 1956, he was eighteen years old, came from Bermondsey and had been a merchant seaman. He had a lot of curly blond hair and a grin as deep and wide as the Grand Canyon.

He was discovered singing in a Soho coffee bar, the 2I's, by a man called John Kennedy, a New Zealander in his late twenties. Kennedy had been around in a variety of trades and had flair, invention and a fast mouth.

Anyhow, he did a good job on Tommy Steele. He started him out as one more poor man's Presley but ballyhooed him with more energy, more imagination than anyone was used to. He swept aside obstacles like so much kindling, wouldn't slow up for anything. He was a truly obsessive man and barnstormed Tommy to number one in six months flat.

Give him credit, Tommy did his best to live up to the spiel. On stage, he squirmed and wriggled in all the right places, strummed his guitar till his fingers went numb, snarled animal, generally did the whole bit. Still he wasn't really cut out for it. The trouble was he wasn't evil enough.

As it turned out, he was natural showbiz. He had instant charm going for him, he was photographed with his mother and he kept right on flashing that bottomless grin. He was all hair and teeth. Adults took one look at him and weren't remotely fooled – the boy was all right. So he moved on from rock as fast as he could and turned to ballads, comic recitations, novelties. He played Shakespeare at the Old Vic and studied tap dancing and squeezed himself into evening dress. He even combed his hair and he was much loved by everyone. He was that all-time showbiz cliché, the lovable Cockney, always merry and bright. He had turned into a pop Max Bygraves.

Compare his saga with Elvis and you have the precise difference between the great American and great British entertainment epic. Elvis became God. Tommy Steele made it to the London Palladium.

Next in line was Terry Dene. He wasn't greatly talented, he had smooth features and he sang rock without giving it any personal flavour at all. What happened to him sums up the fifties very well.

He had bad nerves. Coming from roughly the same background as Tommy Steele, he had emerged out of the Elephant and Castle, but he wasn't anything like as brash or self-assured. He wasn't remotely tough. He was petrified, in fact.

He had a round face, unformed, childish, and he always looked as if he was on the point of bursting into tears. Very often he did just that, which made him ideal maternity-food for those as liked it. No question, the boy was cuddly.

All the time he had troubles. He wasn't much of a singer and often got the bird. This upset him. He'd brood until he got out of control. He'd be told to take a rest and he'd return glowing, earnestly promising reform. Things would go all right for a bit but inevitably he'd slip back. Then the cycle would begin again.

He didn't even get many hits. Factually, he was never more than a minor success but the press found him fascinating, his bring-downs and comebacks, his crises, and they plugged him like mad. This way, even by pop standards, he grew into a figure out of all proportion to anything he'd ever done.

In July 1958, aged nineteen, he married a singer called Edna Savage, a few years older than himself, and it was the fuss wedding of that year. The papers picked it up as a signal that even rockers were human, were capable of finer feelings, and ran it huge. The whole industry glowed with reflected pride. Terry Dene wept with happiness.

The next thing was, Terry got his call-up papers and went off to do his national service.

The press yelled bonanza again. The comparisons with Elvis were most lavishly drawn, the image of pretty young rocker giving up a fortune and selflessly marching away to fight for king and country was nudged home with a bulldozer. Terry himself was quiet and dignified. Edna Savage was proud of him, his mother was proud of him. For one week, he was a hero.

As Rifleman 23604106, he smiled for cameras, waved for weeping fans. He kissed Edna Savage good-bye and flashed a thumbs-up sign. A few hours later, though, having realized exactly what he was taking on, he burst into tears and collapsed. 'It was grim, man, just grim,' he said. 'I was standing up there with my tin tray, having my bit of food plonked down in front of me like all the others. The thought of me in that little bed with fifteen other blokes around – I felt real sick.'

Two months on, he got his medical discharge and made his ritual comeback. This time it didn't work. Edna Savage left him and nobody was proud of him any more. His records didn't sell. 'This time I'm older, sadder and much wiser,' he promised but no one believed him. He retired and came back, retired and came back again. He had a couple of years in badly-paid tours and everything was rough. Finally, he dropped out of sight.

That wasn't all: a couple of years later, he was seen standing on a Soho street corner, preaching the gospel with the Salvation Army. What he preached was repent your sins, change your ways before it's too late. Nobody much stopped to hear him.

He looked much older, greyer. But he said he was happy and fulfilled. He didn't want publicity, he wouldn't give interviews. For some reason, he didn't trust the press.

What's more, he stuck it out, he didn't break down. He went on the road and, as far as I know, he's still out there, preaching as he goes.

If Tommy Steele and Terry Dene were the fifties heavies, Wee Willie Harris and Screaming Lord Sutch provided the slapstick.

Wee Willie had his hair dyed flaming pink and wore a polkadot bow-tie like elephant's ears. Also, baggy candy-striped Big Bopper suits and neon shoes. All set off by an unchanging idiot grin.

Screaming Lord Sutch was nobody's idea of a genius musician either. He didn't need to be because he was a tireless self-publicist instead. Basing himself very much on the antics of Screamin' Jay Hawkins, he pulled all the standard stunts of the time – clambered out of coffins or dressed up like a caveman. What made him a stand-out was his persistence.

His gift was that whenever he looked like fading, he always managed some stroke. He stood for Parliament, got engaged, grew his hair long, tried some new form of fancy dress, hustled like mad. As stunts, they were lousy but they were also endless and, cumulatively, they worked.

He had real staying power. He has never had hits but he's outlasted everyone and still goes out for good money now. He's an institution. These days he has transformed himself into Lord Caesar Sutch and rides on stage in a chariot. Why the change? 'You have to move with the times,' says Sutch.

After the first wave of rock, there was a fast craze for skiffle, which was knockabout American folk song thumped out any old how on guitar and washboard. Its major attraction was that any musical ability was entirely irrelevant. All you needed was natural rowdiness.

Dustbin lids, tin pans, papers and combs – anything went. In no time, there were an estimated three thousand skiffle clubs in London alone. Admittedly, they shut down as fast as they opened, but it was still an impressive statistic.

The cult's leader was Lonnie Donegan, long-time banjoist with Chris Barber's traditional jazz band. He sang emasculated versions of old Leadbelly numbers like *Rock Island*

Line, belting them out with frantic energy and a built-in rasp. Then he moved on to custard-pie comedy routines like *Putting On The Style* and *My Old Man's A Dustman*. Good luck to him – he cashed in fast and didn't get his motives confused. What's more, he held on tight and still does well in, among other things, variety and seaside summer shows.

Much better than anything Donegan did, though, was *Last Train To San Fernando* by Johnny Duncan and his Bluegrass Boys. The genuine American article, Duncan had a wild whining voice, straight from the nostril and, if skiffle hadn't suddenly died an overnight death, he might have done good things.

As it is, *San Fernando* is my nomination for the best British record of the fifties. This isn't such a cosmic claim as it sounds. Check the opposition and you'll see that I'm taking no great chances.

In all this chaos and foolishness, the only person who had any remote awareness of what was really happening was a TV producer called Jack Good. Everyone else saw pop as a one-shot craze and rushed to cash in on it fast before sanity returned and everything returned to normal. By contrast, Good realized it clearly as a major phenomenon.

I suppose he was the first pop intellectual. He'd been to Oxbridge, had letters after his name and could spell words of more than three syllables. More, he knew that pop was going to boss the entertainment industry from here on in, that it was the product of real social change rather than publicity hype, that its possibilities were just about limitless.

As a producer, he was responsible for *Six Five Special*, *Oh Boy* and the other major rock TV shows of the fifties. In the sixties, he emigrated to America and produced *Shindig*, their best pop showcase ever.

He sent P.J. Proby to Britain in 1964. He dreamed up a musical version of *Othello*, Muhammad Ali to take the title part and Proby himself to play Iago. He even made a great record called *I Sold My Heart To The Junkman* by Lyn Cornell, an English version of an American hit, out-of-tune and hopeless but quite amazingly exciting, a little joke masterpiece. In every job he tried, he did something good.

I can remember hearing him interviewed on the radio once, sometime in the late fifties. He said that Elvis Presley was a genius and that he'd go down as one of the major artistic figures of our century. Even now, that would hardly go unchallenged. In its time, it was total anarchy. And his willingness to be outrageous, to shoot his mouth off blind at a sceptical audience was a big help in getting rid of rock's built-in inferiority complex.

The next figure to come along was Larry Parnes, who was a very big-time manager indeed and sold pop in bulk. He handled whole battalions of singers and gave them marvellous Technicolor names – Billy Fury, Cuddly Duddley, Marty Wilde, Vince Eager, Johnny Gentle, Dickie Pride, Duffy Power and so forth.

Parnes was the perfect fifties manager, meaning that he was shrewd, fast-witted and had natural publicity flair but didn't go further. He had limited imagination, didn't plan years ahead and didn't bother his head too much about art or progression. But he made money and avoided mistakes.

His first major property was Marty Wilde, who tried hard, had many hits and was a thoroughly likeable man but didn't have the magnetism to bring him right through. Billy Fury was different.

Fury was the closest that Britain ever got to producing a genuine rocker, someone almost in the class of Eddie Cochran. For one, he was a face, high cheekbones and moody little eyes and a comma of hair drooping down on his forehead. For two, he was a mover, he rolled his hips like he almost meant it.

Originally, he was a scouse called Ronald Wycherley and, when he was in his middle teens, he wanted to wear drainpipe jeans but his father wouldn't let him. So he'd sneak out of the house into the back yard and hide his drainpipes in the outdoor lavatory. Then, when the time came to go out, he'd saunter away all innocent in his baggy flannels, whip round the corner, up over the back lane wall, rescue his drainpipes from the can and finally hit down in full splendour. That was determination. That was his exact difference – could anyone imagine Tommy Steele or Terry Dene going to all that trouble just to be an image rocker?

He was a merchant seaman but did some singing and songwriting on the side, and the way he was discovered was very typical of the period and of the way that Larry Parnes functions. In 1958, he got the ferry to Birkenhead, where Marty Wilde was doing a one-nighter, and played a few songs in Marty's dressing-room. Larry Parnes overheard him.

Five minutes later, Ronald Wycherley was Billy Fury and was playing bottom of the bill. When he came off stage, he dashed back home, packed his case and joined the tour. Real Eddie Cantor stuff – no fuss, no messing about, no nothing. Just go out there and sing and get paid. The rest, as they say, is history.

On stage, he was best at agonized balladeering, face contorted and hand clutching at nothing, thin body all racked and buckled with sadness. When things got going, he'd wrap himself around the microphone like a python and rape it. This got him banned in Ireland and fussed about even in England. So he toned down. Still, just for a moment, he'd been wild in there.

He was strange. When he was at his peak, around 1961, he moved into the country and took up bird-watching. Ornithology became his great driving passion. He said that he couldn't talk deeply about himself to people, couldn't relax with them but he felt much happier with animals. 'I'm an introvert and an extrovert,' he said. 'I'm an exhibitionist on stage but I can't tell anyone about myself, I freeze up. I don't want anyone to know.' When he talked, he mumbled and stared at his hands. He was tense and, in some odd sense, genuinely innocent.

He has lasted well. His records tend not to be hits any more but he has a big following and goes down a storm in cabaret. He's still managed by Larry Parnes and they go along steadily. In the North, even after ten years, he gets mobbed in the streets.

Fury was one prong of the triumvirate that dominated British pop from about 1959 until the Beatles first broke through in 1963. The other two were Cliff Richard and Adam Faith. Of the three, Fury was the most exciting, Faith the most intelligent, Richard the most competent. What they had in common was that they ended up smooth. In every way, they became presentable. They had tidy smiles and non-committal accents and nice manners. They tended not to make fools of themselves in public. Between them, they made pop singers almost respectable.

Cliff was easily the most successful. His great secret was that he was like a magic slate, a pad on which almost anyone could scrawl their fantasies and rub them out and try again. He was the nice boy that girls could be proud to date, the perfect son that mothers could be proud to raise, the good nut that schoolboys could be proud to have as a friend, the earnest youth that intellectuals could be proud to patronize, the perfect flesh that homosexuals could be proud to buy drinks for, the showbiz smile that hipsters could be proud to despise and so on. It was a format that Tommy Steele had used first and that the Beatles were later to perfect. It is the classic British way of making it – be a clean white wall and let everyone write graffiti on you.

At the time when he got his first hit, 1958, he was seventeen. By any standards, he was adult for his age, very cool and knowing indeed. Probably that's why he never let himself be conned or mismanaged. Whenever it counted, he was always shrewd.

He started out as one more computerized rocker, one more sexy mover and sub-Elvis rebel, but this wasn't ever his natural style. He wasn't butch enough for it, he didn't even hint at rape. Instead, he sang in tune and showed many toothpaste teeth. He was sleek, glossy. Most important, he was amazingly scrubbed, he radiated a kind of glowing cleanness that ordinary mortals couldn't even hope for. With all that going for him, rock was out. He was born to sing ballads.

His first ballad hit, *Living Doll*, was by far the most influential British single of the whole decade. It was cute and sweet and bouncy. It was tuneful and ingenuous. It was the British equivalent to highschool – and it was desperate. In months, it took over completely. No rage, no farce, no ugliness left. We had mass-produced faces with mass-produced voices on mass-produced songs. It was as bad as the pre-rock early fifties all over again. That's mostly why the Beatles were hailed as such messiahs when they first started.

It has to be said that Cliff at least did it well. He was unassuming, he worked hard and he came to be very professional. He was insipid and syrupy but he wasn't nauseous. He was modest and thoughtful, essentially decent.

When Beatlemania came along, Cliff took it well. He praised the Beatles' records, refused to bitch back when they were rude about him, held on to his dignity at all times. He just slid neatly into the background and looked benign. After all, he made upwards of a hundred thousand pounds a year and could afford to be kind.

His most lasting influence, however, hasn't been his singing, his conversion, even his white smile, but his speaking voice. Before him, all pop singers sounded what they were, solidly working class. Cliff introduced something new, a bland ramble, completely classless. It caught on – David Frost uses it. So do Simon Dee, Sandie Shaw and Cathy McGowan. Admen and publicists and hangers-on everywhere. Ambitious kids ape it and it has become the dominant success voice. I'm not suggesting that anyone deliberately copied it from Cliff but he was where it first broke through – that's the kind of area in which pop is most genuinely powerful.

The Shadows, who had been his backing group all this time, were almost as successful as Cliff himself. There were four of them, three guitars and drums, and they made records of their own, almost all of which went straight to number one – neat little instrumental, entirely unmemorable and played with total lack of any emotion. On stage, they wore evening dress and the three guitarists shuffled forward and back in unison. At moments of great climax, they'd turn quickly at right angles and kick one leg out limply from the knee. Then everyone would scream.

I've never figured out just why they made it so big. Partly because of Cliff, I suppose, and partly because they shared his clean innocence and partly out of habit. Partly perhaps because they were musicianly, and partly because their tunes were always easy to hum. Most of all, because there were no real challengers around at the time. At any rate, they were fiercely worshipped and imitated and, on the Continent, they were the most influential sound ever.

Even now, if you're traipsing around the backwaters of Morocco and you stumble across a local group, they'll sound exactly like the Shadows, flat guitars and jigalong melodies and little leg kicks and all. In Spain or Italy or Yugoslavia, they're regarded as the pop giants of all time. Elvis Schmelvis, Beatles Schmeatles. Viva los Shads!

The only Shadow I've ever been able to warm to at all is Hank B. Marvin, guitarist and song-writer. He wore huge black spectacles and had many spots and was nobody's idea of beautiful. When he was younger, he must have felt quite self-conscious about it all and to respond by christening himself Hank has always struck me as quite a splendid act of defiance.*

*The Shadows have now disbanded.

There were other big successes at this time: Frank Ifield, a large hunk of Australian baritone with an alarming line in yodelling; Helen Shapiro, who had a truly foghorn voice but was badly over-publicized and didn't sustain; Eden Kane, who growled; David Jacobs, compere of the long-running TV show *Juke Box Jury*, the last word in mister smooth; Emile Ford, who was excellent but he was also coloured and that, ten years ago, was just about that; and Norrie Paramor, a small middle-aged man with glasses, mild and harmless, who produced hits for Cliff and the Shadows and Helen Shapiro and, by his very harmlessness, summed up everything that had gone wrong.

The best of the bunch was Adam Faith, who was at least an original. He was a marvellous face, classic bone structure, but he was also very short and had to wear monstrous high-heeled boots if he wasn't to be dwarfed by his infant fans. He didn't have much of a voice either, he was all nose and tonsils, a poor man's Buddy Holly. What he did have, though, was good management, good song-writing, good plugging and, most important, a certain persistent oddity, a real individuality.

His first number one, *What Do You Want?*, was one continuous hiccough, a dying fit, agonized and agonizing, the words contorted almost beyond recognition. He spewed up the word 'baby' as 'biybee', choking horribly on each vowel, and that was the major hook. So all right, maybe it wasn't any profound insight into the human condition but it was catching; it made him. One word mispronounced and he had his whole career going for him.

Natch, he flogged it hard, spluttering and expiring like a man inspired, and he did very nicely. In retrospect, his big hits – *Poor Me*, *Someone Else's Baby*, *How About That?* – stand up as the best, most inventive British records of that time, the only truly POP music we were producing then. They still sound active now.

But the most important thing he did was to introduce the concept of Pop Singer as Thinker, now so popular with documentaries and the Sunday papers.

Originally, he got interviewed by John Freeman on *Face To Face*, a chore he shared with such as Jung, Gilbert Harding and Tony Hancock. Freeman put up a series of nice slow lobs for him and Adam fended them off very capably – his favourite composers were Sibelius and Dvořák, he said, and his favourite book was *Catcher In The Rye*, sincerity was the quality he would most like to be admired for, that and being an individual; thirty was about the right age to get married. That kind of thing. Hardly sensational but he spoke it neatly, smoothly. He was strictly non-moronic.

Soon, he was to be heard discussing morals, sex before marriage, just about anything solemn that got thrown at him, and this was where pop began to go up in the world. Slowly and humbly, admittedly, but upwards just the same. All through the fifties pop had been desperately unfashionable, the last word in non-chic. Outside its immediate public, it was seen simply as a joke.

Now, mostly because of Adam, it was getting to be accepted. It was becoming something of a fashionable status symbol and that, of course, is where the Beatles cashed in.

Finally in this chapter, Jimmy Savile, who was our best disc jockey. Come to that, to me, he was our only disc jockey.

In America, DJs have always been big business. People like Dick Clark or Murray the K have been superstars, one-man industries, phenomena on a par with anything but the very biggest stars of all. Mostly they have been maniacs, hurricane spielers, throwing out ads and jingles, music and patter and noise like one-armed bandits gone berserk. Their shows are brainstorms and their music is only one part of the attraction. That's what jockeying means.

British jockeys have never been in the same class. Most of them sound like BBC announcers, neat, laundered, boring.

They have nothing to do with pop. They aren't jockeys at all, in fact, they're only men who put on records.

Until Emperor Rosko arrived in the middle sixties, Savile was the only genuine exception. He's a Yorkshireman, an ex-miner of indeterminate age and he has different-coloured hair almost every time one sees him, usually peroxide blond, occasionally pink or striped or tartan.

As an antidote to all the mid-Atlantic that surrounds him, he uses an exaggerated staccato Yorkshire accent and waves his arms, rolls his eyes, hams like mad. He isn't good-looking, smooth or even very funny. But he wears amazing costumes, looks like something from space and works his ass off. His one card is outrage.

He isn't an easy character to unravel. He's shrewd, hard-headed, but he has wide naïve streaks and he can come on horribly sentimental at times. He makes at least fifty thousand pounds a year, lives in a council flat and allows himself only £9 a week spending money. On the other hand, he raises thousands of pounds each year for charity, flogging himself really hard at times. In a way, it makes sense: his hunger is not for owning money but for making it.

Beyond being a jockey, he's a wrestler and keeps himself painfully fit. When he's in London, he lives in a room under the stairs of a small King's Cross hotel, a miserable little box, and he works out endlessly with dumb-bells.

So he's mean, hard-headed, tireless, a marvellous raconteur, truly original. He's crazy like a fox. And with the money he makes, who wouldn't be crazy the same way?

8

RUE MORGUE, 1960

Nineteen hundred and sixty was probably the worst year that pop has been through. Everyone had gone to the moon. Elvis had been penned off in the army and came back to appal us with ballads. Little Richard had got religion, Chuck Berry was in jail, Buddy Holly was dead. Very soon, Eddie Cochran was killed in his car crash. It was a wholesale plague, a wipe-out.

Why didn't rock sustain? Not easy to answer. Partly it was because the vintage rockers were so ill-fated. Partly it was because they weren't flexible – they did what they did perfectly but couldn't progress. But mostly it was because pop is by nature ephemeral, it must change constantly to keep alive and not even the very best things can hold.

New people came up to replace the gone heroes, of course, but they weren't in the same class, they certainly weren't flat-out rockers. Hard rock was done. What had replaced it was a continuation of highschool. Most of them were just as forgettable as their predecessors: Brian Hyland, Jerry Keller, John Tillotson and, a bit later, Bobby Vinton. Bobby Vee was not much better but was given good songs like *Rubber Ball* and *Take Care Of My Baby*. The only stand-outs were Neil Sedaka and Dion Dimucci, two of the most underrated figures in the whole of rock.

There's not much to be said about them, just how good they were and what lasting records they made. Sedaka came from Brooklyn and trained as a classical pianist. Then he knocked off songs for Connie Francis, Clyde McPhatter, LaVern Baker. Then he began to make records of his own. Almost without exception, they were classics.

He was quite some writer. He'd start out steady, build up gradually and then, when he snapped into the chorus, the hook, there'd be a real explosion. It isn't possible to explain it right but he'd come out with a sudden aching, pulling figure that used to make me catch my breath and count. It had nothing to do with words, it was purely musical. Something would burst.

His best sides were *Breaking Up Is Hard To Do* and *Oh Carol* and *Happy Birthday Sweet Sixteen*. Ten years on, they still make me gasp every time I play them.

Dion, who had hits with the Belmonts before he went solo, was simpler. He was just given some hit songs and he did them well – *Little Diane*, *Runaround Sue*, *Ruby Baby*, *The Wanderer*. He was a format singer, meaning that all his singles sounded alike, which was fine by me. They were a bit like catch songs, everyone singing different riffs and chasing each other, and this gave them a curious circular feel. Comforting. His best was *Little Diane*: 'I should knock you down and slap your face – bad girls like you are a disgrace.'*

He went through a long bad patch in the middle sixties but made one beautiful record in 1967, *Mr Moving Man*. And then, out of nowhere, he cut a major 1968 American smash, *Abraham, Martin and John*.

Neither Dion nor Sedaka was strictly a rocker but they were in direct line of descent. That's how they came to be so good – they had drive, guts, when everything that surrounded them was jellyfish and flabby.

*Words of *Little Diane* reproduced by permission of Spanka Music Ltd, London.

Why had everything gone so dead? Really, it was a failure of imagination, a simple inability to think things out from basics.

When rock had come along, it had changed everything, it had seemed the complete answer and the industry had got used to the idea that what you had to do was, say, imitate Elvis, change his format slightly, add a mandolin, take away a triangle and you were automatically made. They weren't far wrong, of course.

But each imitation was a small emasculation of the one before, each rehash took things further and further away from the original hub. Pop ended up as a copy of a copy of a copy. Teenagers got bored, records sold less. In the end, there was just nothing left and that was 1960.

Nineteen sixty was the gap between two separate generations, the changeover, and the reason it was so bad was really that pop moves in very specific generation cycles: there is one breakthrough, followed by maybe three years of great excitement, followed by three years of stagnation, followed by a fresh breakthrough. Each cycle takes roughly seven years to run its course and 1960, of course, was the stagnant bit.

Seven years seems nothing but it's really surprisingly much. After all, one pop generation really only lasts four years, the time it takes to get from eleven to fifteen and, again, from fifteen to nineteen, and a seven-year cycle means that a whole generation gets skipped.

Why does it work like that? Probably because seventeen-year-olds are up too close to things, they don't see straight. When someone like Elvis first explodes, they buy his records and copy his looks but it goes no deeper, it's only imitation.

With fourteen-year-olds, however, it becomes a big part of growing up – Elvis is their great adolescent hero, he's central. They buy their first suit and have their first sex and promote their first hangover with him in the background. And then they have five years in which they can distance him, get him

71

into perspective and absorb him deeply. So when they come to do things themselves, they don't ape him but use him to form their answers.

Roughly, that's why 1960 was bad and, in the same way, that's why 1963 came good.

Also, Tin Pan Alley was back in the catseat. As soon as record sales began to fall, the music publishing world decided gleefully that hard rock was finished and they shut out everything that wasn't highschool. Instead of yakety saxes and greasebox bass, the big black sounds of classic rock, we all got stuck with Disneyland.

Tin Pan Alley, of course, saw this as a clean-up campaign, a repudiation of all that sinful jazz music, a return to decency. Ironically, though, 1959–60 became the ultimate golden age of hype – the only way to make kids accept the prevalent crap was by flat-out payola and so the swing back to godliness was turned into the dirtiest period that pop has been through.

Also, this was the time of the Beach Party movies, made by American International and starring such as Tommy Sands, Frankie Avalon, Annette (ex-Mickey Mouse Club Mouseketeer) Funicello and Fabian.

These were unchanging epics – there were always a lot of cleancut bodies in bikinis and briefs, a few songs, a few bad jokes, much suntan and sand and water, hundreds of flashing teeth and endless cheerfulness. Seen in retrospect, they're camp and they're true Pop Art, they say more about Campbell Soup than Warhol ever did. As 1960 teen entertainments, though, they were nothing but dire.

All of this, the whole 1960 bit, was epitomized by Fabian.

His real name was Fabiano Forte and he came from Philadelphia. When he was thirteen, he was signed up by two local recordmen and computerized.

To start with, he had the basic requirements – olive flesh, duck-ass hairstyle, conveyor-belt features. He had the required passing resemblance to Elvis Presley. On top of this,

his management did the full Professor Higgins bit. They had him groomed, had him taught to speak nicely, had his voice trained. Made him round and flawless like a billiard ball.

One snag: he couldn't sing. He ran through voice teachers the way old-time Hollywood stars once ran through wives. What did that matter? His management launched the biggest publicity campaign ever, besieged the trade papers for weeks on end, howled him from rooftops. Fabian himself only stood still and sparkled.

Once the snowball had got started, it was hardly stoppable. In no time, Fabian was going out for twelve thousand dollars a night and then he sold a million of a record called *Tiger* and then he was into movies. Not just crap movies either – he was in *North To Alaska* with John Wayne. Later, he got married and was duly mobbed. And all the time, he could hardly sing a note. That's highschool. So, all right, he's less than mister big these days but what should he care? He's rich. He made it.

Outside of the prevalent highschool pulp, however, there were three originals from this time – Roy Orbison, Del Shannon and Gene Pitney. They had a lot in common. For a start, they weren't amateurs.

They had good strong voices and none of them did much cavorting on stage, they just stood up straight and did their act without fuss. Then they were song-writers, businessmen and they were built to last. They were shrewd. Between them, they added up to the first major onset of professionalism.

Out of the three of them, Orbison was easily the most impressive. No question, he wasn't a likely-looking pop star but he could cut just the same. He had a pudgy, pasty face, very white and sickly. Then he was chronically short-sighted and had to wear glasses as thick as lemonade bottles. No Mr Universe. But he had a classic voice, perfectly controlled from mumble through to full-blooded yell, and he approached his songs like operatic arias.

Usually he set off almost conversationally then broke into tortured tempo, got gradually more fevered, more tragic and finally wound up in frantic howls of anguish. It was a formalized pattern, used on almost all his best records, and he had it by heart. He never missed a trick.

If your nerves were bad, the unbroken agony of it all might get a bit oppressive. But if you were suckered by schmaltz, Orbison was the very best brew going. Whatever, he attracted great regiments of fans and, in Europe, they've stayed endlessly loyal to him. Outside of Elvis, he has the most unquestioningly devoted following going.

Not that he has stuck exclusively to ballads. In his time, he's rocked harder and longer than most but he always sounds as if he wants to slow things down and, even at his toughest, he's always liable to launch himself into sudden spasms of bug-eyed operatics.

Orbison was born in Texas in 1936, and, by his teens, he was writing Country 'n' Western. In the fifties, he was on to rock and wrote *Claudette*, a million seller for the Everlys. So by the time he recorded *Only The Lonely* in 1960 and finally made it big, he'd been ten years in the business. An old pro, battle-hardened. That's how he came to sustain so well.

He was a quiet man, not flash or imposing, not outstanding in any way. He was polite. When he wasn't touring, he stayed home in Texas with Claudette, who was his wife, and they played motorbikes together. Finally, she had an accident and was killed. Orbison put out a record called *Too Soon To Know*, very much based on her death, and it was a big European hit.

He's still a good performer. The last time I saw him was at the 1966 *New Musical Express* poll-winners' concert and he shared the bill with the Beatles, the Rolling Stones, the Walker Brothers, Cliff Richard, the Shadows, Dusty Springfield, the Who and umpteen others – full flower of British pop. With hardly any exceptions, he cut them into pieces.

74

He wore something like an out-of-work flamenco danc-er's outfit, high-waisted trousers and boots and a tatty little jerkin. Then his puff-pastry face and those impenetrable tinted glasses. All the time he was on stage, he didn't move an inch, didn't even nod his head. He just stamped his foot, stood his ground and belted.

Why was he good? It was something to do with presence. Everyone else was frantic, ran themselves crazy trying to whip up reaction. Orbison just commanded: the big O. He sang nothing that hadn't been a major hit for him – *Running Scared*, *Pretty Woman*, *In Dreams* – and he banged it out so solid, so impossibly confident that he made everything that had gone before seem panicky. He'd been around, had twenty years behind him. Almost on his own, he knew what it was all about.

(Orbison is based in Nashville, Tennessee, and this is maybe the place I should mention Nashville in some detail.

Basically, it's the centre of country music but it handles a lot of pop as well; it carries more recording sessions than anywhere outside New York. Most everyone works there – Elvis Presley, the Everlys, Joe Tex, even Bob Dylan, and then the straight Country 'n' Western acts, Johnny Cash and Chet Atkins, George Jones and Buck Owens and Hank Snow.

It's a strange city, filled to overflowing with guitar pickers by the thousand, all scuffling, and, at its highest levels, the music community there has formed itself into some kind of unofficial club, managers and publishers and artists. To get accepted into this, you have to be very big indeed, you have to be a monster but, once you've made it, you're in for life and you're looked after, you're just about guaranteed work for as long as you can walk. You're in an oligarchy and you can never fall.

Roy Orbison is in this league.)

Del Shannon was along the same lines, meaning that he had a lumberjack voice and never budged. Not as oper-atic as Orbison, he just wound himself up until he roared, from where he gradually got louder and louder and louder, climaxing with a frantic falsetto shriek. All it took was a lot of lung-power and one sharpened stick. Simple but effective.

He has always been one of my heavy heroes. He charges head-on at his songs like some angered bull, mauls them, bangs them against the board until they're shattered. Over the early sixties, he turned out long streaks of worldwide hits and wrote them himself – *Runaway, Hats Off To Larry, Two Kinds of Teardrops, Swiss Maid, So Long Baby.*

On stage, there was the same appeal. Shannon was pretty sawn-off and wore his big guitar slung high across his chest, so that he had to haunch to get at it. That made him look aggressive and he stood square and howled. Beautiful songs, beautiful noise. Pure pop. The backing pounding along like a cavalry charge, all organ and percussion, and Del himself bull dozing through everything. He could have knocked down brick walls, that man, he could have demolished skyscrapers.

There wasn't much more to him – he was originally an out-of-town boy from Grand Rapids, Michigan, but he turned into very much the spruced, smooth-voiced young businessman, shaved and manicured, toting a smile like a slot machine. That didn't matter: he sang like someone else entirely and it was his records I cared about. Raunchy might be the word I need.

If Del Shannon looked like some kind of budding executive, Gene Pitney came on like a full-blown tycoon, which was exactly what he was. He was of Polish extraction, and money interested him deeply. Deals – they lit him up like neon.

The one time I met him, he was in his hotel room and he was talking business on the long-distance telephone. Shirt torn open at the neck, tie twisted, sweat marks under his armpits: classic Hollywood image. As he talked, he moved one hand in small upward circles, as if he was trying to conjure up something tangible out of the air. Like banknotes. So I stood there, waiting to get noticed, and he looked straight through me. I wouldn't say he was ignoring me. I'd really say that he didn't know there was anyone else in the room.

Ballads were his meat. Tearjerkers, monstrous flowerpots that made Roy Orbison's songs sound like Woody Woodpecker symphonies in comparison. And he had a big voice, a fine range and most professional projection, but he chose to sing in a whine like an electric saw. Cutting, needling, excruciating. It has given me more real pain than any other voice I've ever heard. I can't be objective about it: it nags me like a toothache.

Still, he's sharp. His judgements have been cautious, unadventurous but always accurate. And, even forgetting England and America (he has always been bigger in England than in the States), he has huge followings in Europe, in the Far East, in Australasia, almost everywhere. He commutes endlessly. He makes deals, cuts hits, accrues, amasses.

On stage, he looks small and has a schoolboy's face, round and unused, his hair slicked flat across his skull. He stands still in a single spotlight, all lost and lonely, one hand in his pocket, the other extended towards his audience, and he wades through heartbreak ballad after heartbreak ballad. Between numbers, he sits on a stool and reads out sentimental letters from his fans. His audience hushes for him as if he were making a funeral oration. Then he sings more ballads and he looks sad as hell, trapped inside his spotlight, and everyone feels sorry for him. Mothers adore him.

It's all a bit like a recital, he carries himself like an updated Richard Tauber. Everyone is miserable. When he completes each song, he looks down and stares stonily at his feet. You almost expect him to let drop a rose. Anyhow, his control is remarkable, he never drops a stitch. By the time he's through, even those who hate him most, even me, we feel like we've been swimming in a cement mixer.

Most important of all, there were the Four Seasons.

In pop terms, the Seasons were freaks – they were four bodies of ill-assorted shapes and sizes, all getting on a bit, and they looked like bank clerks, accountants, floor managers, they looked like anything on earth but they never looked like any pop group.

As it happened, they weren't only pop, they were the most POP pop ever. I mean, if I had to explain pop to anyone in one throw, I'd just play them a Four Seasons record – *Sherry*, *Rag Doll*, *Big Girls Don't Cry*, *Let's Hang On* or *Dodie*.

The thing was, they had a lead singer called Frankie Valli and he had the most piercing falsetto ever, a monster, an excruciating screech and, whenever he really let it go, he'd shatter plate windows all across the city. It was the ultimate deterrent and it was also beautiful, it was a thing of true wonder. It would scream out of your hi-fi like some insane air-raid siren and it deafened you, destroyed you, turned you blind. So you'd stumble and shake in the sheer wildness of it. You'd be tripped out on sound alone.

They had two ultra-shrewd hustlers behind them, Bob Crewe and Bob Gaudio, producers and writers who kept them fed with natural hit songs and, from 1961, they've peddled a string of American smashes, they've hardly looked like slipping. Almost every time they've walked into the studio, they've cut some major classic. Altogether, they've probably turned out more mind-snappers than any other group in the world and it's only in the last year or so that they've finally hit trouble.

There's not much to say on them, they're not analysable. They're perfect, that's all.

Then there was Brenda Lee, who didn't make sense. Just five foot tall, she looked like an all-time peak in highschool teenybop. She wore wide party dresses, very likely with frilly petticoats underneath, and she had an unformed elfin face, hugely grinning at all times. She chewed gum, read comics. Had outbursts of adolescent spots and pimples. Wore high heels and nylons on big nights out. For Chrissake, she was even her school cheer leader.

She came from Atlanta, Georgia, a real Southern girl, and she was making hits by the time she was eleven: Little Miss Dynamite. Right through her teens, she alternated singing and going to school. Her songs were just what you'd expect, bouncy little routines, halfway between rock and country. And the only thing that didn't make sense about her was her voice, which was freakish, making her sound thirty at least and sexual, knowing, very world-weary indeed. By the time she was seventeen, she had a ballad style along the lines of Edith Piaf, as used and bravura as that.

She could be magnificent. She conjured up real three in the morning visions, ashtrays full of ends and lipstick smears on the coffee cups, small rancid rooms, off-hand desperation. Then she'd come out and she'd be like some kewpie doll, all sheen and varnish and eyes that really roll. It was this woman/child contradiction that made her happen. Myself, I couldn't ever take it.

When she grew up, the greatest part of her appeal inevitably fell away. She got married and had a child. Still, she looked amazingly innocent, she wore the same bobbysoxer uniform as ever, but it just wasn't the same thing. So her records stopped being hits.

Her voice hasn't changed, still feels like bad whisky. Sometimes she puts out new singles and they're not good songs, not well produced or anything but, herself she cuts through it like a laser beam. If only she didn't look so precisely like Little Orphan Annie.

In any case, she made no difference. Nor did Del Shannon or Dion or Orbison or Neil Sedaka. Nineteen hundred and sixty meant doldrums just the same.

The point is that pop doesn't work around good records or pretty voices or cute people – those are only details. Really, it happens off superheroes and superdollars, off hyped mass hysteria and deepdown social change, off short-term collective insanities. People aren't relevant.

79

9

THE TWIST

'I'm not easily shocked but the Twist shocked me . . . half Negroid, half Manhattan and, when you see it on its native heath, wholly frightening . . . I can't believe that London will ever go to quite these extremes . . . the essence of the Twist, the curious perverted heart of it, is that you dance it alone.' Spot the mystery voice? Right first time: Beverley Nichols reporting from New York in January 1962.

It's strange the way the Twist got so fussed about. Realistically, it was the least sexual dance craze in forty years. With old faithfuls like the jitterbug and the jive, after all, the girls spun like tops and everyone got fast flashes of knicker. With the Twist, you got nothing. Just Chubby Checker telling you to imagine that you'd had a bath and were towelling your back. Approximately as carnal as cornflakes.

Well, pop was now sunk neck-deep in pigshit and it needed something violent, something quick to pull it out again. Never mind if it be real or phoney, straight or hyped, just so long as it could hit. And it happened that there wasn't anything real available at the time, so hyped it had to be.

And the Twist was lying around. Most of it would have been a scraped grade-C fad, maximum span of six months. Another hula hoop. But 1961 was parched, was really desperate. So first Chubby Checker had a hit record. Second,

New York smart society decided that the Twist was cute and started to hang out in the Peppermint Lounge. Third, the gossip columnists jumped aboard. Fourth, the whole industry started hyping. And fifth, madness set in.

At this point, enter something like Beverley Nichols on a white horse and suddenly you get visions of kids copulating on dance floors, mass national debauch and the breakdown of all known moral standards, the collapse of Western civilization. Strong stuff: that's the way the money grows. So now you finally have a story, a phenomenon. All right, so nobody really gives a damn and nobody ever will. That isn't quite the point.

The Twist wasn't even new. Hank Ballard, who had been around on the R&B scene ever since the early fifties, wrote the original song in 1958 and had a specialized hit with it. Dance-craze records have always been a stable part of the Negro market and nobody paid much attention.

Two years on, Chubby Checker re-recorded it and got himself a national breakout. Checker was Ernest Evans from Philadelphia and had been a chicken-plucker. He looked something like a young Fats Domino and he played it up, he even bowdlerized the fat man's name (Fats Domino = Chubby Checker: do you dig it?). Truthfully, he wasn't much talented but he was shrewd, he found himself with a hit on his hands and he hammered it. He twisted like a maniac. Demonstrated it on television, diagrammed it in the papers. Lost thirty-five pounds in a year just pretending to towel his back. So the Twist seemed almost fun and it caught on. Journalists satirized it gently, how ludicrous and freak it was. The Peppermint Lounge, just off Times Square, hired a group called Joey Dee and the Starliters and they played Twist all night every night. Chubby Checker cut *Let's Twist Again*. Even Elvis had a twist song, *Rock-A-Hula-Baby*. This was all getting to mean big business.

Here's where something odd happened. New York social-ites, truly smart people, started to haunt the Peppermint

Lounge. Elsa Maxwell and Greta Garbo and Judy Garland, Noël Coward and Tennessee Williams, the Duke of Bedford. Everyone, as they say, who was anyone. All of them twisting like there was no tomorrow and looking very foolish indeed. Inside weeks, you had to spray twenty-dollar bills like confetti even to catch a glimpse of the dance floor.

This was only odd because no jetsetter had ever shown any remote interest in pop before. Not a flicker. In the fifties, it had seemed hip to like the more refined end of modern jazz – Miles Davis, the Modern Jazz Quartet, even Thelonious Monk. But not rock and roll music. Anything but that. The thing to be was cool and there was nothing cool in pop. Certainly not in fat Negro chicken-pluckers from Philadelphia.

But the sixties were something different and it was suddenly fashionable to be frantic again. It was like the twenties, the Scott Fitzgerald thing, the Charleston, all that dazzle and fevered decadence. So pop was permissible. Amusing. Jackie Kennedy was rumoured to twist. In London, Margot Fonteyn shook it down in public. In Paris, so did Jean Cocteau.

This is where it started, the hysterical adulation of pop singers by the rich and trendy all over the world. It became hip to know Joey Dee, hipper to know Checker. Huge status to be publicly snubbed by Phil Spector. A bit later it was paradise to be entirely ignored by the Beatles. And by 1966, Mick Jagger was the most wanted guest in the world, the final face, the ultimate. For one pout of his red lips, any millionaire hostess would have promised away her life.

Why pop? Because the yen was all for youth and beauty and, if nothing else, pop was always young, always beautiful. Because pop made its money for itself. Because it spoke so coarse ('common as dirt, darlings, isn't he divine?'). Because it was what's happening, babydoll. What more reason does anyone need?

Out of this arose a whole new superclass and how did you qualify? You only had to be a face. And what was a face?

82

Roughly, it was when you walked into any snob restaurant anywhere and everyone sensed you come in behind them and automatically turned round. You were young, flash, international *Vogue* said you were. Now. Exactly, you were the beautiful people. Names: Terence Stamp and David Bailey and Jean Shimpton and Terry Donovan, Rudolf Nureyev or Margot Fonteyn, Andy Warhol, Baby Jane Holzer, Justin de Villeneuve, Twiggy. Not Truman Capote or Norman Mailer or Elsa Maxwell or even Marlon Brando. But definitely not. This was a most exclusive league. Muhammad Ali was its patron saint. Princess Margaret and Antony Armstrong-Jones were its recognized monarchs. Most super of all superstars.

Anyhow, once the faces had showed at the Peppermint Lounge, the Twist ballooned almost instantaneously from a fad into an industry. The papers pissed themselves. Big money got invested. Very quickly, there were Chubby Checker T-shirts and jeans and ties. Chubby Checker dolls. Or Twist skirts and Twist raincoats and Twist nighties. Conveyor-belt Twist movies. Ballrooms had their biggest boom in decades. Everyone cleaned up. And the insanity was that, even now, nobody really cared. Try finding one truly hooked twister and you'd have had quite some search. No competition, the Twist was the most total hype ever.

The one thing remotely interesting about it, as Beverley Nichols noted, was that you danced it alone. Suddenly, dancing wasn't anything to do with romance any more, nothing to do with fun or companionship or any stuff like that. Instead, it became pure exhibitionism, a free platform for sexual display and, down among the teenybops, that passed for kicks.

Certainly, the Twist's appeal was nothing to do with its music, which was always drab as hell – its cuteness was simply that it allowed kids to do something that would have got their faces slapped for them in any earlier generation, namely to stand up in public and promote their ass. And all right, so it looked foolish, but it felt illicit – that was the full equation.

It didn't last long. Well, it wasn't really meant to. In any case, it was replaced by other dances, other campaigns and the same people went on making money. In the absence of any dominant individuals, dance-crazes bossed pop right up until the Beatles broke. There was the Hully Gully, the Madison, the Fly, the Pony, the Popeye, the Mashed Potato, the Dog, the Monkey. A bit later, the Slop and the Waddle and the Frug. The Jerk and the Block. Right on into these last years and the Boogaloo, the Philly Skate, the Sanctification, the Beulah Wig. The inspired Funky Broadway. That's not all. Endless and interchangeable steps. Go to a club one week, go back the next and everyone is moving differently. There are kids who devote all their lives from sixteen to twenty-one in mastering dances that nobody else is up to yet. It's a full-time career. More than a career – an art almost. At the least, a vocation.

Dancing was a focus. So was radio. Between them, they made up the hard centre of early sixties American teen romance. They bossed.

Millions of kids up in front of their bedroom mirrors, getting hip to the Pony with the Good Guys on station WMCA. Or out in the park on the Hully Gully from the All-Americans on WABC. Or sipping coke through Murray the K's Monkey on 1010 WINS. That's the way the fantasy went. It was a self-contained cycle, twenty-four hours each day, DJs spieling like maniacs all across the nation and music splintering and feet shuffling, butts twitching by the megaton. It didn't ever have to end, it needed no improving. It was perfection.

Radio was a big surprise comeback. Television had completely taken over in the forties and fifties, but now steam was huge all over again. Not to be listened to, not like before TV, but as an endless burble background for teenage daydream. It was all music, no speech and no interruptions allowed – kids didn't like talk, they flipped dials fast to another station. So the only way a DJ could survive was to develop a spiel so fast, so smooth that it became music on its own. No message, no sense to impart. It was pure noise: 'So hit me one time, that's a groove, that's nice baby, ooh mammy-o, lay it down, sock it to me, John, George, Paul and Ringo, Fab Four, babydoll, it's what's happening, baby and bam bam bam –' starting as a rumble and rising gradually to an unending Hitlerian scream. It was like electricity, it was like glass. It was just there.

Murray the K was king jockey. Of all DJs ever made, he spieled hardest, fastest, loudest and longest. Hustled the biggest deals and pulled the biggest strokes. In his hysteria and unflagging speed, he entirely epitomized the phase.

He was an American Jimmy Savile, meaning that he wasn't hip or heroic in the least but that he won out on brashness alone. He was in his late thirties, a sturdily-built businessman, and he wore Stingy Brim straw hats, tight pants, lurid shirts. He could have been a successful insurance salesman from Ohio going berserk on Hawaiian vacation. But still he talked blind streaks and never ran out of wind.

His catch phrase was 'It's what's happening', he used it all the time. And he rocked in his seat, he roared and hollered, pounded, went purple in the face, but he never once stumbled in his spiel. Never ever. He was surrounded by tapes: commercials, one-shot interviews, trains, cavalry charges, explosions, weird-beard laughs, end of the world screams. In between, he even played records. Everything was impetus. Murray the K, wham bam thank you mam. Interminable shows like roller-coaster rides: he's what's happening.

He outstayed all rivals, beat them blind when it came to cunning. In the very early sixties, he was unchallenged top dog and then naturally, because American DJs hardly ever last, he began to flag. By early 1964, he was definitely on the slide.

Right then the Beatles flew in for their first American tour. At this moment, they were at their utmost peak, they had the top five records on the American charts and they were the hottest properties ever. And when they touched down at Kennedy Airport, they went straight into press conference, there to be interviewed by the cream of the nation's journalists. And, strangely, by Murray the K.

It wasn't ever a fair contest. The journalists huddled together and fired questions. But Murray the K somehow wriggled through their legs and got right to the Beatles' feet, crouched there and just about crawled up them. Stingy Brim hat, maniac leer and his stick mike pushing upwards, ever upwards. His mouth shooting questions all the time. And he stole it, he broke it up. He turned a formal occasion into a face. So Paul McCartney looked down at him. 'Murray the K,' said Paul. 'Cut out the crap.'

Immortality: the nation's pressmen got routine, Murray the K got exclusives. 'Cut out the crap.' That's all. Nirvana. Quite possibly, it was the scoop of the century.

From there, he hounded the Beatles like Charlie Chan. He roomed with George Harrison and taped his thoughts just before going to sleep, just after waking. Dubbed himself the Fifth Beatle and got away with it because who could resist such nerve, who could fail to be secretly impressed? So Murray came back to New York with a mountain of exclusive tapes and played them endlessly. Sample:

Murray the K: 'What's happening, baby?'

Ringo Starr: 'You're what's happening, baby.'

Murray the K: 'You're happening, too, baby.'

Ringo Starr: 'O.K., we're both happening, baby.'

By the end of the tour, Murray was right back on top again and stayed that way. He made one hundred and fifty thousand dollars a year. Sold Murray the K T-shirts and hosted albums of Murray the K's Golden Gassers. And his resourcefulness is such that he might never end. He summed it up himself. 'I'm not riding the Beatles' coat tails,' he told Tom Wolfe once. 'If they go, I'm going to be ready for the next person that comes along.'*

Crude stuff maybe but it was something, at least it was action. It wasn't 1960 and blackness. Everyone was up and running again. We were back to pop.

*The Kandy-Kolored Tangerine-Flake Streamline Baby by Tom Wolfe (Jonathan Cape, London 1966).

10

SPECTORSOUND

So Phil Spector is in some plush night-club and he's dancing with his wife and he's doing no harm to anyone. He's around twenty-two years old and he is five foot seven, nine stone, and he has long ratty hair hanging all down his shoulders and he has a high-pitched mincing voice and he's wearing totally outrageous clothes. At this time, in the early sixties, he is a freak. But he has made about twenty straight hit records and earned two million dollars and he's the hottest thing in the whole of pop. And he dances with his wife and minds his own business.

Suddenly he feels something tugging his hair from behind and he turns round and there is this large man. The man starts calling him filthy names, terrible dirt, right in front of Spector's wife. The man is an animal and he keeps tugging Spector's hair. Spector stops him. 'I'm going to tell you this one time, that's all,' says Spector. 'Don't ever try that again.' And he fixes the man with terrible eyes, he burns him, assassinates him with one look.

So what happens? So the man reaches out and knocks Spector halfway across the room.

'I mean, I've studied karate for years,' said Spector later. 'I could literally kill a guy like that.'

Spector was born in the Bronx and his father died when he was nine. So his mother took him out west to California, teen paradise, and he grew up small, runtish, with bad hair and unhealthy skin. But he was clever, he was really talented and he had imagination. So when he was about seventeen, he wrote a song called *To Know Him Is To Love Him* and formed a group called the Teddy Bears and the record sold around two and a half million copies across the world.

The title? Spector remembered it off his father's tombstone: 'To Know Him Was To Love Him.' That was very typical.

This was in 1958 and two years later he was a major producer at Atlantic Records and very soon afterwards he had his own label, Philles Records, and was cutting huge hit records every time he walked into the studio. *He's A Rebel* and *Da Doo Ron Ron* and *Then He Kissed Me* by the Crystals, *Be My Baby* and *Baby, I Love You* by the Ronettes, *Zip-A-Dee-Doo-Dah* by Bob B. Soxx and the Blue Jeans – every one a beautiful noise and every one a monster smash.

He was a real breakthrough. Before him, it might have been allowed for kids to turn into stars and get their names in the papers but they never managed, produced or hyped, they were never in control. Pop was still overwhelmingly a middle-aged industry. Then Spector came through and knocked all that down.

He was a tycoon: he gave orders, made things happen, was responsible to nobody but himself. What's more, he was disgustingly successful. On nothing but energy and knowledge of what records were about. At one throw, he destroyed forever the concept that pop took experience, that you had to be a long-time businessman. And he showed up the business as slow and flabby and hopeless, an industrial joke. For this revelation, the middlemen – distributors and pluggers and hypers and publishers – never forgave him.

But he was more important than that. What he really spelled was huge good news for losers. There he was, seventeen years old. He wasn't tough and butch and boorish, he wasn't one of the boys. He thought that most Americans were

89

animals and he became agonized at the very first hint that he was being crowded. Simply, he wasn't equipped.

So he went into pop and became a millionaire. Just like that. From start to finish in five years. Insulated himself against everything that he loathed. Grew his hair long and wore fancy dress and adopted a falsetto. Was outrageous in every way possible. Then not only did he get away with it but he even became famous for it, he was celebrated. So all right, he was talented, very talented indeed. Just the same, he'd done something extraordinary.

Except, of course, that he was dancing in a night-club once and a large man knocked him halfway across the room. It's not so easy, that's America. Then he had to hire bodyguards. Even with two million dollars, he still couldn't get left in peace.

Anyhow, Phil Spector was the first man to see pop as the new natural refuge of the outsider. The place you could make money and cut yourself off from filth and also express whatever you wanted without having to waste half your lifetime looking for breaks. The way he saw things, America was sick and pop was healthy. It was uncharted territory and its potential was endless. It was teenage property. In all these ways, he was an important signpost for the hippies that followed him.

Otherwise, though, he wasn't so much in any dada-beat-hippie tradition as a pop bowdlerization of Oscar Wilde. Meaning that he was sharp and bitchy, fastidious, vulnerable, and that he was a culture snob, that he had great style and that you always felt he was doomed. He even looked rather like Wilde, he had exactly that kind of ostentation.

His most persistent image of himself was paranoid – creative Phil Spector hemmed in by cigar-chewing fatties, beautiful Phil among the uglies, groovy Phil versus hair-tugging America. His records were his best revenge.

They were dirty great explosions, guerrilla grenades. They were the loudest pop records ever made.

90

Spector himself was a prodigy, knew more about the actual mechanics of recording than any other producer before or since. Most producers say what they want and their engineers provide it but Spector ran it all, understood every last insignificant dial or switch in his control box and bossed it. So what he did, simply, was to assemble all of the noise in the world and then ride it.

He was demoniac. He'd take one good song and add one good group and then he'd blow it all up sky-high into a huge mock-symphony, bloated and bombasted into Wagnerian proportions. Magnificent, chaotic din: he'd import maybe three pianos, five percussion, entire battalions of strings. Drums and bass underneath like volcanoes exploding. Tambourines by the hundredweight. And he looked down from his box and hurled thunderbolts. Added noise upon noise, explosion on top of explosion. Until it wasn't the song that counted, the voices, nothing like that but only the sound, Spectorsound, and the impetus. Momentum, lurching and crushing and bursting, and it couldn't possibly be stopped.

That's my image of him: he's up and burning in his box, his long hair wet, his face collapsing and, under him, there's impossible sound but he drives it, he keeps adding to it and still he can't ever make it finally loud enough. So when you bought Phil Spector records, you were buying no throwaways but huge frantic outpourings of spite and paranoia, rage and frustration and visioned apocalypse. And if you were teenage, you probably felt exactly the same way and you loved it. That's how Spector came to make two million clear at the age of twenty-two.

At any rate, everything was good to him for a time but then he wasn't cut out for serenity, it wasn't his style and he couldn't hold. For one, he'd made it, he'd achieved everything possible and what in hell did he do next? For two, the Beatles came along, early 1964.

Spector had been number one pop phenomenon in America and now the Beatles replaced him. He wasn't the youngest, the newest, the wildest any more. He was definitely last year's model. Life was drooping. Stung, he made his best throw yet, *You've Lost That Lovin' Feeling* by the Righteous Brothers, and it was also a world monster. It was also endlessly brilliant.

Still, he wasn't made happier. He was more capricious all the time. He was afraid and had premonitions. (There's a famous story about how he stopped a plane just before take-off and wouldn't fly in it because he felt something creepy about it. Something wiggy.) And he had always been hooked on image but now he was getting obsessive: he plunged his whole office into darkness and, when anyone went to do business with him, all they could see was his shape in the gloom, all they heard was his voice squeaking out of nothing.

Early in 1966, he made his best cut, *River Deep – Mountain High* by Ike and Tina Turner, and it failed in America. Very possibly, it was the best pop record of all.

It was total brainstorm – Spector was louder, wilder, more murderous than he'd ever been and Tina Turner matched him, big earth woman, one scream of infinite force. At one time, there's an instrumental chorus and everything thunders, crashes, gets ready for final dissolution. Tina snarls and wails in the background. Then she screams once, short and half-strangled, and everything goes bang. That's the way the world ends.

In England, it made number two but what's England? In America, it bombed, got nowhere. Spector was destroyed. He wrote off American record-buyers as finally moronic and stomped off into the California desert to make art movies. Nothing much came of this. After about a year, rumours came filtering through that he was about to make a comeback. He made one more record with Ike and Tina, *I'll Never Need More Than This*, and it duly bombed. After that, nothing.

What else can he do? He has made money but he has spent a lot. He hasn't taken root in movies, right now he's making records again but he's been through all that already. Most of all, he's only approaching his late twenties and he has his life to fill in.

It's been quite a melancholy little story. Poor little rich boy perhaps but still a sad saga. After all, he has real talent, he is one of those very few who've genuinely had what it takes. Spector and Elvis and Charlie Rich. Mick Jagger and Pete Townshend. P. J. Proby. Then who?

His big stumbling-block has been the problem that every major pop success faces and hardly anyone solves: when you've made your million, when you've cut your monsters, when your peak has just been passed, what happens next? What about the fifty years before you die?

11

CALIFORNIA

California is teen heaven. It is the place that pop was created for. Chuck Berry did a song about it called *The Promised Land* and, like always, he knew what he was talking about.

This California is hugely enlarged reality, verges on complete fantasy. In pop, it is the joob-joob land far beyond the sea, where age is suspended at twenty-five and school is outlawed and coke flows free from public fountains and the perfect cosmic wave unfurls endlessly at Malibu. The home of the lotus eaters. And it has been made like this when kids live in grey cities, tenement blocks and it keeps raining and they know this can't be right, there must be something better. California is the something better.

No drag lives there but only sun, sun, sun. Surf in the morning, hotrod later and maybe a barbecue at night – isn't that the way that life should be? Surf city, two girls for every boy. Drive-ins and Muscle Beach Party. California dreaming: that's what Chuck Berry meant.

To fit these fantasies, California pop has always been like comic strips, continuing images of sand and sea and sun, everything drawn bright and clean and simple.

It hasn't ever properly grown out of highschool. As late as the middle sixties, West Coast heroes were still pictured sitting in class all term, passing sly notes to the school iceberg.

At night, they went to drive-ins and necked. At weekends, they bombed up and down the coastline in their hotrods. Eddie Cochran would have understood it perfectly. And when summer came and school was out, they went down to the beaches, surfed, barbecued steaks and danced barefoot in the sand. That's when they also fell in love, happily or unhappily, and they stayed that way till fall. Then they went back to school and started all over again.

It was a tightly limited world, very compact, very secure, and there are people around who see it as a vision of hell but I'm not one of them.

Anyhow, it was a storyline that never seemed to run out of steam and, from 1960 on, which was about the time that California developed a specific pop identity, separate from all other highschool, it was variously used by the Beach Boys, Jan and Dean, the Hondas and the Rip Chords and the Rivingtons, Ronnie and the Daytonas, Dick Dale and umpteen others. The market was inexhaustible. All you had to do was throw in the right dream words, wipe-out and woody and custom machine, and you were home. Californians bought you out of patriotism and everyone else bought you for escape. The more golden your visions, the more sun-tanned your sound, the better you sold. It was almost that simple.

Musically, as well as emotionally, it was all updated highschool, big bass voice at the bottom and careening falsetto up above. All that was new was the efficiency with which it was done.

Because California pop tended to be competent. Sometimes it even used quite complex arrangements, lines interweaving, voices unexpectedly juxtaposed, even a bit of counterpoint. More, nearly everyone sang in tune. As pop, it was light and flexible and fast. Vastly attractive. And it was perfected by the Beach Boys.

In the first place, the Beach Boys were three brothers, Brian and Dennis and Carl Wilson, and one cousin, Mike Love.

Rounded out by a local boy soprano called David Marks. All five of them lived in Hawthorne, California, and went to school and surfed.

This was the beginning of the sixties and surfing was everything, it was the maximum West Coast cult. It had been a major world sea-sport ever since the war, a bottomless box of myths and remembered afternoon heroics, but it had been mostly post-teen, mostly the property of hairy athletes in their mid-twenties. Now, by the early sixties, schoolboys had finally got wise to it and they were altogether hooked.

It was understandable hysteria – imagine yourself riding waves, everyone watching you, girls gawking, and you have this one small board under your feet, that's all, but still you swoop and soar, fly free and nothing can bring you down. You walk the water. And so fast, what speed, what poise, what godlike splendour. No wonder bikinis pop. No wonder your classmates turn their heads away (boy, were their faces ever red?!?). And at the end, you tuck your surfboard under your arm like some briefcase and walk up the beach so cool and easy, not looking to left or right, not even caring. Still the greatest. Then you lay down in the sand and starlets queue to feel your muscles. That's surf fantasy. No more peacock sport was ever invented.

Anyway, the Wilsons surfed like everyone else and Dennis, who was a light golden colour, who was good-looking and fit and always made out with girls, was very smart at it. But Carl and Brian were overweight and weren't so hot. Carl was the youngest and even-tempered by nature and he didn't mind too much. But Brian was the eldest, the most intelligent, the most talented and he didn't like fatness one bit.

Around 1962, the Wilsons formed themselves into a group – their father was a long-time song-writer and it was almost inevitable that they'd get involved with pop – and Brian, being the cleverest, became their writer. What he wrote about was surf.

Amazingly, this was the first time that any specifically surf music had been written, the first time that California was given its own pop identity. Out of nowhere, though, Wilson wrote songs with titles like *Noble Surfer, Surfin' Safari* and *The Lonely Sea,* and they were wild.

He worked out a loose-limbed group sound and added his own falsetto. Then he stuck in some lazy twang guitar and rounded it all out with jumped-up Four Freshmen harmonies. No sweat, he'd created a bona fide surf music out of nothing. More, he had invented California.

He adapted Chuck Berry's *Sweet Little Sixteen* and called it *Surfin' U.S.A.* This was the great surf anthem, the clincher: a hymn of unlimited praise. Next, in 1963, he did *Surf City* for Jan and Dean and it was a national number one. So surf was suddenly American big business and Brian Wilson ruled it.

It made sense. Maybe he did have flab problems, maybe he wasn't Mister Surfing Universe but he wrote the songs, did the real work and Dennis just sat at the back playing drums. Other kids surfed better but gremlin Brian Wilson articulated it all, made pop poetry from it, got rich off it. Inside very few years, he could afford to hide his belly inside a Rolls-Royce he'd bought from Brian Epstein.

Very quickly, he expanded from surf to hotrod, the other major West Coast obsession, and then further into generalized pop. He handled things well, kept progressing all the time. By the time that any fad burned out, the Beach Boys were inevitably long long gone.

His car songs were beautiful. Hotrods brought out a huge sentimental streak in him and he wrote real flowerpots. When his cars won, he celebrated them like monster heroes and, when they broke down, he mourned them like dying lovers. His great maudlin falsetto quavered and ached, the harmonies behind him went dirge-like.

There was no subject too soap-opera for him to take on. He churned out *A Young Man Is Gone,* an ode to the departed

James Dean, and *Spirit of America* and *Be True To Your School*. At the same time, he did some fine rejoicings, full of energy and imagination – *Shut Down*, *409*, *Little Deuce Coupe*. Fine rock and roll music but brought up to date, kept moving and not left to atrophy. Best of all was *I Get Around*.

What Brian Wilson was doing now was making genuine pop art. No camp word-plays on pop but the real thing. He was taking the potential heroics that surrounded him and, not being arty, not being coy in the least, turning them into live music. Simply, he'd taken highschool and raised it to completely new levels, he'd turned it into myth. As far as I'm concerned, this was his best period.

By now, he had established the Beach Boys as the most successful group going and he was tired. He had all the songs to write, all the decisions to make and, at the same time, he was on the road, travelling and losing sleep, huddling in cockroach dressing-rooms. Generally hustling himself half to death. Then, from late 1964, he was under pressure from Beatlemania and the Beach Boys went through a bad patch, their records sold less. So he thought he needed time to reflect, space to stretch in and he decided he'd stop touring, leaving the rest of the group to keep on gigging without him. He'd stay home in California and write masterworks instead.

Since that time, he has been increasingly withdrawn, brooding, hermitic. He has developed strong mystic traits, runs in no gangs. And occasionally, he is to be seen in the back of some limousine, cruising round Hollywood, bleary and unshaven, huddled way tight into himself.

Musically, meanwhile, he has travelled a long way, most of it backwards. As he has become more and more of a recluse, so he has got increasingly hooked on the concept of Wilson as creative artist. No more surfboards and hotrods, no more amateur mythmaking. Instead, he has emerged as a full-blown solemn romantic, turning out successions of near tone-poems, fragile pools of sound, very limpid. Small choirs running through mock-fugues and rambling boy sopranos. Sad songs about loneliness and heartache. Sad songs even about happiness. Sometimes it works and then it's exquisite – *Caroline No, Here Today, Don't Talk (Put Your Head On My Shoulder)*. More often, it's just sloppy.

On *Heroes and Villains*, for instance, he worked nine months and came up with a product lasting for a couple of hours or so. The record company took one small snippet from it and released it as a single. Net result: a medium hit, a medium record, not bad by any means, but certainly not in the same class as the stuff he'd once knocked out on a lazy afternoon.

It wasn't so hard to understand what had gone wrong. When the Beach Boys first started out, pop wasn't too complicated, it was mostly a knack, a certain game to be mastered. Either you could do the trick or you couldn't. Brian Wilson could do it perfectly. The way he wrote car songs, so simple and obvious but still so improbable, it was something like the way Muhammad Ali fights, Elvis moves, Brigitte Bardot looks sexy. That's rating him too high but it isn't grotesque. By any standards, he had instincts, strange talents and you couldn't explain them.

Later on though, after he stopped touring, he wasn't doing tricks any more, he was playing no inspired game. He was being an artist.

This was fine: it was good that he should progress, that he should attempt outside his depth. But he took himself too solemnly, he was mildly megalomaniac about it all. Almost, he was ashamed of pop. He got snob. Running so fast and precious, his hat got away from his head.

(This wasn't his only problem. His other trouble was that, like all talented and intelligent pop writers, he found himself stuck in an entirely phoney position. Understandably, writers want to grow up and progress. But their crucial audience, the people who finally buy their records, are maybe sixteen years old and by no means hooked on experiment. Pop is always teen music. People in their twenties may be interested, may think it is smart to namedrop but, basically, they aren't consumers. They don't spend. So you have stalemate: the writers aren't allowed to go forward, don't want to stand still, can't go back. They're wedged from all sides. Their big failing is only that they're too intelligent. If they were robots, things would be forever simple.

Given all this, how can pop ever move? How can it be adult and still sell? How can it make itself understood to teenagers and not be stagnant? Probably, it's the most urgent dilemma in the industry and I'm not very sure that there's any real answer.)

Brian Wilson is hardly a loser. He still writes big hit records and the Beach Boys still go out for fortunes. But that's not the whole object: he has real talent going and it isn't working itself out right. The pace has gone off him and, off-hand, I'd lay money that *I Get Around* will be the best record he'll ever make. Partly that's his fault, partly it's pop's, partly it's nobody's. Whatever, it's a waste.

California pop, in general, happened mostly in Los Angeles and Hollywood (San Francisco, at this time, still thought that pop was maybe vulgar), and a whole new breed of young West Coast hustlers was emerging, managers and artists and producers, and they were sharp, they took California over.

These weren't the beautiful people. They were hard nuts one and all, and they got very rich very quick. Hardly lovable, but they did understand pop, they made good records and they made things happen. No time wasted, they turned California into the most hip centre in world pop.

Almost invariably, they were obsessed by image. They spent the most part of their lives competing for cool, racking up points in some undefined but desperate struggle for gloss. How did they sit and how did they move and how did they speak? How did they pull? Who did they sleep with? How did they look when Phil Spector walked in? How was their high?

Did they sweat? Was the TV in their car black-and-white or colour? The battlegrounds were endless and the competition deadly. Blow your cool just once and you were gone.

You can't really play image unless you're well surrounded at all times, stooged and bodyguarded, set off like some precious stone, things arranged and the people sit and light cigarettes for you. You must do nothing yourself. Just sit there and project. Just ooze out cool. And because of this, the West Coast produced hangers-on even more abject, more agonized than other places. It was the bottom.

Hollywood is always like that. Losers by their thousands: once they'd have been around movies and now they used pop, the true Pat Hobbys of their time. Promotion men, all toupee and seersucker suit. Publicists and pushers and just bodies. The Rolling Stones got them quite right: 'I'm sitting here thinking just how sharp I am – I'm an under-assistant West Coast promo man.'*

Most of these aforesaid hustlers were pretty boring but not Nick Venet. He had managed the Beach Boys once but hadn't quite kept it, had made definitely erratic progress from there on in. Still, he always kept going. He made some surfing records, did records with Timi Yoro. Produced and directed a documentary on Mississippi peace marches. Really, he was an amazing stayer, the kind of man who's always around, never beaten.

Dark and florid and flash inside camel-hair coats, he looked the eternal operator, a B-feature heavy, and he talked entirely in declamations, slogans, odd little sayings. I had lunch with him once. 'I'm known as the Gutsy Greek,' he told me. 'I got where I am by hustle, bustle and elbow-grease.' Everything he said was ornate, an attempted proverb. 'Even stopped clocks are right two times a day' or 'The music is the maestro' or

*Words of *West Coast Promotion Man* by permission of Mirage Music Ltd, London.

'When the Gutsy Greek strikes, he never miss.' I was most impressed, liked him enormously. 'Baby,' he said. 'Unto thine own self be true.' With advice like that, how could I possibly miss?

The centre of Californian hip was Lou Adler. He managed Johnny Rivers and Jan and Dean (later he also discovered Barry McGuire, P.F. Sloan and the Mamas and the Papas but they belong in another chapter). He owned Dunhill Records, too, the most astronomic of all independent West Coast labels. And he was a millionaire.

Jan and Dean had a streak of surf and hotrod hits, mostly written by Brian Wilson, and acted as something like Adler's lieutenants, his Rosencrantz and Guildenstern. They weren't notably talented but they were pure California, all clean and golden, and they were given hit songs to record.

Johnny Rivers was a small roughneck from Louisiana and he was America's first major discotheque star. Discos were an early sixties development, an improvement on big impersonal concert halls. The idea was that you had an intimate night-club atmosphere and played mostly records, with only occasional live acts. First and last, discotheque records had to be dancing records and that's just what Rivers turned out.

He played Hollywood's Whisky A Go-Go and laid down a most solid beat, nothing fancy, just four-square all the way. Sang old classic rockers like Chuck Berry's *Maybellene* and Willie Dixon's *The Seventh Son*. Chalked up hit after hit. Never smiled once.

He epitomized the Hollywood cool. Slouching and shrugging and looking mean, he gave me the toughest interview I ever did in my life. Every question I asked, he answered by grunting. High grunt for Yes, low grunt for No. And all the time I was there, he looked straight past me at Lou Adler and Adler looked back at him, both of them expressionless. This wasn't being moronic, this was being cool. This was image.

After some time, he left the room and came back with shades on. Nothing changed much, nothing improved. When I left, he did shake hands with me and moved his mouth. 'I'm Johnny Rivers,' he said. 'Who are you?'

Adler himself was a very successful man and a very tough one. Tough and cool and clever. From the whole Californian image race, he emerged as the runaway winner, a walkover. If you were a would-be face and you got accepted on his team, you were making out fine.

The nucleus of this team was his contracted product – Jan, Dean and Johnny Rivers. Brian Wilson, whenever he came out of hiding, tended to string along. Then a few lesser lights to make up the numbers.

They were perfectionists. They were the most rigid of all possible societies. Every last detail was studied, checked and rechecked. No clumsiness, no fractional uncool allowed. Mistakes simply didn't happen. No one laughed out loud, no one waved his arms, nobody ever made fools of themselves. Everyone was watchful. The etiquette was crippling.

I have a photograph of the Adler team in London. They have tried to get into a hotel restaurant and have been told that they can't sit down without ties. So they're all sitting around a corner table – Adler, Johnny Rivers and assorted flunkies and girls – and the men are wearing T-shirts, flash jackets and so forth but they're wearing completely incongruous ties, old school models supplied by the restaurant. They look quite ridiculous. But they're not smiling, they're deadpan. They see nothing remotely funny. Well, that's California cool entirely summed up.

Obviously, this was all a long way from the original 1960 dream. Wasn't innocent or highschool whatever. Just the same, California has remained the great pop Utopia: let's all go to San Francisco.

The semi-illusion still survives that West Coast life is somehow essentially freer than anywhere else. If I ever get there, the dream goes, I'll live in a penthouse and drive Cadillacs and spend my money without thinking. More, I'll develop perfect flashing teeth and my body will go a light golden colour. I'll become oddly fascinating. And I'll even be able to adopt slouching Brando cool without being ludicrous.

The California promise, then, is that you won't be a person any more, not just a slow and boring human being like all other humans, but you'll be somehow magnificent. Overnight, you'll be transformed into something heroic.

12

SOUL

In its simplest terms, soul was only updated rhythm 'n' blues, a rehash of the same old format that has dominated Negro music for the past thirty years, and the only thing new about it was that it has been gingered with a big fat shot of gospel.

In the thirties and forties, big-city coloureds had used their music mostly in first-degree escape. If they lived in the ghetto, if they were poor and badly housed and hopeless, they could at least look flash on Saturday night and shake down to Cab Calloway or Chick Webb, Stick McGhee or Louis Jordan or Wynonie 'Mr Blues' Harris, or whoever else happened to be big at that particular time. The musicians fitted themselves sensibly to the situation – they kept things light and flip and sexy and, if they had sense, they did nothing to remind their audience of what was really going on outside the dancehall.

Good-time music, loose and amiable and, by comparison, gospel was purest poison. It was archaic, primitive, and it was determinedly down-home. It reminded Northern Negroes of everything they most wanted to forget. Older generations liked it all right but their kids, hip and sharp-shooting, got embarrassed by it and thought it was somehow Uncle Tom.

With the fifties and the upsurge of some kind of organized Negro militancy, things began to change. The coloured public was no longer so keen to ignore its past and, instead of being something vaguely shameful, gospel came to be seen as a real part of the black tradition, private black property. Also, its flat-out emotionalism was an exact expression of the new rage and aggression in Negro life.

So around the middle fifties, Negro pop started grafting gospel feel on to the existing R&B styles. The beat didn't change, neither did the subject matter, but everything dug deeper, more passionate and everyone sweated. That was soul.

Soul has always been bossed by James Brown. Born 1928, he was a hysterical blues screamer out of Atlanta, Georgia. Very down-home, he had got his training in a Southern gospel quartet and used the same technique when he turned to pop.

It's just about impossible to over-estimate how big a figure James Brown has been. For more than ten years now, he has criss-crossed America in endless ninety-day barnstormers and, in that time, he has gone far beyond being just a singer. Really, he's the final symbol of everything that Negroes can do, of the money they can make, the style they can achieve, the arrogance they can get away with. More even than Muhammad Ali, James Brown has been the outlaw, the Stagger Lee of his time.

Beyond having had maybe fifty straight American hits, he has a show that's made up of a twenty-one-piece band, four drummers, a boy and a girl singer, Elsie, TV Mamma, and anyone else he feels like hiring. He owns three music companies, five record companies and, when he goes out on tour, he sends out a team of interior decorators ahead of him to redesign all the hotel rooms that he'll have to stay in. In these ways, he's a Sultan, an unreachable, and whites simply don't come into it.

He's a small man, rather ugly, but he is a beautiful dancer and he has a freak voice, hysterical and piercing and quite unnaturally loud. Little Richard, Arthur Brown, John Lennon, P. J. Proby – they're all whisperers by comparison.

And basically, what he does is set up some very simple pattern, one deepdown riff, and then he hammers it, hits it over and over, calling a phrase and having his band answer it, building on infinite repetition, piling it on until the tension gets to be almost physically painful. It's the call-and-response gospel thing, the same old preach, only hyped into line with the sixties.

His stage act lasts one full hour and, all that time, he's doing nothing but working up panic, hammering and hitting, shrieking, falling to his knees in fake anguish like some cry-man Negro Johnnie Ray, striding the stage on bandy legs like some dwarfish Negro Groucho Marx. And his band grinds on behind him and his dancers pirouette and his drummers lay about them. Then he goes into some dancing, a faster Mick Jagger, tight black pants and legs like propeller shafts, and he's only beautiful.

On *Prisoner of Love*, he walks away from the mike and calls the title in the darkness. Very thin and distant, repeating just these three words over and over. And then he comes back into the light, up to the mike, and he lets out a series of screams, mad anguished shrieks that last ten seconds each. Probably they're the loudest sounds you've ever heard any human being make and, physically, you can't not be moved by them. That's the way he works on you. That's the way he hurts you and beats you up.

Right at the end of his hour, on *Please, Please, Please*, he pretends to collapse and is hustled offstage by an attendant, his shoulders covered by a blue cloak. When he gets into the wings, he suddenly breaks loose and rushes back to the mike, screams a few more bars and falls right down again. This time a red cloak gets used. He goes through silver and gold and leopard-spots. Never gets off until his fifth attempt.

It's terrible ham, of course, so calculated and precise that Brown fines his musicians each time they make a mistake, even each time their shoes aren't brightly polished enough.

107

But under all its gimmickry, it's sexual and menacing and genuinely meant. It is also a black show, an Apollo show, and no white man could ever fully join in with it. More than anything, that's what has made him so crucial.

He's such a tycoon. Beyond all of his companies, he has organized his musicians into something like a cooperative society: they pay in a part of their wages and hold shares in the organization and, between them, own real estate and businesses and so forth. When anyone opts out, Brown has him replaced by someone unknown and struggling, someone who really needs the break. Uncle James – everyone gets looked after.

Talking to white journalists, he is withdrawn. Not mean or boorish but always guarded. He can be helpful, most courteous but he doesn't stretch out. Why should he? He has no need of us. We don't count.

Next in line was Ray Charles.

If James Brown got the soul train moving in the Negro market, Charles was responsible for breaking it around the world and, at his vocal peak, he has always made his rivals look straight silly.

Born in Georgia in 1932, blinded at six, orphaned by fifteen, he had it hard in every way possible and took a long time to get going. Into his twenties, he sold himself as a carbon Nat King Cole and hicked from town to town with a trio, playing a bit of piano, singing the good old good ones. Settling himself down for a lifetime of safe mediocrity.

But around 1953, for no good reason that he or anybody else has ever explained, he just suddenly upped and quit. Threw Nat Cole out the window and hit for himself. What he changed into was purest gospel. The real thing and no padding allowed.

He got himself a big band that could play the blues, hired a solid tenorman called Fathead Newman, added a girl group called the Raelets and topped it all up with his own new voice,

108

which was curdled and hurt and quite magnificent. Raw, very agonized. Crabbed and ugly and unmusical but it carried a kickback like a mule. All you could say – it sounded right.

Anyhow, he was very successful. He sold massively among Negroes, gradually built up a following among whites and, by 1960, had emerged as a definite world force. Remember: this was the dead time, the phase when rock 'n' roll had run out of steam and the charts were dominated by the detergent inanities of Frankie Avalon and Connie Francis. Pop was sicker than any time before or since and, coming when it did, a record like Charles's 1959 hit, *What'd I Say?*, was pulverizing. So strong, so fierce, so sexy. Simply so real. More than just a one-time smash, it was a rallying point, a trampoline from which pop began its climb back.

Apart from anything else, he was a musician, good on piano and adequate on alto sax, and this was something almost entirely unknown in pop. He did albums of instrumentals. He took solos. He recorded with Milt Jackson, the MJQ vibist, and wasn't disgraced even then.

All of this seemed so extraordinary at the time that his publicists promptly dubbed him the Genius and, what's more, many people believed it. Coming after Pat Boone or Fabian, who was to argue?

He was in no pop tradition. More, he was in the line of doomed jazz heroes – Billie Holiday and Charlie Parker. He was black and blind, and, as such, he appealed not so much to any mainline pop crowd as to students and schoolboys and teen rebels of all shades. Kids like myself who were snob, who thought that pop was nice but maybe a bit banal and Ray Charles was the real thing, smashed and tortured, the soul-cry of an oppressed people. So if you thought yourself at all hip, you automatically worshipped him. Beat poets and hipsters and jazzmen everywhere preached him as messiah: Allen Ginsberg, Jack Kerouac, Charlie Mingus. In those times, he was hip status symbol number one.

He had great presence. He'd grope his way out on stage, wave into the blackness around him and then you couldn't look away from him. You just watched him all the time. Not that he did anything – he only sat and played. Still, he was mesmeric, he had it.

And his voice, when it soared, it chilled you and you sweated. He twisted you and hurt you. The first time I saw him, he stretched me so tight that I sicked up all my tea. All right, I was sixteen at the time and romantic. All the same, I didn't spew for anyone.

Of course, it was too good to last – he signed up with the giant commercial complex of ABC-Paramount and promptly had all his natural force smothered in great wads of candyfloss. In 1962, he committed virtual hara-kiri by cutting a slop Country 'n' Western ballad, *I Can't Stop Loving You*, complete with strings and background choir. Predictably, it sold upwards of two million and was followed by sundry other abortions in the same style. But, apart from being lousy, they were bad long-term commercial policy, alienating him from his blues public and leaving him without any stable following.

The next step was to put him in a movie called *Ballad In Blue*, a back-dated weepie in which he played himself as an all-time caricature of the folksy, lovable, cornbread-and-molasses nigger, and the softening-up process was complete. When he's given his head, he can still outsing anyone and some of his last records have been brilliant again but it's a bit late now and hits have been hard to come by.

Ray Charles, in many ways, goes down as a black Elvis Presley, a great natural vitality strangled and aborted by the mechanics of showbiz. That's too melodramatic an image but it isn't untrue.

Sam Cooke had charm.

He came from Chicago, son of a minister, and he spent years touring with a gospel group called the Soul Stirrers.

When he finally went solo, he sang soul gently, melodically. Sometimes he softened down so much that he was hardly soul at all, he was straight pop. Watered-down or not, he was sweet without being sickly and he wrote some fine songs – *You Send Me, Cupid, Bring It On Home To Me, Havin' A Party*.

He was infinitely professional. He'd been through the smalltime American night-club bit and knew his business backwards. When he toured Britain in 1962 with Little Richard and Jet Harris, he got up against solid rocker audiences and they wanted to hate him. Every night he'd go out cold and work his ass off, keep right on pushing until they finally broke and, absolutely without fail, he'd wind up slaying them. By the time he got through, they'd all be up on their feet and waving white handkerchiefs at him. Very corny, of course. But still it took some getting and he got it. He never missed once.

Offstage, he was sharp, self-confident, fast on his feet. He was a close friend of Muhammad Ali, among the first into the ring to congratulate him after first beating Sonny Liston. In every way, he was smart. Too smart for his own good, in fact, because a woman shot him in a hotel, December 1964, and he died.

The word Soul had originally come out of modern jazz. Negro musicians like Charlie Mingus, Cannonball Adderley, Les McCann and Bobby Timmons reacted violently against the West Coast cool, white and gutless, that had bossed jazz through the fifties and, by 1960, they had taken things right back to the roots again. Amens, built-in funk, straight-ahead twelve bars – all the tricks of down-home or gospel got dragged back in. Black blues, black musicians, black traditions and it showed in the titles: *Better Git It In Your Soul, Work Song, Wednesday Night Prayer Meeting, Moanin'*.

Somewhere along the line the word Soul got used, sounded right and stuck. In no time, it had become the most over-used

111

cliché in the whole range of popular music. It has stayed that way ever since.

Jazz soul got copied by pop. All of the riffs and patterns and catch-words off a thousand commercial hits were first used by jazzmen. Very often, jazz and pop were indistinguishable anyhow: didn't Ray Charles play jazz? Didn't the Adderley brothers flirt with pop? And which was Jimmy Smith, where did Brother Jack McDuff belong? The easiest answer was that they were sometimes jazz, sometimes pop and mostly a bit of both. Really, the distinctions didn't matter much.

Across the past decade, pop or jazz, soul has become progressively stylized, formal even, and now tends to be as ritualized as some religious festival.

This is the ritual: the groups wear silk suits, comb their straightened hair into quiffs, concentrate obsessively on synchronized hand gestures, and the soloists sweat hard, yell themselves hoarse and are usually fast, tricksy dancers. Groups and soloists alike indulge in standardized bouts of dialogue with their audience. ('Is everybody all right?' 'Yeah.' 'Let me hear you say Yeah.' '*Yeah*.' 'No, let me hear you say Yeah louder.' 'YEAH.') Everyone grins a lot. In these ways, soul is as crisp and pat as a recorded message.

What makes all of this such a bring-down is the total lack of any real involvement. Most soul singers come on like wind-up dolls, they almost sleep-walk and they smirk, leer and grimace like so many nigger minstrels. They don't act like people and they don't treat their audience like people either. It's all depressingly Tom.

At any rate, if soul really has become Uncle Tom, it's largely traceable back to the Tamla Motown and Atlantic Records combines, the first soul companies to wake up to the obvious proposition that, since white kids have more spending money to waste than black ones, they're a vital market. In the light of this discovery, the music has been made gradually less harsh, less racial and more accessible to half-baked white taste.

112

The worst offender like this has probably been Tamla Motown, which is a pity because it has also dug up a lot of very heavy talent and turned out some really marvellous music. Apart from anything else, it has been one of the most romantic success stories in pop.

In 1959, Berry Gordy Jr, a Detroit song-writer and ex-auto assembly-line worker, launched Gordy Records on a loan of seven hundred dollars. This was fair enough: there are hundreds of small-time coloured labels all across the States, turning out minor local hits and just ticking over. They don't make fortunes but they usually don't go broke either. They survive.

But Berry Gordy somehow exploded: he wrote some good songs, little beauties, and turned them into national hits by sustained flat-out hustle. Then he formed two more labels, Tamla Records and Motown Records, and wrote some more songs, had some more hits and, by now, he was a snowball. In 1961, he got his first million sellers, the Marvellettes' *Please Mister Postman* and the Miracles' *Shop Around*. So suddenly he was an industry.

From there, he just expanded like mad. Signed the Supremes, the Temptations, Little Stevie Wonder, Marvin Gaye, Mary Wells, Martha Reeves and the Vandellas, the Velvelettes, the Four Tops, Brenda Holloway, the Contours and sundry others, all of whom clocked up monster hits for him. Unearthed two writing machines, Smokey Robinson and Holland/Dozier/Holland. Anyway, by 1964, he was selling upwards of twelve million records each year. Five years, out of nowhere, and now he bossed the first real shrine of soul. He'd been running fast.

The format was, and still is, simple – the songs are all written with one obvious hookline, to be repeated and hammered home *ad nauseam*, and the beat is kept heavy and the individual voices stay secondary to the overall sound. The rhythm sections are invariably magnificent, the singers strong and professional. Most times, the records sound as though they've been put together by computer but, just every so often, a little more trouble is taken and then a classic pop record comes out.

At its worst, Tamla has always churned out good noise for dancing, and, at its best, it has been superb. At its norm, it has put out more slick, well-made, commercial foot food than any other company in the world.

The one drag is that, once he's broken an act in the soul market, Gordy invariably converts them into cabaret turns. Puts them into the white night-club circuit and has them make like family entertainers. Which is fine for the acts themselves, because they make more money, but a bit rough on their long-time followers, because the music turns lousy.

Again, I'm being too prissy: pop is a business first and last. It has always been full of false messiahs and bring-down is an essential part of the game.

I'm not going to go into any detailed analyses of the individual Motown acts. Most of them are excellent but they're also largely interchangeable. The Supremes are the best looking, the most astronomically successful ('America's Sweethearts'), and Diana Ross, their lead singer, has the sexiest voice. The Temptations have the best sound and are almost my favourites. The Four Tops are the most passionate and Stevie Wonder is the most individual. Gladys Knight sings the best blues. Brenda Holloway is the most under-used. So on and so on.

They all have regular, almost automatic hits and if anyone should happen to miss out three or four times running, then everyone thinks a bit straighter, works a bit harder next time out and a giant is made.

The only real stand-outs are Smokey Robinson and the Miracles, who have been around almost longest of all. Smokey is lovely. He sings lead in a perfect woman's soprano, not a falsetto shriek or anything so vulgar, but a finely controlled warble, full of its own small subtleties. Pop's first female impersonator, original *prima donna*.

The Miracles grunt away in the background and Smokey is everything. Most of his best songs, things like *Tracks Of My Tears* and *Ooh Baby Baby* and *I Second That Emotion*, are begging letters for love and he pleads, he sobs, he keens. Torments of one teenage girl-child, operatic agonies, and his voice breaks, bends and trembles on every last note. Sometimes it's a cry of pure pain and sometimes it's only a sigh. Either way, it would like to break your heart. So high and soft and busted. Such fractured sound: *Ooh Baby Baby* is likely the most long-pumping ballad in pop.

How could I criticize him? He only has to open his mouth and I'm melted.

Still on Motown, I really can't dismiss the Supremes in one line. They have, after all, been the most consistently triumphant American act of the last five years. Every time they walk into the studio, they sell a million.

First and last, they're professional. They sing the right notes, smile the right smiles and move like three synchronized robots. They're lookers, politely sexy, and they open their big eyes for all the people, show their teeth, even wriggle their shoulders. Pink tongues and false eyelashes: they're cute.

They paraphrase the whole Motown saga. In the start, they were rough and noisy and they made good commercial soul music but, when they got to be successful, they cooled it and now they play only white night-clubs and sing standards, film songs, blockbusters out of musicals. They're clean. They give the politest, blankest, most boring interviews in the world, real showbiz stuff about being glad to be back in our wonderful country again and aren't London policemen just gorgeous? So what about black power? What about it, indeed – despite their schmaltzy monologue on *Somewhere*, which so shook up the 1968 Royal Command Performance, they remain as Tom as they could get.

Atlantic Records, Tamla's major rival, pre-dates pop.

It's run by the Ertegun Brothers, Ahmet and Nesuhi, and it has been going for upwards of twenty years now. In that time, it has always been the most perceptive, tasteful and committed label around.

Over two decades, it has pushed Joe Turner, Stick McGhee, the Clovers, Ruth Brown, Ray Charles, LaVern Baker, the Drifters, the Coasters, Solomon Burke, Wilson Pickett, Aretha Franklin and whole regiments besides. Everything that has been new and worth shoving. And not only pop but much good jazz: Charlie Mingus and the MJQ, John Coltrane and Ornette Coleman, often when rival companies were still running scared of them. It's not a list that any other combine could even approach.

The Erteguns are clever men, civilized and urbane, even sophisticated. Not obvious hustlers by any means. Ahmet, who has been the more dominant, looks like a Turkish diplomat – he has a billiard-ball skull, a goatee, a squeaky voice, and he comes on like an all-time playboy. Inside the image, he has shrewdness and staying power. Not long ago, he sold Atlantic to Warner Brothers for twenty million dollars and that just about rounded everything off.

Again, there's not much point in going into any individual breakdowns – Atlantic's major strength has always been its professionalism and the Erteguns have invariably used the best writers, producers, engineers or session men going at any given time.

The most cosmic singles have probably been *Drinkin' Wine Spo-Dee-O-Dee* by Stick McGhee and his Buddies (1947) and *Hello Stranger* by Barbara Lewis (1962). Outside of that, it's simply been steady brilliance right through.

Their ablest lieutenant has been Jerry Wexler, about whom there's not much to say except that he's probably played producer on more great records than anyone else in the industry.

The only other of their associates who rates a mention is the late Bert Berns, who write such enduring stuff as *Twist and Shout, Hang On Sloopy, Here Comes The Night* and *I Don't Want To Go On Without You*. Well, he wasn't owned by Atlantic but he did a lot of work for them and this is where he fits in best.

Really, I bring him in only because I never met anyone who understood pop so well. Who agreed so much with me, that is.

He was an identikit American recordman, canny and tough and flash, always money conscious and he wasn't a beautiful person but he was intelligent, articulate and he made some good lines.

One time, in my innocence, I asked him what pop was about. At the time, we were sitting in some restaurant and, straight off, Berns swung round at our table and yelled the one word: 'Waiter!'

Immediately, three waiters burst out of the wings at a canter and dashed to our table. Berns asked for a match and was faced by a sudden wall of flame, by three flickering hands. When the waiters left, Berns looked at me and wasn't even smug about it. 'Wouldn't you say,' he asked, 'that's what pop's about?'

Aretha Franklin has been different class.

Out of all the many people in this book, she's the only talent I can rave about without making reservations or schnideries of any kind.

Simply, she's magnificent. She's infinitely the best voice that pop has produced.

Really, she's the newest in the great line of Ma Rainey, Bessie Smith, Mahalia Jackson, Dinah Washington – big women, classic women, and they've all had voices of infinite strength and command. And they've none of them messed about. They've just stood up and hollered. Foghorn lungs that could shatter plate-glass windows at twenty paces, no microphones required. Simple white dresses and slaughter-house shoulders. Big legs and big breasts and big hands. There's been nothing remotely girlish about any of them but they've all been marvellous women.

Aretha herself is nothing new. In the first place, she led the choir in her father's church. New Bethel Baptist, flat-out gospel, and she used to be a happening all to herself. Then she turned secular and things didn't go so well any more. She was lumbered with nothing songs, third-rate producers and not much progress was made. Not that she starved: she played night-clubs and built herself a tidy reputation. Still, she wasn't an explosion. Not the way she should have been.

She wasn't finally signed to Atlantic until 1967 but, since then, everything has come together fast. Most every single she's made has done a million. And it has been so easy, so straight-ahead: Jerry Wexler, her new producer, has thrown out all clutter, all fuss and bombast, and has only let her voice ride free, blazing like a six-gun, so fierce and bossy and bottomless that it doesn't seem possible.

She has repose. Massive certainty – she has an infinite sweep in her phrasing, great size, a crippling ferocity and she hits even mediocre songs so hard that they're smashed, gouged, entirely annihilated and then renewed. Given some crap to sing, she lays into it like mad and simply tears it to pieces, scattering strings and brass and angelic choirs like some avenging thunderclap. And where her rivals panic and have to climax each number in strangled hysteria, she unrolls one steady steamroller progression from first chorus through to last. From an opening of monumental queenly calm right through to final apocalyptic break-up. Aretha roaring and whooping and snarling like a Holy Roller. Then she's some amazing natural force, not stoppable, and she rips through brick walls like candy-floss, destroys skyscrapers, tramples the city underfoot. But when she's quite finished, she only smiles slightly and doesn't sweat, doesn't even perspire.

More than anyone else in pop, it's irrelevant what she's like offstage or what she eats for breakfast. She's only music. She is a talent that's hardly possible and she exists to be wondered at.

Her only possible rival is Tina Turner, whom I've already mentioned when I was talking about Phil Spector. On *River Deep*, she came across as a voice of vast potential, a hurricane, but she must have been Svengalied by Spector because she's never been quite so good again. Usually, she's wallowed in exactly that kind of strangled hysteria that Aretha disdains and it becomes boring. Really, she wastes herself.

Never mind, she's sexy. She's a great woman with long black hair right down her back and a beautiful snarling animal face and a truly cosmic arse. Not pretty but sexual as hell. And her energy is endless, she flings herself about the stage like some maniac and her hair flays her flesh and her butt, always her butt. Then the sweat rolls off her in sheets and her lips peel back from her teeth and she's quite murderous.

All this time, Ike Turner, her husband, plays guitar behind her and looks mean, a neat little man with a goatee and sad cynical eyes. He looks like some elegant black magician, so calm and sinister, and Tina his spell, his servant possessed by spirits.

I remember seeing them in a London club one time and I was standing right under the stage. So Tina started whirling and pounding and screaming, melting by the minute, and suddenly she came thundering down on me like an avalanche, backside first, all that flesh shaking and leaping in my face. And I reared back in self-defence, all the front rows did, and then someone fell over and we all immediately collapsed in a heap, struggling and cursing, thrashing about like fish in a bucket.

When I looked back up again, Tina was still shaking above us, her butt was still exploding, and she looked down on us in triumph. So sassy, so smug and evil. She'd used her arse as a bowling ball, us as skittles, and she'd scored a strike. Smart woman: her flesh dissolving and her hair all flying and her big man-eater teeth flashing. She ate us all for breakfast.

Outside of Tamla and Atlantic, there are other major American soul labels, notably Chess, Bell and Mint. And outside of these, there are maybe five hundred minors. If you like soul music, they're all fine and, if you don't, they're boring. There's not much more I could say on them.

The thing about soul is that a quite astonishing number of American Negroes are good at it. They tend to have naturally strong voices and they sing in tune, keep time and are loud. Usually, they have no individuality whatever but they're at least competent. So they come streaming out of the South in their thousands and hassle. Most often, their records never make the national charts but they're still regional R&B sellers and money gets made just the same. Huge complicated networks of labels and artists and radio stations all across America – it's a self-contained business within pop and is independent of all trends outside itself.

Because the supply of singers is so limitless, coloured labels can afford to get tough and they do.

A bargain they make is that they'll get an artist a hit, they'll start him off but that's all: they get him known and he can then make money out of live shows. And if he doesn't accept that, he can drop dead.

Of course, there's sometimes trouble. Maybe the artist accepts the bargain at first, chalks up hits, gets himself established and then turns difficult. The companies don't like that. They even hate it.

But if his mind stays straight, if he isn't foolish, then everyone gets on fine. It's rational – except for pro football or boxing, soul is usually the only chance that Southern coloureds ever have of escape. The companies give them that chance. In return, they want only humility.

The only other label I'm going to go into detail about is Stax/Volt, which is Memphis-based and has a roster including the deceased Otis Redding, Sam and Dave, Eddie Floyd, Carla Thomas, Arthur Conley, plus sundries. It is also the heart of the sweat-and-Tom syndrome and has much to answer for.

The basis of Stax is its house rhythm section, Booker T. and the M.G.s, and they're the best engine room around, they make everything burst. Booker T. Jones plays organ and Steve Cropper plays guitar and Duck Dunn plays bass and Al Jackson plays drums. That Memphis soul stew. They're all tremendous.

The biggest Stax seller yet has been Otis Redding and there are plenty of people around who'll tell you that he was a genius. He was from Macon, Georgia, and started out very much in the style of Macon's other chosen son, Little Richard. All huff and puff and sharp sticks.

In the early sixties, he went on a soul kick and was very good at it. He had a fine anguished sound, blues-drenched, full of attractive little tricks and mannerisms, and his early hits were most convincing – *Mr Pitiful*, *Respect*, *I've Been Loving You Too Long*. Meaty stuff, full of guts, and he seemed as if he really meant it.

In person, he wasn't so hot: paunchy, baggy-trousered, white-socked and ham as hell. He stomped about the stage on his heels, waved his arms, grinned, sweated. He sang well and used good songs. But he was monotonous – he approached every number the same and all those mannerisms that had once been cute were now very stale indeed. Face it, he was typical soul, a bit Tom. Still, he wasn't bad. He just didn't slay me.

He was very popular with white kids, with hippies especially, and he played along with them, making small folksy speeches on Soul and Love and Brotherhood. At the 1967 Monterey Festival, the great Love happening, he was the only soul singer to show. Others stayed away because it was a white event and because they were expected to appear unpaid, a condition entirely counter to the whole spirit of Negro

121

entertainment. Otis himself hesitated but finally turned up. And he did himself a lot of good, he became the hero of the whole bonanza.

He was worshipped. Well, after all, he was black. And not just brown black, Northern black, but a real rich Georgia black.

He made good records and sang nice and was perfectly fine. But he wasn't the greatest soul artist in the world, not nearly, and that's what the hippies thought he was. Aretha Franklin, James Brown, Smokey, Tina Turner – they were all, in their different manners, more impressive performers but none of them sued for white favour, and Otis won out.

Just as he was at his peak and had won an English poll for World's Best Male Singer, he was killed in a plane crash, along with his backing band. He was said to be only twenty-six. Maybe it was true.

Just before he died, he'd cut a record called *Dock Of The Bay* and it was his best, his least fake work in ages. More thoughtful and more felt again. So, the signs were he would have improved.

Myself, I've always much preferred Joe Tex to any of the Stax crowd. He's a soul Chuck Berry, and he's all very big-hearted and avuncular on top but, way down deep, he's sly, he stands a lot of watching.

He comes from Baytown, Texas, and he's been around a whole long time. Nobody is quite sure exactly how long but he certainly had years of scrabbling, hassling and surviving before he ever got a hit. Maybe a full decade. And now that he's finally made it, he's hanging on like a limpet. He is notoriously hard, wary, and he does nothing unless he gets paid for it.

He writes his own material, halfway between country and the blues, softer and subtler than most soul and, according to his hand-outs, he makes 'songs of kindness, compassion and humility'. Maybe so, but such kindness I could easily live

122

without. Like, for instance, *I Believe I'm Gonna Make It*, his Vietnam song:

> When I got your letter, baby,
> I was in a foxhole on my knees,
> And your letter brought me so much strength
> (Tell you what I did, baby, you won't believe it)
> I raised up and got me two more enemies.*

He's a great one for handing out advice. The way he poses himself is as benevolent Uncle Joseph, forefinger wagging and his head shaking in quizzical puzzlement at the boundless foolishness of man. And his songs are folksy little sermons, things like: *Lying's Just A Habit, John* or *Hold What You've Got* or *Don't Make Your Children Pay*.

He has a cunning voice, real back-country Texas, and he's hugely smug. Most of all, he enjoys doing spoken monologues, extended debates on the state of the world. Or, more particularly, on man's responsibility to woman. All of this he delivers in a very humble mumble. Impressive: Uriah Heep is quite outclassed.

Still, he's cute. He has great greasy charm, much wit and inventiveness, and it just isn't possible to hold out against him. He's so transparent about it all. (In *Don't Make Your Children Pay*, for one, it turns out that he's against us starving our children, not on any moral grounds, but because we might need them some day and it wouldn't do to have them hate us then. Investment and repayment. Self-interest right along the line.) And he's funny, he really is, and he obviously enjoys himself. So his records turn into good clean dirt and you can't resent them. You keep trying to disapprove but your principles slip. That's how you get corrupted.

*Words of *I Believe I'm Gonna Make It* by Joe Tex by permission of London Tree Music Ltd, London.

123

Finally, in this chapter, I have to say something about B. B. King, who has nothing much to do with soul, who is hardly pop at all but has been a major figure just the same. Most simply, he's the blues.

He's a tubby man in middle age and he plays maybe the best blues guitar in the world. Originally, he comes out of a Mississippi plantation and is Bukka White's cousin. And there's no hyped-up gospel about him, no commercial sixties hysteria, but he plays pure blues, the real thing, and makes no compromises with anything.

Even though he's from the South, what he peddles now is Northern big-city stuff, tough and cynical. He uses organ, trumpet and tenor behind him, a small rough-edged band, and he only sings a bit, plays a bit. His voice is harsh, mean-sounding, and his guitar wings way over the top, simultaneously brutal and incredibly delicate. So he sells nothing to a white audience but, among Negroes, he's one of the genuine giants and has been for the last fifteen years.

His songs are mean and humorous and boastful. Very full of B. B. King's importance. And he trusts nobody, he rates women very low indeed and takes no jive, no mess. Still, he laughs at himself.

His music is mostly simple twelve bars, straight ahead, and he doesn't ever change. Just the blues, only the hard blues. You learn him off by heart: it's so casual, so static, and it only works because he's just naturally riveting, because he can play some chorus you've heard one hundred times before and somehow make it new again.

The biggest influence he's had, outside of other black blues guitarists his own age, has been among the young intellectual whites – Eric Clapton, Mike Bloomfield, Peter Green. The way they see him, he's the last hero of a long romantic tradition and they revere him just as much as trad jazzmen once worshipped Bunk Johnson. They're truly in awe of him. Not, of course, that he's much interested: he has his own black public, he has owned them for two decades now and earnest white cults are so much jam. All he does is play the blues.

Inevitably, this chapter has been a bit of a ramble: I've had to cover quite a long period, a range of styles, a variety of approaches, and still make them seem as if they had something in common.

The odd thing about soul up to here is that, having started out as a great return to roots and reality, having brought some desperately needed guts into pop during the early sixties, it has grown into something even more phoney than the stuff it replaced. It is exciting or sexual or even moving but does it reflect a new black pride, does it hell? It is commercial. It is professionally servile. And all the impulses that created it in the first place have long since been forgotten. Now it's only a sleep-walking factory.

13

THE BEATLES

Next came the Fab Four, the Moptop Mersey Marvels, and this is the bit I've been dreading. I mean what is there possibly left to say on them?

In the beginning, I should say, the Beatles were the Quarrymen, and then they were the Silver Beatles, and there were five of them – John Lennon, Stuart Sutcliffe, Paul McCartney, George Harrison and Pete Best. All of them came from working-class or lower-middle-class backgrounds in Liverpool and the only ones with any pretensions to anything were Paul McCartney, who had racked up five 'O'-levels, and Stuart Sutcliffe, who painted.

The heavies at this time were Sutcliffe and John Lennon, who were at art school together.

Sutcliffe was something like an embryo James Dean, very beautiful-looking, and he wore shades even in the dark, he was natural image. Of all the Beatles, at this stage, he was the most sophisticated and the most articulate and Eduardo Paolozzi, the painter, who taught him for a time, says that he was very talented indeed.

As for Lennon, he was a roughneck. His father, who was a seaman, had left home when Lennon was still a small child, his mother had died, and he'd been brought up by his Aunt Mimi. And by the time he got to art school, he'd grown into a professional hard-nut, big-mouthed and flash, and he rampaged through Liverpool like some wounded buffalo, smashing everything that got in his way. He wrote songs with Paul McCartney. He had hefty intellectual discussions with Sutcliffe. He was rude to almost everyone, he was loud and brutally funny, his put-downs could kill. A lot of people noticed him.

The Beatles, at this time, were still total Teds: they wore greasy hair and leather jackets and winkle pickers, they jeered and got into fights and were barred from pubs.

The music they played then was souped-up rock, much influenced by Eddie Cochran and Buddy Holly, not notably original, and they were less than an explosion. In 1960, they managed a tour of Scotland with Johnny Gentle, one of the lesser figures in the Larry Parnes stable, but mostly they alternated between random gigs in Liverpool and seasons at the Star Club in Hamburg, where they played murderous hours each night and halfway starved to death.

At this point, Stuart Sutcliffe left the group to concentrate on his painting and, soon afterwards, died of a brain tumour. He was twenty-one. Meanwhile, the Beatles had begun to move up a bit – they'd made some records in Germany, bad records but records just the same, and they'd built themselves a solid following, both in Germany and at home. And musically, they'd become competent and they had their own sound, a crossbreed between classic rock and commercial R&B, and they were raw, deafening, a bit crude but they were really exciting. At least, unlike any other British act ever, they didn't ape America but sounded what they were, working-class Liverpool, unfake, and that's what gave them their strength, that's what made Brian Epstein want to manage them.

Epstein was the eldest son in a successful Jewish business family and he ran a Liverpool record store. In his early twenties, he'd wanted to be an actor and he'd gone to RADA but now, approaching thirty, he'd resigned himself to being a businessman. Intelligent and loyal and neurotic, painfully sensitive, he was nobody's identikit picture of a hustler but he was civilized, basically honest, and he had capital. So he asked the Beatles to let him be manager and they agreed.

Soon after this, Pete Best, the drummer, got flung out and was replaced by Ringo Starr. Best had laid down a loud and clumsy beat, quite effective, but he'd been less sharp, less clever, less flexible than the other Beatles and they'd got bored with him, they wanted him out.

Ringo Starr's real name was Richard Starkey and he'd been playing with Rory Storm and the Hurricanes, Liverpool's top group of that time. Actually, he wasn't too much of a drummer and he had rough times at the hands of vengeful Pete Best fans; he was given a fierce baptism. But he had his own defences, a great off-hand resilience and a deadpan humour, and he survived.

Meanwhile, Epstein acted like a manager. Privately, he had huge inhibitions about hustling, but he fought them down and sweated. So he had demos made and touted them round the record companies; he pleaded and spieled and harangued. And having been first turned down by Dick Rowe at Decca, the King Dagobert of pop, he finally got a contract with E.M.I. and everything began.

From there on in, it was fast and straight-ahead: the first single, *Love Me Do*, made the thirty and the second, *Please Please Me*, made number one and the third, *From Me To You* also made number one (louder) and the fourth, *She Loves You*, made the biggest hit that any British artist had ever cut. All of them were written by Lennon and McCartney.

By spring of 1963, they had taken over from Cliff Richard here and, by autumn, they were a national obsession. At the beginning of 1964, given the most frantic hype ever, they broke out in America and stole the first five places solid on the chart. Summer, they released their first movie, *Hard Day's*

Night, and it smashed and that just about rounded things out. Altogether, it had taken two years from first big push to last.

At the end of all this, they had become unarguably the largest phenomenon that pop had ever coughed up and, even more remarkably, they've hardly slid since. To the time of writing they have sold upwards of two hundred million records and they're coming up for their twentieth straight number one.

Beyond that, they had made millions of pounds for themselves and many more millions of pounds for the Government and, in reward, they were all given the MBE for their contributions to the export drive. This was a clincher – assorted worthies sent their own medals back in protest but everyone else was delighted. That's how respectable pop had become and it was all the Beatles who'd made it like that.

Beyond their music itself, their greatest strengths were clarity of image and the way they balanced. It's a truism that no pop format is any good unless it can be expressed in one sentence, but the Beatles went beyond that, they could each be said in one word: Lennon was the brutal one, McCartney was the pretty one, Ringo Starr was the lovable one, Harrison was the balancer. And if Lennon was tactless, McCartney was a natural diplomat. And if Harrison seemed dim, Lennon was very clever. And if Starr was clownish, Harrison was almost sombre. And if McCartney was arty, Starr was basic. Round and round in circles, no loose ends left over, and it all made for a comforting sense of completeness.

Completeness, in fact, was what the Beatles were all about. They were always perfectly self-contained, independent, as if the world was split cleanly into two races, the Beatles and everyone else, and they seemed to live off nobody but themselves.

There is a film of their first American press conference that expresses this perfectly. Hundreds of newsmen question them, close in and batter and hassle them but the Beatles aren't reached. They answer politely, they make jokes, they're most charming, but they're never remotely involved, they're private. They have their own club going and, really, they aren't reachable. They are, after all, the Beatles.

Throughout this, they are very subtly playing image both ways – they are anti-stars and they're superstars both. They use Liverpool accents, they're being consciously working class and non-showbiz and anti-pretension but, in their own way, they're distancing themselves, building up mystique for all they are worth. With every question that gets thrown at them, they spell it out more clearly: we are ordinary, modest, no-nonsense, unsentimental and entirely superhuman.

For some reason, such built-in arrogance hardly ever misses – it's the same equation that the inherited rich sometimes have, the way that they can be charming, gentle, humble as hell and still you know you can't ever get to them, they're protected and finally, they only function among themselves. They're in their own league and you're insulted, you sneer but you're hooked and, kid, would you ever like in.

This is the superstar format, the only one that really works, and the Beatles had it exactly, they were a whole new aristocracy in themselves. And, of course, they'd have been huge anyway, they'd have come through on their music and their prettiness alone, but it was this self-sufficiency, this calm acceptance of their own superiority, that made them so special.

Between them, the four of them being so complementary, they managed to appeal to almost everyone.

Lennon, for instance, trapped the intellectuals. He started writing books and he knocked out two regulation slim volumes, *In His Own Write* and *A Spaniard In The Works*, stories, poems, doodled drawings and assorted oddments. Mostly, they were exercises in sick, sadistic little sagas of deformity and death, written in a style halfway between Lewis Carroll and Spike Milligan.

130

Predictably, the critics took it all with great solemnity and, straightaway, Lennon was set up as cultural cocktail food, he got tagged as an instinctive poet of the proletariat, twisted voice of the underdog. He himself said that he only wrote for fun, to pass time, but no matter, he was turned into a heavy Hampstead cult.

Meanwhile, he sat around in discotheques and tore everyone to pieces. He was married and had a son. He lived in a big suburban mansion in Weybridge and he was sharp as a scythe. He wrote songs as if he was suffocating. Still, he was powerful and he generated a real sense of claustrophobia, he had great command of irony and he owned one of the best pop voices ever, rasped and smashed and brooding, always fierce. Painful and obsessive, his best songs have been no fun whatever but they've been strong: *I Am The Walrus*, *A Day In The Life*, *Happiness Is A Warm Gun* and, most racked of all, *Strawberry Fields Forever*.

On stage, he played monster and made small girls wet their knickers. He hunched up over the mike, very tight because he couldn't see an inch without his glasses on, and he'd make faces, stick his tongue out, be offensive in every way possible. On *Twist and Shout*, he'd rant his way into total incoherence, half rupture himself. He'd grind like a cement mixer and micro-bops loved every last dirty word of him. No doubt, the boy had talent.

Paul McCartney played Dick Diver. He was stylish, charming, always elegant and, whenever he looked at you, he had this strange way of making you feel as if you were genuinely the only person in the world that mattered. Of course, he'd then turn away and do exactly the same thing with the next in line but, just that flash while it lasted, you were warmed and seduced and won over for always.

He was a bit hooked on culture: he went to all the right plays, read the right books, covered the right exhibitions and he even had a stage when he started diluting his accent. No chance – Lennon brought him down off that very fast indeed. Still, he educated himself in trends of all kinds and, when he was done, he emerged as a full-blown romantic, vastly sentimental, and he wrote many sad songs about many sad things, songs that were so soft and melodic that grannies everywhere bought them in millions.

In their different styles, then, both Lennon and McCartney had gotten arty and their music changed. In the first place, their work had been brash, raucous, and the lyrics very basic – *She Loves You, Thank You Girl, I Saw Her Standing There*. Good stuff, strong and aggressive, but limited. From about 1964 on though, they got hooked on the words of Bob Dylan and their lyrics, which had always been strictly literal, now became odder, quirkier, more surreal. Message and meaning: suddenly it was creative-artist time.

My own feeling is that Lennon has heavy talent and that McCartney really hasn't. He's melodic, pleasant, inventive but he's too much syrup.

Still, they do make a partnership: Lennon's toughness plays off well against McCartney's romanticism, Lennon's verbal flair is complemented by McCartney's knack of knocking out instantly attractive melody lines. They add up.

Of course, when McCartney runs loose with string quartets, some horribly mawkish things happen – *Yesterday, She's Leaving Home* – but he has a certain saving humour and he's usually just about walked the line.

At any rate, he looks sweet and more than anyone, he made the Beatles respectable at the start and he's kept them that way, no matter what routines they've got involved in. Even when he confesses to taking acid or bangs on about meditation, he invariably looks so innocent, acts so cutely that he gets indulged, he's always forgiven. Regardless, he is still a nice boy. Also, not to be overlooked, he is pretty and girls scream at him.

More than any of the others, though, it was Ringo Starr who came to sum the Beatles up.

America made him. In England, he was always a bit peripheral, he always sat at the back and kept his mouth shut but, when the Beatles hit New York, they were treated very much like some new line in cuddly toys, long-haired and hilarious, and Ringo stole it.

Big-nosed and dogeyed, he had a look of perpetual bewilderment and said hardly anything: 'I haven't got a smiling mouth or a talking face.' He only bumbled, came on like some pop Harry Langdon and women in millions ached to mother him. In fairness, it has to be said that this was not his fault – he looked that way by nature and couldn't change.

Every now and then, out of deep silence, he'd emerge with some really classic line. No verbal gymnastics like Lennon, not even a joke – just one flat line, so mumbled and understated as to be almost non-existent.

My own favourite was his summing-up of life as a Beatle: 'I go down to John's place to play with his toys, and sometimes he comes down here to play with mine.'

He's solid. When he got married, he chose no model, no starlet, but a girl from Liverpool, a hairdresser's assistant. He'd known and gone steady with her for years. And when all the Beatles went meditating in India with the Maharishi, he said that it reminded him of Butlins and came home early.

Really, he summarizes everything that's best in the English character – stability, tolerance, lack of pretension, humour, a certain built-in cool. He knows he's not a great drummer and it doesn't upset him. Not very much upsets him in fact: he only sits at home and plays records, watches television, shoots pool. Simply, he passes time.

He is hooked on Westerns and he loves new gadgets and he spends a lot of his time just playing. He sits with his wife and his children. Well, he may be slightly bored at times because he has nothing much to do any more but he isn't too bothered and, quite genuinely, he would make out all right if the

Beatles went broke on him and he had to get a nothing job again. No matter what, he ticks over.

George Harrison is more problematic.

To begin with, he wasn't much more than a catcher, a trampoline for the others to bounce off. On stage, he'd set himself a little way back from the mike and play along without smiling. He hardly moved and he'd look cut off, vaguely bored.

His big moment used to be when he and Paul McCartney would suddenly bear down hard on the mike together and, cheeks almost touching, they'd shake their heads like mad. This gesture used to provoke more screams than almost anything else. But when it was over, Harrison never followed it up, he only dropped back and looked bored again.

In interviews, too, he was less than impressive. He was slower than the rest, less imaginative, and he tended to plod a bit. In every way, he was overshadowed by Lennon/ McCartney.

At this stage, his most publicized interest was money and he got very tight with Epstein, who used to explain the complexities of Beatle finance to him. Epstein, who worshipped the Beatles and was greatly afraid of losing touch with them, loved this and used to speak of Harrison as his most favourite son.

Still, as Lennon/McCartney got increasingly arty, Harrison was stung and he began chasing. He went on a heavy intellectual streak himself.

First up, he got interested in Indian music and took lessons on sitar from Ravi Shankar. Second, he was to be seen flitting in and out of London Airport wearing beads and baggy white trousers. Third, he started writing Indian-style songs, all curry powder and souvenirs from the Taj Mahal, very solemn. And finally, he went up a mountain with the Maharishi Mahesh Yogi, guru to the stars, and came down again a convinced mystic. From here on, he was a philosopher, a sage, and his interviews were stuffed full of dicta, parables and eternal paradoxes. Sitting crosslegged in Virginia Water, he hid his face behind a beard, a moustache, two Rasputin eyes and he was almost unrecognizable as George Harrison, guitar-picker.

Ringo apart then, all of the Beatles had gone through heavy changes. In 1963, they'd epitomized everything that was anti-pretension: they'd been tough and funny and cool, merciless to outsiders, and they'd had the most murderous eyes for pomposity of any kind. That was one of their greatest attractions, their total lack of crapola and, even after they'd made it so huge, they didn't lose out. Well, maybe they read more books, went to more theatres and so forth but, basically, they stayed as hard as ever. Paul McCartney wrote a few sentimental ballads, Harrison learned sitar. Lennon put smoked windows on his Rolls but the wit was still dry, the put-downs fierce, the lack of sell-out total.

It wasn't until the release of *Rubber Soul*, Christmas 1965, that the cool first began to crack. Musically, this was the subtlest and most complex thing they'd done and lots of it was excellent, *Drive My Car* and *Girl* and *You Won't See Me*, but there were also danger signals, the beat had softened and the lyrics showed traces of fake significance. One song at least, *The Word*, was utter foolishness and hardly anything had the raw energy of their earlier work, there was nothing as good as *I Saw Her Standing There* or *I'm A Loser*. Simply, the Beatles were softening up.

The next album, *Revolver*, was further on down the same line. Again, there was a big step forward in ingenuity and, again, there was a big step back in guts. *Eleanor Rigby* was clever but essentially sloppy. Harrison's *Love You To* wasn't even clever. And then there was *Tomorrow Never Knows*.

What had happened? In general, it was probably the inevitable effect of having so much guff written about them – they got told they were geniuses so often, they finally believed it, and began to act as such. In particular, it was acid.

In the context of this book, it doesn't matter much whether acid was good or bad for them. All that counts is that it greatly changed them. Right then, they quit being just a rock group, Liverpool roughnecks with long hair and guitars and fast mouths, and they turned into mystics, would-be saints.

Soon after he'd owned up to using acid, early summer 1967, I did an interview with Paul McCartney and he was into a whole different level from anything I'd ever read by him before. No put-downs, no jokes, no frivolity whatever – he was most solemn and his eyes focused somewhere far beyond the back of my head. 'God is in everything,' he said. 'People who are hungry, who are sick and dying, should try to show love.'

Having gone through acid, the next inevitable step was that the Beatles went into meditation: George Harrison climbed his mountain with the Maharishi and soon the others had swung behind him, they'd renounced acid and devoted themselves to lives of total spirituality.

Undoubtedly, all of this was a major triumph for Harrison: it must have been sweet indeed to have Lennon and McCartney follow his lead, he made the most of it, he came out on TV and looked beatific and scattered dicta like chaff. 'This is going to last all our lives,' he said, and he sat crosslegged on the floor.

Meanwhile, during the first weekend that the Beatles spent with the Maharishi, September 1967, Brian Epstein had died, aged thirty-two.

Inevitably, being so successful, he'd been the butt of much schnidery within the industry and, generally, he'd been rated pretty low. Paraphrased, the party line was that he was really a less-than-averagely shrewd businessman but he'd gotten lucky one time, very lucky, and he'd happened to be hanging round as the Beatles came by.

Also, beyond incompetence, he was meant to be weak, vain and maudlin. Most of this was true. Just the same, I liked him.

The main thing about him was that he wasn't moronic, he wasn't even entirely fascist. He wasn't much criminal and he didn't have people beaten up and he didn't automatically scrabble on his knees each time someone dropped sixpence in a darkened discotheque. More, he read books and went to theatres and understood long words. No use denying it: he was intelligent.

By the conventions of British management, this was all eccentric to the edge of insanity and it changed things, it set new standards. After Epstein, managers became greatly humanized: they weren't necessarily any more honest but they were less thuggish, altogether less primitive and, sometimes, they even liked pop itself.

Beyond the Beatles, of course, Epstein had handled whole Liverpudlian armies – Gerry and the Pacemakers, Billy J. Kramer, Cilla Black, the Fourmost, Tommy Quickly. In the beginning, around 1963–4, these were all hugely successful but, mostly, they were light on talent and, Cilla excepted, they didn't sustain. Still, Epstein always stayed remarkably loyal to them, never kicked them out. Partly this was due to injured pride, but partly it was conscience, principle, integrity – the whole bit.

Just how much did the Beatles really owe him? Well, he was no Svengali, no alchemist and, obviously, they would have happened without him. He wasn't greatly imaginative, he pulled no outrageous strokes for them but he was steady, painstaking, and he didn't flag. Occasionally, his inexperience betrayed him into raw deals but, taken overall, he worked well for them.

Most important, he was a mother figure – he cared for them, reassured them, agonized on them, nagged them, even wept for them. He needed them. Even towards the end, when they'd outgrown management and would no longer take orders from anyone, he was always there, always available, devoted and doggy as ever. He could always be fallen back

137

upon. And, most of the time, his advice was good and they took it rightly. After all, in all the time he managed them, they never once made fools of themselves.

His major problem was anti-climax.

Having managed the Beatles, having helped make maybe the biggest entertainment phenomena of this century, he still had to manage the rest of his stable and he'd been a lonely, neurotic man at the best of times but, in his last two years, he got quite frantic – he financed bad plays that flopped and promoted tours, sponsored a bullfighter called Henry Higgins, turned the Saville Theatre into a would-be pop shrine, and he kept thrashing about for new diversions to keep himself amused. Nothing worked. Everything bored him.

Already, in the last days of Epstein's life, the Maharishi had been taking his place as resident mother, as adviser and comforter in chief (a development that must have struck him as a betrayal), and now, with Epstein dead, the guru had the field all to himself. Like I said earlier on, meditation was a logical progression from acid, just because it did the exact same things for you as acid did, except that acid-love was artificially-induced and nirvana was natural. And so, when the Beatles jumped, half the hip end of pop followed dutifully behind them. Donovan and the Beach Boys and Mick Jagger, Eric Burdon and the Doors, and the Maharishi's Indian headquarters got all clogged up with hair and hippie beads.

As for the guru himself, he was less than impressive and, by spring 1968, the Beatles had left him.

Meanwhile, Christmas 1967, they'd shown *Magical Mystery Tour*, their first self-produced film, and it was bad; it was a total artistic disaster. It was the first real failure they'd ever had but still it made profits and hardly weakened them at all. That's just how secure they'd become – they were establishment, institutionalized, and nothing could touch them.

More important, they launched Apple. In the beginning, this was conceived as a huge artistic and business complex, covering records and films, merchandizing and electronics and music publishing, TV and literature, plus any other assorted media that might arise, and it was going to straddle the world in one vast benevolent network, handing out alms to anyone and everyone that deserved them. Young poets that couldn't get published, musicians and designers and inventors, unrecognized talents, everyone, they were to come straight to Apple and the Beatles would review their case in person, the Beatles would help.

Inevitably, such saintliness was short-lived: the Beatles promptly found themselves besieged by massed no-talents and maniacs and charlatans, bummers of all descriptions, and they began to cut back fast. Within a year, the whole Utopian structure had boiled down to not much more than one indie record label, no better and no worse than any other.

Undeterred, the Beatles plunged on headlong into project after abortive project – there was a full-length cartoon film, *Yellow Submarine*, which did nothing much in England and cleaned up in the States, and there was a stage adaptation of John Lennon's *In His Own Write*, which was successful, and there was also a John Lennon art exhibition, which wasn't, and there was an excursion into boutique-management, which was a mistake, and, finally, there was a mammoth double-album ninety minutes and thirty tracks long, which was mostly just boring. And John Lennon got divorced from his wife and took up with Yoko Ono, a Japanese lady, and, between them, they came up with an album full of squeaks and squawks, *Two Virgins*, with nude pictures of themselves all over its cover. And Paul McCartney called Lennon a saint. And George Harrison wrote further mock-Orientalisms on the soundtrack of a film called *Wonderwall*. And Ringo Starr, of course, went right on shooting snooker.

In America and in England, they have become two entirely separate things: in the States, where pop is followed with great solemnity by almost everyone intelligent under the age of thirty, there are still many people who take them seriously, who see them as divinities and hang upon their every utterance, while in England, where pop remains mostly entertainment, they're seen as cranks, millionaire eccentrics in the grand manner, vaguely regrettable, maybe, but quite harmless.

Either way, they continue to sell records in millions, they're still flying, they're up so high by now that nothing can bring them back down again. Simply, they've gone beyond.

The thing that fascinates me most in all this is that it's happened so fast, that it's taken only five years for ultimate hard-headedness to get changed into ultimate inanity, and I'm puzzled. There are, of course, lots of easy explanations – too much acid, too many ego-trips, too much money and success and wasteable time – and maybe the easiest answers are the right ones after all but, myself, I'm not so sure, I sense that there's something here that I don't yet understand, that's only going to become clear in retrospect.

In any case, they're still young, they have time to return inside their skulls and then, just possibly, they'll do what they promised in the first place, they'll purge pop of pretension. Meanwhile, though, they've only killed off one style in bullshit to replace it with another.

From here on in, I have only one or two final evaluations to make and then I'm through. First, their music.

What do I say? They're good. They have talent and Lennon/McCartney are the most inventive, wide-ranging and melodically ingenious writers pop has produced. They've added whole new dimensions to pop, they have introduced unthought-of sophistications, complexities and subtleties. And *Sergeant Pepper's Lonely Hearts Club Band*, their best album, really was quite an impressive achievement.

For all this, I don't enjoy them much and I'm not at all convinced that they've been good for pop. So all right, the Beatles make good music, they really do, but since when was pop anything to do with good music?

140

Sergeant Pepper was genuinely a breakthrough – it was the first ever try at making a pop album into something more than just twelve songs bundled together at random. It was an overall concept, an attitude: we are the Lonely Hearts Club Band, everyone is, and these are our songs. It was ideas, allusions, pastiches, ironies. In other words, it was more than noise. Some of the songs were dire (*Lucy In The Sky With Diamonds, She's Leaving Home, Within You Without You*) and others were pretty but nothing (*When I'm 64, With A Little Help From My Friends*) and a few really worked out (*Lovely Rita, A Day In The Life, I'm Fixing A Hole* and *Sergeant Pepper* itself). In any case, the individual tracks didn't matter much – what counted was that it all hung together, that it made sense as a whole. Added up, it came to something quite ambitious, it made strange images of isolation, and it sustained. It was flawed but, finally, it worked.

So, if *Sergeant Pepper* passes, what am I grousing for? Well, it did work in itself, it was cool and clever and controlled. Only, it wasn't much like pop. It wasn't fast, flash, sexual, loud, vulgar, monstrous or violent. It made no myths.

And why should the Beatles limit themselves to pop? Why can't they just expand and progress as they want, not thinking about categories? No reason – they're responsible only to themselves and they can work whichever way they like.

The only thing is that, without pop, without its image and its flash and its myths, they don't add up to much. They lose their magic boots and then they're human like anyone else, they become updated Cole Porters, smooth and sophisticated, boring as hell. Admittedly, the posh Sundays say they're Art and that's true but, after all, what's so great about Art? What does it have on Superpop?

The way I like it, pop is all teenage property and it mirrors everything that happens to teenagers in this time, in this American twentieth century. It is about clothes and cars and dancing, it's about parents and highschool and being tied and breaking loose, it is about getting sex and getting rich and getting old, it's about America, it's about cities and noise. Get right down to it, it's all about Coca-Cola.

And, in the beginning, that's what the Beatles were about, too, and they had gimmick haircuts, gimmick uniforms, gimmick accents to prove it. They were, at last, the great British pop explosion and, even when their songs were trash, you could hear them and know it was mid-twentieth century, Liverpool U.S.A., and these boys were coke drinkers from way back.

They've changed. They don't belong to their own time or place any more, they've flown away into limbo. And there are maybe a million acid-heads, pseudo-intellectuals, muddled schoolchildren and generalized freaks who have followed them there but the mass teen public has been lumbered.

What's more, because the Beatles are so greatly worshipped by the rest of pop, most every group in the world pursues them and apes them and kneels at their feet, and that's why there's no more good fierce rock 'n' roll music now, no more honest trash.

And at least, with the Beatles, there has always been a certain talent and wit at work but, with their successors, there's been little but pretensions. Groups like Family and the Nice in England, the Grateful Dead and Iron Butterfly in America, they're crambos by nature and that's fine, they could be knocking out three-chord rock and everyone would be happy. But, after the Beatles and Bob Dylan, they've got into Art and so they've wallowed in third-form poetries, fifth-hand philosophies, ninth-rate perceptions. And, who've lost out? Teenagers have.

In America, admittedly, kids have tended to take anything they've been given and like it, they've come to talk in the same crapola terms as their groups. But in England, they've mostly shrugged and walked away, record sales have crashed and everything's gone stale.

It's bad: originally, in the fifties, the whole point about rock was its honesty, the way it talked so straight after all those years of showbiz blag, and now it's become just as fake as Tin Pan Alley ever was.

So it isn't really their fault, you could hardly blame them, but, indirectly, the Beatles have brought pop to its knees. It'll get back up again, it must do because somehow it's needed, but I don't think it'll be the Beatles who'll revive it, I think it's already too late for that.

In some sense, they have opted out and they can hardly come back in again. They'll keep progressing, they'll make better music yet and they won't ever fall. Only, in thirty years, I don't think they'll have meant so much as Elvis Presley.

In the end, Bert Berns may still have summed them up better than anyone.

As I mentioned in an earlier chapter, Berns was a most shrewd man and he understood pop perfectly. And one afternoon, about three years ago, he sat in some decaying West Hampstead café and looked gloomy over a picture of the Beatles. Then he shook his head in infinite sage sadness. 'Those boys have genius,' he said. 'They may be the ruin of us all.'

14

MERSEYBEAT

The Beatles had been the turning point and, after them, every-thing was changed. Pop stopped being straight noise and now it was full of dogma, full of complex theory, and it was hefty, obsessive, altogether neurotic. It was almost religious and that's the way it has remained.

The Beatles, of course, have dominated everything. They've stood in the middle and everyone else has ebbed and flowed around them – they have been at the heart of all things.

Predictably, the first thing they were at the heart of was hysterical boom in Liverpudlia. Two days after *Please Please Me* had crashed number one, the collected managers and agents of Britain hit Merseyside like a plague and they didn't leave again before every last able-bodied guitar-picker in town had been hijacked. They were pure Hollywood and they smoked cigars, drove limousines, waved shiny contracts and conned everyone blind. They slavered greed from their throats, lust from their nostrils, hype from their eyeballs and, inside six months, they'd run the city clean. Nobody left but women, children and crips. Total wipe-out.

In the first wave alone, there were the Searchers, Gerry and the Pacemakers, Billy J. Kramer and the Dakotas, the Mojos, the Swinging Blue Jeans, the Undertakers, Tommy

Quickly, the Merseybeats and the Big Three. Without exception, they had a few fast hits and, without exception, they then faded.

Liverpool is a strange town, it gets obsessed by everything it does. It is a seaport and it's made up of different races, it is a city full of neighbourhoods, full of gangs and, outside of Glasgow, it is the rawest, most passionate place in Britain.

It has a certain black style of its own, a private strength and humour and awareness, real violence, and it is also grim, very much so. After the pubs close down, everyone stands out on corners and watches what happens and has nowhere much to go. Clubs are small, sweaty and dumb. Kids don't move by themselves or they get nutted by the guerrillas. This is America in England: a night out ends almost inevitably with a punch on the nose.

In such an atmosphere, hungry and physical, pop could hardly miss. It exploded. It took over completely, it turned everyone fanatic and, by the early sixties, there were upwards of 350 groups around, more getting born each day. Almost always, they were musically dire, quite dreadful, but that wasn't the point – they were loud, crude, energetic, and they weren't faked.

Of course, in the normal run of things, almost none of them would ever have happened but this was no normal run, the Beatles had smashed, Liverpool was a national obsession and, suddenly, they couldn't lose.

Quality wasn't remotely relevant here – all they had to do was open wide, let those lush scouse accents out and they were home in one, they had walkovers. In this way, the charts got filled with musical assassination but it was a fierce time, at least it was rowdy, and nobody was bored.

Individually, nobody came to much – the Searchers were the most melodic, the Swinging Blue Jeans the most frantic, the Merseybeats somehow the most archetypal.

The one figure that fully sustained has been Cilla Black.

Cilla was really called Priscilla White and she was a Catholic girl from the Scotland Road, hot contender as Liverpool's most grimy slum of all. When she got out of school, she worked in the cloakroom at the Cavern Club, a hang-out much celebrated as the birthplace of the Beatles, and she did some singing on the side. Then, out of nowhere, she got herself signed by Brian Epstein.

At first glance, she was all problems.

When she sang soft, for instance, she was fair but, when she let fly, her voice turned into a monstrous foghorn blare, the melody got lost and all hell broke loose. Also, she was quite plain, not ugly but not possibly glamorous, and she was gawky, clumsy, and she couldn't move right. And she was a chatterbox, and she kept giggling. Definitely, she was the girl least likely.

In the light of all this, Epstein played it very clever. No question, he showed shrewdness.

He wasted no time on turning her into any sequined toothpaste robot but let her giggle, let her dress wrong, let her do anything she wanted, and he was right because, the more gauche she seemed, the more schoolgirlish and gauche, the better she was loved.

It's true – the British don't like their girl singers to be too good, they think it smacks of emancipation, and Cilla at least seemed safe. Obviously, she was a nice girl. Also, she was respectful and reliable, very clean and quite unsexy, and she played daughter or maybe kid sister, steady date or fiancée, but she played nobody's mistress at all. She wasn't like that.

Everyone patronized her like hell, waiting for her to fall, but then she didn't fall after all, she floated instead and she's still up there now. She won't ever come down, either – she still can't sing much, she still comes on like a schoolgirl but she's liked like that and she can't go wrong.

Genuinely, she's warm and she makes people glow. In her time, she will grow into a pop Gracie Fields, much-loved entertainer, and she'll become institutionalized.

Anyhow, getting back to the point, Merseybeat was huge for a time but Liverpool was a limited city, it only hid so many guitarists and, once they'd all been snared and signed, the business had to look somewhere else for its meat. In any case, the whole thing had only been a one-time craze and, inevitably, it finally blew up. When that happened, thousands of guitarists all over England dropped their scouse accents like gangrened legs and shuddered.

So Merseybeat is now seen only as a farce, an embarrassing lapse from sanity, and being scouse is possibly the heaviest cross that any would-be pop star can bear. Still, I enjoyed it. Right here, I wouldn't mind swapping.

15

THE ROLLING STONES

In Liverpool one time, early in 1965, I was sitting in some pub, just next to the Odeon cinema, and I heard a noise like thunder.

I went outside and looked around but I couldn't see a thing. Just this noise of thunder, slowly getting closer, and also, more faint, another noise like a wailing siren. So I waited but nothing happened. The street stayed empty.

Finally, after maybe five full minutes, a car came round the corner, a big flash limousine, and it was followed by police cars, by police on foot and police on motorbikes, and they were followed by several hundred teenage girls. And these girls made a continuous high-pitched keening sound and their shoes banged down against the stone. They ran like hell, their hair down in their eyes, and they stretched their arms out pleadingly as they went. They were desperate.

The limousine came up the street towards me and stopped directly outside the Odeon stage door. The police formed cordons. Then the car door opened and the Rolling Stones got out, all five of them and Andrew Loog Oldham, their manager, and they weren't real. They had hair down past their shoulders and they wore clothes of every colour imaginable and they looked mean, they looked just impossibly evil.

In this grey street, they shone like sun gods. They didn't seem human, they were like creatures off another planet, impossible to reach or understand but most exotic, most beautiful in their ugliness.

They crossed towards the stage door and this was what the girls had been waiting for, this was their chance, so they began to surge and scream and clutch. But then they stopped, they just froze. The Stones stared straight ahead, didn't twitch once, and the girls only gaped. Almost as if the Stones weren't touchable, as if they were protected by some invisible metal ring. So they moved on and disappeared. And the girls went limp behind them and were quiet. After a few seconds, some of them began to cry.

In this way, whatever else, the Stones had style and presence and real control. They are my favourite group. They always have been.

To begin with, they used to play the Crawdaddy Club in Richmond and they laid down something very violent in the line of rhythm 'n' blues. They were enthusiasts then, they cared a lot about their music. Really, that was the only thing that linked them because they'd come from different backgrounds, very different situations, but they'd all grown up to the blues and, for a time, they got along.

At this point, they were only archetypal drop-outs. I mean, they weren't art students but they should have been, they had all the symptoms, that aggression, that scruffiness and calculated cool, that post-beat bohemianism. And in these very early sixties, before the age of T-shirts and baseball boots, the heavy art-school cults were Ray Charles and Chuck Berry and Bo Diddley, Muddy Waters, Charlie Mingus and Monk, Allen Ginsberg and Jack Kerouac, Robert Johnson. If you were pretentious about it, you might stretch to a paperback translation of Rimbaud or Dostoyevsky, strictly for display. But the Stones weren't pretentious – they were mean and nasty, full-blooded, very tasty, and they beat out

149

the toughest, crudest, most offensive noise any English band had ever made.

(Up to this, the British R&B scene had been desperately thin: Chris Barber, the trad trombonist, had started a few sessions in the late fifties but, by 1960, the obvious boss was a harmonica-blower called Cyril Davies, who died just as the blues boom was finally lifting off the ground.

Davies was an earnest man and a good musician but he mostly rehashed the Americans, he made almost no attempt to translate things into English terms and that limited him. Still, he laid foundations.)

At any rate, the Stones were at the Crawdaddy, peddling stuff about midway between the bedrock Chicago blues of Muddy Waters and the pop-blues of Chuck Berry, and they built themselves a following. Naughty but nice, they were liked by Aldermaston marchers and hitch-hikers, beards and freaks and pre-Neanderthal Mods everywhere. Simply, they were turning into the voice of hooliganism.

As groups go, they were definitely motley: Mick Jagger, who sang, came out of a solid middle-class background and had been to the London School of Economics; Keith Richards came from Tottenham and was quite tough; Brian Jones wasn't tough at all – he was from Cheltenham, very safe, but he was insecure, neurotic, highly intelligent.

Charlie Watts had worked in an ad agency and, being a drummer, never talked; Bill Wyman was older, was married – he didn't quite belong.

Anyhow, the thing about them was that, unlike the Beatles, they didn't balance out but niggled, jarred and hardly ever relaxed. At all times, there was tension to them – you always felt there was a background chance of a public holocaust. That was partly what made them exciting.

In 1963, Andrew Loog Oldham became their manager.

Oldham, without doubt, was the most flash personality that British pop has ever had, the most anarchic and obsessive and imaginative hustler of all. Whenever he was good, he was quite magnificent.

His father having been killed in the war, he'd grown up with his mother, quite rich, and he was sent to public school. By the time he was sixteen, he was doing window displays for Mary Quant, the clothes designer, and then he spent a year bumming round the South of France before he came back to work in the cloakroom at the Ronnie Scott Club and be a publicist with Brian Epstein's NEMS. And that was the whole sum of his achievement at the time he first met the Stones. He was then nineteen years old.

What he had going for him was mostly a frantic yen to get up and out: he loathed slowness and drabness, age and caution and incompetence, mediocrity of all kinds, and he could not stand to work his way up steady like anyone else.

Instead, he barnstormed, he came on quite outrageous. He slabbed his face with make-up and wore amazing clothes and hid his eyes behind eternal shades. He was all camp and, when he was batting off nothing at all, he still shot fat lines and always played everything as ultimate big-time.

The great thing was the way he pushed himself, he could either clean up or bomb completely. He couldn't possibly get caught by compromise.

Anyhow, the Stones were obviously just his meat. He caught them at Richmond and got hooked by their truculence, their built-in offensiveness. Also, he struck up immediate contact with Mick Jagger, who was greatly impressed by him and became almost his disciple, his dedicated follower in the ways of outrage.

So Oldham brought in Eric Easton, who was his partner and had capital. Easton, a stock businessman who handled such showbiz stuff as Bert Weedon and Julie Grant, wasn't unimpressed. 'But the singer'll have to go,' he said. 'The BBC won't like him.'

151

As manager, what Oldham did was to take everything implicit in the Stones and blow it up one hundred times. Long-haired and ugly and anarchic as they were, Oldham made them more so and he turned them into everything that parents would most hate, be most frightened by. All the time, he goaded them to be wilder, nastier, fouler in every way and they were – they swore, sneered, snarled and, deliberately, they came on cretinous.

It was good basic psychology: kids might see them the first time and not be sure about them, but then they'd hear their parents whining about those animals, those filthy long-haired morons, and suddenly they'd be converted, they'd identify like mad.

(This, of course, is bedrock pop formula: find yourself something that truly makes adults squirm and, straightaway, you have a guaranteed smash on your hands. Johnnie Ray, Elvis, P.J. Proby, Jimi Hendrix – it never fails.)

So their first single, *Come On*, got to the edge of the twenty, and then *I Wanna Be Your Man* was number ten, and *Not Fade Away* was number three and, finally, *It's All Over Now* was number one. Their initial album did a hundred thousand in a week and, by this time, they were running hot second to the Beatles and they kept it like that for two years solid. Later on, in America, they even temporarily went ahead.

All this time, Oldham hustled them strong: he was hectic, inventive, and he pulled strokes daily. Less obviously, he was also thorough, he worked everything out to the smallest spontaneous detail. Well, the Stones were really his fantasy, his private dream-child and, healthy narcissist as he was, he needed them to be entirely perfect.

The bit I liked best, about both Oldham and the Stones themselves, was the stage act. In every way, both individually and collectively, it expressed them just right.

Charlie Watts played the all-time bombhead drummer, mouth open and jaw sagging, moronic beyond belief, and

152

Bill Wyman stood way out to one side, virtually in the wings, completely isolated, his bass held up vertically in front of his face for protection, and he chewed gum endlessly and his eyes were glazed and he looked just impossibly bored.

Keith Richards wore T-shirts and, all the time, he kept winding and unwinding his legs, moving uglily like a crab, and was shut-in, shuffling, the classic fourth-form drop-out. Simply, he spelled Borstal.

Brian Jones had beautiful silky yellow hair to his shoulders, exactly like a Silvikrin ad, and he wasn't queer, very much the opposite, but he camped it up like mad, he did the whole feminine thing and, for climax, he'd rush the front of the stage and make to jump off, flouncing and flitting like a gymslip schoolgirl.

And then Mick Jagger: he had lips like bumpers, red and fat and shiny, and they covered his face. He looked like an updated Elvis Presley, in fact, skinny legs and all, and he moved like him, so fast and flash he flickered. When he came on out, he went bang. He'd shake his hair all down in his eyes and he danced like a whitewash James Brown, he flapped those tarpaulin lips and, grotesque, he was all sex.

He sang but you couldn't hear him for screams, you only got some background blur, the beat, and all you knew was his lips. His lips and his moving legs, bound up in sausage-skin pants. And he was outrageous: he spun himself blind, he smashed himself and he'd turn his back on the audience, jack-knife from the waist, so that his arse stuck straight up in the air, and then he'd shake himself, he'd vibrate like a motor, and he'd reach the hand mike through his legs at you, he'd push it right in your face. Well, he was obscene, he was excessive. Of course, he was beautiful.

The weird thing was, Jagger on-stage wasn't like Jagger offstage but he was very much like Andrew Oldham. Andrew Loog Oldham. I mean, he was more a projection of Oldham than of himself. (This happens often. For various obvious

153

physical reasons, most managers aren't capable of getting out and being stars themselves. So they use the singers they handle as transmitters, as dream machines. Possibly, that's the way it was with Jagger and Oldham.)

Anyhow, what I was saying, the Stones had a wild stage act and, at that time in Liverpool, the night I mentioned before, they put on maybe the best pop show I ever saw: final bonanza, hysterical and violent and sick but always stylized, always full of hype, and Jagger shaped up genuinely as a second Elvis, as heroic and impossible as that.

After the show, I hung around in the dressing-rooms. The Stones were being ritually vicious to everyone, fans and journalists and hangers-on regardless, and I got bored. So I went down into the auditorium and it was empty, quite deserted, but there was this weird smell. Piss: the small girls had screamed too hard and wet themselves. Not just one or two of them but many, so that the floor was sodden and the stench was overwhelming. Well, it was disgusting. No, it wasn't disgusting but it was strange, the empty cinema (chocolate boxes, cigarette packs, ice-lolly sticks) and this sad sour smell.

Throughout this chapter, I've kept on saying how great the Stones were but all I've shown is evil and the question finally needs to be asked: what's so good about bad?

No question, of course, the Stones were more loutish than they had to be but then, after all, each pop generation must go further than the one before, must feel as if it's doing everything for the first time. Always, it must be arrogant and vain and boorish. Otherwise, it's not being healthy and the whole essential teen revolt gets dammed up, that whole bit of breaking away and making it by oneself, and then it's stored up in frustration, it twists itself and, most likely, it comes out ugly later on.

The best thing about the Stones, the most important, was their huge sense of independence, uncompromised.

In the first chapter, I said that pop had originally been just that, a movement towards teen independence, and that Elvis was its first great leader. Well, compared to Elvis, the Stones were entirely different class: they were as far ahead of him as Elvis himself had been ahead of the young Sinatra.

No mashed banana sandwiches, middle-aged managers, G.I. blues, teddy bears, Gods or obediences – the Stones were a teenage industry all by themselves, self-contained, and the adult world simply wasn't relevant. That's why they were so loathed inside the business, because they threatened the structure, because they threatened the way in which pop was controlled by old men, by men over thirty.

That's also why they mattered, that's why Andrew Oldham mattered in particular, because they meant that you didn't need to soften up to make it any more. You didn't need to be pretty, you didn't need to simper or drool or suck up – the old men might hate you in every way possible and you could still make yourself a million dollars.

Really, the Stones were major liberators: they stirred up a whole new mood of teen arrogance here and the change was reflected in the rise of Mod, in Carnaby Street and Radio Caroline, in Cathy McGowan and the Who and, later, in Twiggy. These weren't purely teenage happenings, of course, but most everyone involved in them was under thirty and none of them could possibly have happened in the fifties. For the first time, England had something like a private teen society going and, myself, I think it was the Stones rather than the Beatles who led it.

Certainly, the Beatles were the bigger group but, until they turned to Love in 1967, they never greatly changed the way that anyone thought. They were self-assured, cocky, and they took no shit but they were always full of compromise and they appealed as much to adults as to kids. They weren't committed. The Stones were.

In this way, then, the Stones were the final group of the sixties and their image was the final image, Jagger was the final face and their records were the final records. More than anyone, more even than Bob Dylan, they became their time.

Apart from anything else, they made marvellous music.

In the early R&B phase, they were wildly exciting but also crude, derivative, very limited, and they shaped up only as a short-term craze. But then, just as things were wearing thin, Jagger and Keith Richards suddenly upped and exploded as writers. Out of nowhere, they started churning out monsters: *The Last Time, Satisfaction, Get Off Of My Cloud, Mother's Little Helper, Under My Thumb, Paint It Black*.

They weren't much on melody, their words were mostly slogans, and a lot of their songs were simply crap. None of that mattered. All that counted was sound – an adapted Spectorsound but less symphonic, less inflated – and the murderous mood it made. All din and mad atmosphere. Really, it was nothing but beat, smashed and crunched and hammered home like some amazing stampede. The words were lost and the song was lost. You were only left with chaos, beautiful anarchy. You drowned in noise.

Their best record was probably *Satisfaction*. Their most archetypal was *Get Off Of My Cloud*, which sloganized the sixties just as *Blue Suede Shoes* had the fifties.

According to the storyline, Jagger lives in an apartment on the ninety-ninth floor of his block and sits alone by the window, imagining the world has stopped. He plays records incredibly loud, makes holocausts of noise, and nobody can reach him, nobody can turn his volume down. People from below try to shut him up but he takes no notice. He sits and plays records and watches and floats. He can't be touched. He's on his cloud.

From autumn 1966, though, the Stones began to slide.

Basically, they'd become too familiar. They'd come to be accepted and new people came along (the Who, Jimi Hendrix, the Mothers of Invention), who went beyond them in outrage and made them look tame. Suddenly, when the Stones came out to do their thing, they looked dated and a bit comic – Jagger's cavortings even had a certain period charm to them. That's how fast pop is: the anarchists of one year are the boring old farts of the next.

Beyond that, they'd gone badly stale in themselves, they'd lost pace and direction. Like the Beatles, they'd stopped touring. Unlike the Beatles, they didn't use the extra time to make better music – their records went flabby and gutless instead.

Finally, they made an album called *Their Satanic Majesties Request*, very experimental, and they commissioned a 3D cover and they pushed the whole operation like mad, they peddled it as a major musical breakthrough. And it was only boring. It wasn't freakish or dire or nauseous – it was a drag. It had no rage or arrogance left, no image. In every way, it was toothless.

Also, they weren't too much of a group any more: Watts and Wyman were married and settled, Brian Jones was going through big neurotic troubles on his own, only Jagger and Richards were still close.

Fatally, they'd made no films and, without movies, nobody can really sustain. The Stones had had chances – they'd bought a property, they'd had deals set up but they'd never brought anything through. The right moment went and still they fannied about. When they finally got straight, it was already too late.

In the summer of 1967, Jagger and Richards were given jail sentences on drug charges and, later, they got off on appeal. Shortly afterwards, Brian Jones went through roughly the same thing.

That could have saved them: they'd been made martyrs again and they were hounded by authority, by jobsworth, by the uglies in general. They were saints in the true cause of pot, teen symbol of that year, and they were most dignified,

157

and they held their cool. In theory, they should have won everything back.

It didn't work – they rushed out a new record, *We Love You*, complete with sound effects of prison doors slamming, and it badly failed to hit number one. Well, it was a lousy record but that wasn't the point. In such a situation, it should have scored regardless. Obviously, the time for dramatic savers had gone.

The same winter, Andrew Oldham stopped being their manager.

No question, the second half of his management had been infinitely less impressive than the first. Really, he'd run out of targets – after all, he'd come out of nowhere and found the Stones and made them happen, he'd earned himself a million dollars and started Immediate Records, his own independent label, the first indie in England. He'd cleaned up. He'd entirely made it and he was now twenty-one years old.

Not surprisingly, he turned a bit aimless. He hung out in Hollywood a lot and squandered much money. Whenever I saw him he looked bored, vaguely unhappy.

The Stones weren't much pleased by this and relations got very strained indeed. The clincher came when Oldham didn't fly back from Hollywood for the Jagger/Richards drug trial. Even Jagger, who'd always been closest to him, was finished by this and, not long afterwards, the split was made official.

Oldham does all right – he still owns Immediate on which he has the Amen Corner and Fleetwood Mac, and he has the Beach Boys' publishing in England. At the worst, he's suffering from anti-climax. But he is much changed, very much deflated.

At the time of his bust-up with the Stones, he went through some quite bad times. When he came back on the scene, he was almost unrecognizable. No make-up, no camp, no outrage – he'd turned into a businessman.

He wasn't objectionable. He was quiet and thoughtful, very polite, and he wasn't even rude to waiters. He wanted to get into films, he wanted to be solid inside the pop industry and, on his office wall, he had a small photo of himself and his partner, Tony Calder, solemnly shaking hands with some middle-aged American record chief.

In every way, he was a more adult, responsible and admirable man but, myself, I'd preferred the ancient monster. He used to be messianic. And now he was a merchant. So Andrew Oldham lived but Loog was very dead.

And the Stones? At the time of writing they've appeared in a Jean-Luc Godard film, *One Plus One*, and they've done a few televisions, a few records, and that's just about all.

Musically, they've veered away from the artiness of *Their Majesties Request* and gone back to the basics, the bedrock aggression that they've always been so good at. In this style, they've produced one marvellous album, *Beggars Banquet*, and two fine singles, *Jumpin' Jack Flash* and *Street Fighting Man*. No question, they still have what it takes, they remain the best rock band in the world and, if only they'd concentrate, they could rescue rock single-handed.

Tactically, though, they've wasted themselves – there was a time when they could have been as heavy and powerful as the Beatles, when Jagger could have become bigger than anyone since Elvis, when the Stones could have led their whole generation but now it's not going to be like that, there have been too many miscues and culs-de-sac, too much unused time, too much assorted fucking about.

They're hardly suffering. They still sell records and make headlines and, even now, they probably run second behind the Beatles. The only thing is, they could have been more than that.

Predictably, Jagger has come off best. He's settled himself down nicely as an international gossip-column face, a trusty, and he's seen at the opera and the theatre, he makes trends and he gets his face in the papers every time he catches a plane.

He'll always be around. He'll make it in the movies and he'll guest on TV shows and he'll go to premieres. Gradually, he'll lose his hair. Never mind, he's safe.

On the whole, things have worked out well.

So all right, the Stones could have been smarter, they could probably have upped their status a bit but, finally, what would be the point? They could slowly twist themselves into family entertainers (a song, a dance and twenty-two tricks with a banana) or they could hang on to become elder statesmen in pop, sage old maestros like the Beatles will be. What for? Either way, they'd bore everyone stiff.

The way things are, they most likely won't last and I'm pleased. I think that's right. They weren't meant to, they weren't made to get old. They existed only to go bang one time, and then disappear again. And if they have any sense of neatness they'll get themselves killed in an air crash, three days before their thirtieth birthdays.

16

R&B ENGLAND

Outside of mainstream pop fans, there is a separate sub-breed of English teenager, roughly classifiable as the Art Student, which goes in for violent bouts of musical insanity, one-shot fads that come out of nowhere and explode into huge obsessions and then drop dead quite suddenly, never again to be mentioned.

Along this tradition, there was Skiffle in the mid-fifties and Trad around 1960 and R&B in 1964 and, in the summer of 1967, of course, there was Flower Power.

The symptoms haven't varied much: the subject regards itself as several cuts above teenagers in general, being more intellectual and altogether more soulful, and it gets very scornful about any pop outside of its own cult of the moment. Mostly, it isn't an art student at all, it's only a weekend dropout, but it has the mannerisms off, even the uniforms, and you have to be a bit fly to spot the difference.

Over the years, it has usually gone for beards and nuclear disarmament, hitch-hiking, all-night raves, pop and getting its picture in the *News Of The World*.

Numerically, of course, it has only been a small minority, a stable hundred thousand or so, but it has always been fanatic, it has punched much more than its fair weight, and I'd be wrong not to give it space.

161

Anyhow, its most golden age was the early sixties. First, it got itself hooked on Trad, a definitely dire bowdlerization of New Orleans jazz, all banjos and fancy waistcoats and boozy vocals and there was much assorted high jinking on Aldermaston marches. Everyone wore jeans and baggy sweaters, dirty toenails, and Mr Acker Bilk was king.

In due course, Trad died its death and, after a seemly pause, R&B took its place. The Rolling Stones were the major sponsors of course, and Saturday-night Soho used to be jammed tight with mean boys and moody girls, all long-haired, singing infinite choruses of *I've Got My Mojo Working* and blowing mouth-organs out of tune.

What did R&B add up to? In English terms, it was most anything from rock to bedrock country blues, from Chuck Berry and Bo Diddley through Muddy Waters, John Lee Hooker and Little Walter, all the way along to the gutbucket stumblings of Sonny Boy Williamson. Stirring times – old bluesmen kept getting dug out of their Delta obscurity and they'd be shipped across in bulk to bang out a few random chords, sing us their forgotten favourites, get drunk out of their heads and finally lose their teeth in the middle of their acts.

Like you'd expect, most of our home-grown bluesmen were lousy. They'd come out of Surbiton, their hair down in their eyes and their Mick Jagger maracas up by their ears, and they'd sing their blues, dem lawdy-lawdy blues, all about those cottonfields back home: the Dagenham Delta.

The most classic were the Pretty Things, who'd been deliberately designed to make the Rolling Stones look like that proverbial vicarage tea party. Man, they were ugly. I mean, really ugly – Phil May, the singer, had a fat face, entirely hidden by hair, and he'd bang about the stage like some maimed gorilla. The others looked even badder. And their music was all chaos: the big bad blues. Actually it wasn't either big or the blues. Bad it was, however.

162

The Animals were something different again.

I spent my early teenage years in Newcastle and the Animals were my local group, only they were still called the Alan Price Combo then, and they used to play Saturday all-nights at the Downbeat Club. Later on, they moved to somewhere more elegant, the Club A Go-Go, but I always liked the Downbeat best.

It was stuck on top of some kind of disused warehouse, down towards the docks, and the railway bridge ran right outside it, making it shake. It was cramped, wet, ratty and music made its walls buckle. And it was a fierce atmosphere, it burned, and I used to go dancing there with two short-sighted sisters. I never had quite such good nights again.

The Animals sounded good then. Musically, they were quite limited but they came across angry, they hit so hard. Nothing else mattered much but the drive. Also, Alan Price played very tough organ. Then there was Eric Burdon, who sang, and he was odd.

Burdon was small and round, looked like Just William, and he didn't sing in tune much but he had a wild passionate yell.

Always, he was fanatical. He'd been to art school and he worshipped Ray Charles. No other word applies – worshipped him. And he fell about on stage like some exploding doughnut, tubby and ecstatic, howling the blues, and he was a good boozy boy then, he had real talents.

In due course, they went south to London and made it: Alan Price did a new arrangement for *The House Of The Rising Sun* and Burdon sang it quite beautifully and, inevitably, it turned into a worldwide smash. So they had a couple of lush years in there and they made fortunes in America. But somehow they never got around to making another good record, they lost it and, in the end, they came to be just another group.

What went wrong? Nothing very much – they used up their talents, they hung out in too many discotheques and they went flabby. Alan Price left to form his own group and got successful all over again. John Steel, the drummer, went back to Newcastle. Finally, the whole group broke up.

Eric Burdon himself is greatly changed.

He used to be an early-morning madman, hard drinker and hard talker, always bursting out of himself, and he collected war relics, guns and helmets and so forth, but now he preaches Love and smiles angelic smiles for everyone. He went through acid and that changed him, that softened him up. Then he toted beads and bells and San Francisco, the whole bit, and he turned prophetic. These days, his records are tracts and his interviews are gospels. He sermonizes endlessly. Kid, he's pious.

The strange thing is, he's always been trendy and painfully sincere, a tough combination to handle. Whatever has been fashionable, Ray Charles or Newcastle Brown or acid or love, he's moved with it but he's absolutely believed in it. He is the instant sixties saint.

Also, there was the Yardbirds (Most Blueswailing).

There were five of them and they took over from the Rolling Stones at the Crawdaddy Club. In the beginning, their big strength was Eric Clapton, who played the best blues guitar in England and, for me, just about disguised the fact that the rest of the group was stone cold. Never mind, they built up a strong following around the clubs and then they went commercial, swallowed the blues and had hits instead.

Eric Clapton cut out – he wanted to play the blues, nothing but, and the Yardbirds played mostly pulp these days.

Again, there was Manfred Mann.

Manfred Mann himself was a South African organist, an earnest jazzman with a beard and horn-rimmed glasses, and he ran a band that played around one third blues, one third jazz, one third straight pop. They were musicians, what's more. Nothing earth-shattering but they knew their stuff and, over four years, they've churned out one automatic hit after

164

another. Off-hand, I can't think of anything I've liked much but then I can't think of anything I've disliked much either. They're professionals, that's all.

Their singer, Paul Jones, turned into pop's most resident intellectual. He's done a year at Oxford, you see, and he wore a nuclear disarmament badge and he read books. He was nicely spoken, he even used long words. By pop standards, he was truly deep.

The thinking man's pop star: very soon, he was writing articles for the posh Sundays and punditing on TV shows. Later, he went solo and talked some more and finally starred in *Privilege*, Peter Watkins' art movie. By this time, he had the solemnity stakes all wrapped up.

He was ideal. He allowed left-wing intellectuals to feel hip without scaring them, without making them sweat at all. He was a varsity man, after all, and quite civilized. So they could go to him, ask him about Vietnam, and they were safe, they risked no unpleasantness of any kind. No clowning, no yobbism, no embarrassment: that nice Paul Jones, he only smiled and answered them well, a clean machine. In this way he became the Sidney Poitier of pop. It was hardly his fault, but he did. The only trouble was, in the process, he bored his fans to death and they quit buying his records.

Finally, in this batch, there were the Kinks, who started out like they'd be the worst of all but who wound up being easily the best.

They came out in ridiculous red hunting coats and they had long ratty hair like everyone else and, live, they didn't sound good. Their first records were predictable dogs. But then Ray Davies, the singer, started writing their singles for them and he was good.

Davies has never been fashionable, he has always been greatly scorned by hipsters and hippies everywhere, but almost always everything he's done has been a hit and, myself, I'd rate him very high indeed.

165

Whatever else, he's been an original: he has his own areas, his own private progression, and nothing intrudes, nothing deflects him. At all times, he is entirely separate from the rest of pop, he does his walkabouts by himself and, as pop in general has got more complex, so he's got simpler, always more childlike, until his songs have become as pared as nursery rhymes.

His lyrics are all understatements, small simplistic slogans, with bass lines like trombones, trundling along like so many elephants, and his own voice is flat, and awkward, quavering along like some pop George Formby. The whole thing is lopsided, crablike, one step from chaos, but somehow it balances out, it makes sense.

He writes about nothing much, streets and houses and pubs, days at the seaside, little bits of love, drabness and things that don't change, stuff like that. Mostly, he writes about small lives, small pleasures, and he's an open romantic but there's always a slyness in it, some self-mockery.

With his gappy teeth and his grin all twisted, he looks clownish and he seems always doubtful, unsure of himself, so that you expect him to split his pants or trip over his feet at any time. He even wears white socks. And he's childlike (not childish): he has the most intense butterfly concentration, he'll get all wrapped up in something one moment and then he'll be equally obsessed by something new the next.

He gets horribly brought down by the smallest things, he can't stand hassle and has to hide. He's depressive, exhausting. But he's also funny. Myself, I like him immensely.

Anyhow, he has his own style in backhanded logic going for him. We were talking about politics one time and he said he'd admired Anthony Eden, he'd liked his solidity. 'Surely,' I said. 'Didn't Harold Macmillan do all that much better?'

'Macmillan?' he said, all scorn. 'He turned out to be a right Vince Taylor, didn't he?'

166

So that was English R&B, a far cry from the real American article, but it was quite enjoyable, a good and filthy time was had by all. Four years ago, it was, but I walked into a Northern club not long ago and the group was still doing the blues, long hair and maracas and all. I couldn't believe them, I could hardly believe myself. Only four years and, already, they were like a walking museum.

17

BOB DYLAN

First of all, some basics: Bob Dylan was born Bob Zimmerman in Minnesota, 1941.

He came out of a Midwest Jewish background, quite straight and, through his teens, he ran away seven times from home and highschool and college and, according to the legend, which may well be true, he was on the road at eighteen, a hobo in the romantic Beat tradition, a teenage Sal Paradise. He played guitar, he wrote poems, he travelled. When he changed his name, for instance, he called himself after Dylan Thomas.

He was a folksinger by trade and, when he came East in 1961, he sat by the bedside of the dying Woody Guthrie. Then he went down inside Greenwich Village and joined the circuit.

Folk, at this time, was going through a major revival: there was a whole new generation coming through, young and political and ardent, people like Joan Baez and Tom Rush and Phil Ochs, Judy Collins and Tom Paxton, and they'd already established strong colonies in Boston and the West Village. They were radical, romantic, full of beliefs. Between them, they made up quite a powerful movement and Dylan became part of it, he hung around the bars and coffee houses and, very quickly, he got noticed.

He was strange. Technically, he was nothing at all, he played bad guitar and blew bad mouth-harp, he hardly ever sang in tune and his voice was ugly, it came through his nose and whined. Still, it was oddly mesmeric, it wriggled inside your head. Even when you didn't like it, it bruised you.

As for his songs, they started out immensely worthy – they were anti-war and anti-establishment and anti-mammon, full of easy answers and, stylistically, they were a mingling of very many things, folk/blues and Beat and Dada, Woody Guthrie and Robert Johnson and Allen Ginsberg, Big Joe Williams and Rimbaud. 'Open your ears,' said Dylan, 'and you're influenced.'

Fifth-form propaganda apart, he was impressive. He had imagination and energy and sweep, a fast way with words, a vivid feel for imagery and, coming out of nowhere, aged twenty, he seemed like something special. And down in the Village, he grew into a cult, he began to dominate and, already, there were people who called him a genius, a primitive prophet.

Himself, he was cute: he had curly hair and smooth flesh, he seemed shy and shuffled his feet and acted gently. Just sometimes, he'd turn around and be vicious instead but, mostly, he was immensely charming and Allen Ginsberg thought he was sweet, Joan Baez thought he had true inner beauty.

In this style, he took New York and made records and then he wrote *Blowin' In The Wind*, which became a hit for Peter, Paul and Mary, and he sold a lot of albums and, by late 1963, having torn up that year's Newport Festival, he'd emerged as the new leader of American folk.

But then, he went beyond being a folksinger, he became more important than Woody Guthrie or Pete Seeger or Joan Baez ever were, just because he sold outside the normal folk audience and got through to a mass teen public, to kids who'd probably never even listened to folk before but who'd come to look down on Top Forty pop as pulp and wanted music that was honest, halfway intelligent.

Ten years earlier, they might have been modern jazz fans and they'd have worn shades, they'd have covered their bedroom walls with pictures of Bird, but, by the sixties, jazz had gotten boring or incomprehensible or both. Dylan filled the gap.

He was young and pretty, very cool, and he wasn't manufactured, he was no part of any system. Instead, he came on like a Dharma Bum, most romantic, and his songs were filled with all the right kinds of dissent. Above all, he used words, his lyrics went way beyond the slogans of rock 'n' roll (Awopbopaloobop). For the first time, he fed kids with songs that actually meant something, that expressed revolt through something more complex than a big cock and, many of them, the kids liked this.

In all of these ways, Dylan was natural hero-food and, by 1964, he'd come to be the mouthpiece of teen discontent all over the world. As teen discontents go, what's more, the 1964 strain was fierce.

In the past, in the times of Sinatra and Johnnie Ray and Elvis, mass pop dissent had mostly been as crude and superficial as a brick thrown through a plate-glass window: my dad's a square, I hate him, I hate you too, I'll smash your face in.

In '64 that kind of revolt still survived, came through in groups like the Stones and the Who, but now it had been joined by something new, something much more radical, which was a basic contempt for the whole Americanese lifestyle, for its greed and smugness and stupidities, its wars and its ghettoes, its heroes and villains.

Agreed, this was expressed in great starry-eyed generalizations, it was all naïve, but it mattered just the same, it carried weight, just because it wasn't only a small intelligentsia that felt this way any more but mainline kids as well, millions of them.

In this way, Dylan at the helm, *Blowin' In The Wind* became the first anti-war song ever to make the charts and truthfully, it was possibly the worst song that he's written, it was embarrassing in its mimsiness, but that wasn't the point: it changed

170

things regardless, it changed the whole concept of what could or couldn't be attempted in a hit song. Suddenly, pop writers could go beyond three-chord love songs, they didn't have to act mindless any more. Mostly, they could say what they meant.

By any standards, this was a heavy breakthrough and all kinds of people moved in behind it. The Beatles, the Stones, Sonny and Cher, Donovan, P. F. Sloan – everyone had hits with songs that would have been inconceivable before, everyone took to peddling politics and philosophies and social profundities by the pound and, inevitably, most of it was a joke, most of it was total foolishness but, just the same, it moved pop forward into its second phase, it shut down rock and roll, the golden age of pulp.

Right then, pop began to be something more than simple auto-noise, it developed pretensions, it turned into an art form, a religion even and, in all of this, Dylan was the answer.

At the time when the Beatles were still the Mersey Moptop Marvels, when the Rolling Stones were still a Crawdaddy blues band, Dylan was writing verse and getting hits with it. Good verse, bad verse, what did it matter? The point was that, without even trying, he'd put pop through bigger changes than anyone since Elvis.

As for himself, most of his early hits – *Masters Of War, The Times They Are A-Changin'* – were tracts, very simple-minded but then, as he got more and more successful, he grew out of his innocence fast and his music turned tough.

In place of the Minnesota boy scout, a whole new face emerged, watchful and withdrawn, cold and arrogant and often mean, full of conscious hipnesses. In particular, he became secret – he stonewalled and played games and pulled faces, let nobody intrude and, when he decided to put someone down, he'd stare at them without expression until they crawled, he'd be merciless. Definitely, this machine could kill.

Still, mixed in with all the enigmatics, he was also subject to spasms of great sudden gentleness, odd tenderness and then, without warning, he'd be so charming it wasn't possible, he'd get himself forgiven for almost anything.

At any rate, if his changes made him paranoid, they also improved his writing out of all recognition. No more schoolboy sermons and no more good intentions, his songs now were sharper, fiercer, stronger in every way. His melody lines got less hackneyed, his imagery less obvious, his jokes less cute. Instead, he was harsh and self-mocking and hurt, he laughed with his teeth, he packed real punch.

So all right, he was maybe less than the cosmic genius that his supporters claimed and if, like me, you were turned off by the physical sound of him, by the changeless wail of his mouth-harp and by his voice itself, it was still possible not to dig him as a performer. As a writer, though, he was getting formidable.

Mostly, his best songs were also his cruellest, the ones where he let paranoia run wild, where he did nothing but bitch, both at his ladies and at himself. There were, of course, still times when he played his love songs straight – *Just Like A Woman*, *She Belongs To Me* – but more often he was malicious, he sounded disgusted and it suited him.

More exactly, he sounded tired. Where his earlier work had been so full of certainties and self-congratulations, his new songs were sunk in distaste, a sense of waste. And he was still only in his early twenties but there were times when he sounded quite defeated.

Inevitably, as his influence on pop grew, he got influenced back and he rode in limousines, surrounded himself with an entourage, ran around with the Beatles, had a fast intense friendship with John Lennon, did the entire superstar thing, in fact, and, finally, he hired a rock 'n' roll backing band.

By this time, having got so full of sass, he'd managed to alienate most of his friends in folk and him getting hooked on pop was the clincher. When he brought his rock group out on stage with him, purists everywhere booed out loud.

It didn't matter: any ethnic following that he'd lost was swamped by the vast new pop markets he'd opened up and, in any case, his rock group was tough, they did him great good and he came up with his best and most powerful records yet – *Subterranean Homesick Blues*, *Positively 4th Street*, *Like A Rolling Stone*.

By this time, deliberately or not, he'd turned himself very much into the Elvis of the sixties, remote and unreachable, and most everyone you met had some strange story about him, some monstrous saga that at once explained all of his secrets, except that each new story entirely contradicted the one before.

All that anyone could say for sure was that he had image, lots of it and, late in 1966, he was said to have had a motorbike crash and broken his neck and took a whole year to get better again.

He went into hiding and wrote a novel called *Tarantula* and saw nobody, not the press, not his record company, not his friends, not anyone.

When he emerged again, he got friendly with Johnny Cash, the C&W singer, and showed much of his influence in *John Wesley Hardin*, his first comeback album. This had a couple of fine songs in it – *Dear Landlord*, *All Along The Watchtower* – and went further down the line he'd drawn earlier, was more secret and more hurt and more paranoid than ever. Even with its overtones of Nashville, hoedown and Grand Ole Opry, it was grim.

And that, to the time of writing, is the saga just about complete. He's done a few further recording sessions, he appeared at a Woody Guthrie Memorial Concert and, every so often, he suddenly shows, maybe in New York, maybe out West, and spends a night or two in public and then he hides again. In a house in Big Pink, outside of New York, he sits and doesn't smile at visitors.

How do I rate him? Quite simply, I don't – he bores me stiff. Under pressure, I can see that he's an original, that he writes good melodies and makes some funny jokes, that he has a pretty face, that his influence on pop has been immense but still I can't enjoy him, he turns me off. Just the noise he makes, his whine and his sneer, he loses me.

As a poet, he's had his moments of real vision – *Gates Of Eden*, *Visions Of Johanna* – but, more often, I've found him flabby and sentimental, much overblown.

Really, I suppose it's been more his supporters' fault than his own: if he'd been put forward merely as a good young song-writer, a clever lyricist, a heavy image, I'd have been all sympathy. Well, I still wouldn't have bought his records, perhaps, but I'd never have put him down.

What I can't take is the vision of Dylan as seer, as teenage messiah, as everything else he's been worshipped as. The way I see him, he's a minor talent with a major gift for self-hype, for amateur myth-making, which is the same equation that Elvis had, or Mick Jagger, or Jim Morrison, or anyone else that's broken rock up. The only bring-down is, Dylan's been pushed as so much more than that.

At any rate, that's why I haven't attempted any detailed evaluation of his music and that's why I haven't tried to explain him, simply because there's nothing helpful I could possibly say on him. In my own life, the Monotones have meant more in one line of *Book Of Love* than Dylan did in the whole *Blonde On Blonde* – what hope could there be for me?

Just the same, his effect on pop remains enormous: almost everyone has been pushed by him – the Beatles and the Stones, Jimi Hendrix and Cream and the Doors, Donovan and the Byrds – and almost everything new that happens now goes back to his source. Simply, he has grown pop up, he has given it brains.

In the end, he hasn't so much changed rock as he's killed off one kind and substituted another. And if the kind he killed was also the kind I love, well, that was hardly his fault.

18

THE WHO

Quite likely, the Who are the last great fling of Superpop.

I mean, most of the people one calls pop really aren't pop at all any more: they've variously opted out and they hardly make teen music now, they've moved on to something altogether more solemn. The Who remain.

They have it both ways. They're intelligent, musical, they do keep moving forward, but they're also flash and they come on with all the noise and nonsense of some back-dated rock 'n' roll group. They make good music and they're still pop. That's almost a contradiction in terms, but, somehow, they make it.

In the first place, they came out of Shepherd's Bush and they were Mods.

Mod came in from the beginning of the sixties and reached its peak in 1964. Very much, it was a reaction against the yobbishness of the Teds in the fifties.

Mods were small strange creatures, very neat and delicate, and they rode scooters, chewed gum, swallowed pills by the hundredweight. Most of all, they were hooked on clothes. Any money they got, it always went on making themselves look beautiful.

It was the Mods who first made Carnaby Street happen, 1962–3, and they used to change their clothes maybe four times each day. It was fierce, dedicated stuff. If you got caught in last night's sweater, you were finished, you were dead. (By 1964 Carnaby Street was no longer Mod – they'd moved on.)

Anyhow, Mod was a strictly male world and you'd see them mooching around in big tribes, their girls trailing forgotten behind them, and they'd dance all by themselves, sunk deep in narcissistic dreams. They didn't smile. And if there was ever a mirror in the club, there'd be a frantic rush to get in front of it and everyone would pose, pout, ponce about, and they'd get high on themselves, they'd go lost.

So Mod was a new peak of decadence but it was hard work, intense, truly obsessive, and that's the kind of atmosphere that breeds good pop. And Shepherd's Bush was one of the most major Mod citadels and the Who became the great Mod group.

The first thing, they were loud: on stage, they worked between great fortresses of amps and they made that kind of noise that makes your eyes blur, that hits you and hits you, that halfway destroys you.

Always, they were murderous: Pete Townshend used to smash his guitar full into the amps, shattering it like kindling, and the amps would scream out feedback, would squeal and explode. And Roger Daltrey, who sang, used to swing his mike like a lariat and crash it against the drums, and Keith Moon used to play drums with twenty arms, mouth gaping and eyes bugged, flailing and thrashing like some dervish, and John Entwistle used to play bass like Bill Wyman, bored as he could be, and he bound them down or else they'd have flown away. Or Townshend used to swing his arm in a great slow circle like a windmill and he'd handle his guitar like a machine-gun, he'd move very slowly along the faces of the audience, mowing them down one by one, and the people at the end of the line would cringe and cower, try to hide themselves. They didn't want to die. And by the end, the stage would look like a battlefield, all strewn with drum kit and busted guitar and bits of shattered amp, covered by smoke. Everybody sweated. The Who were wild in those days.

The second thing, they had image.

Moody bastards, the lot of them – they used to act like so many spoiled children, they threw tantrums and spat at each other and had fights on stage. They were violent. Well, they were only silly. They'd be obnoxious to most everyone and they'd cause endless hassle. But they spent a lot of money on clothes. Pete Townshend used to spend maybe £80 each week, just to make himself look right. They weren't pretty but they had style.

From the beginning, Pete Townshend was the one that counted most.

His father had played in a dance band and, himself, he'd always hung around the fat fringes of the industry. He wrote songs. He had a nose like a trowel and he didn't enjoy it. The way he explained it, his nose had got laughed at when he was a child and, later, he thought he'd maybe take some revenge, he'd have his nose plastered all across every paper going, he'd push it right back in our faces. So he did. And when he got up on stage and machine-gunned his audience, it was camp but it was also meant; it carried real rage.

No matter what, he would have led a pop group and made them happen and been famous. He had that kind of drive, he couldn't miss.

As it was, he found Daltrey, Entwistle and Moon, and they all called themselves the Hi-Numbers. This was 1963, when everyone was banging out R&B, but the Hi-Numbers used a mixture of Townshend's own songs and Tamla Motown things, all very advanced stuff in its time, and they were immediately good.

At this point, Kit Lambert and Chris Stamp came around.

Lambert was the son of Constant Lambert, the composer, and had been to Lancing and Trinity, Oxford; Stamp was the son of an East End tugboatman and the brother of Terence, a film actor.

Both of them had gone into films, become quite successful as assistant directors. In due course, they met and became friends and went into partnership together.

Lambert was extrovert and insomniac and highly intelligent, too generous, and Stamp was hard, commonsense, approximately ruthless: they made a working combination, they rounded each other out. Anyway, they heard the Hi-Numbers in the back room of some pub and dug them and became their managers.

As solemn management, it's always been farcical. Lambert is neurotic. Townshend is neurotic. Keith Moon is neurotic. Most everyone involved is a maniac, most everyone is extremely bright and, for years, hardly a week would go by without some kind of major trauma. Either the Who were going to break up, or the Who were going to leave Lambert/Stamp, or Lambert/Stamp were going to leave the Who, or everyone was just going to freak out regardless. Of course, nothing ever happened. It got to be something like a pop *Coronation Street* (Lambert as Elsie Tanner? Townshend as Annie Walker?), and the whole pantomime has always been the most inventive, comic and entertaining set-up in English pop. Why? Because they've had fun. Because they're all clever people and they've never let things go dead.

The thing was, Townshend was intellectual and Lambert wasn't exactly intellectual but he had the jargon off. Between them, they looked at the things the Who did and analysed them and thought up sassy names for them. If the Who smashed up their instruments and used feedback and acted like apes, was that violence? Certainly not: it was auto-destruction.

In the same way, if they wore jackets made out of Union Jacks and freaky T-shirts, that wasn't outrageousness, that was Pop Art. No less, Pop Art.

Well, it was all blag, of course, but they wrapped it up pretty, they talked most solemn, and it brought in vast publicity, it was a real stroke. Pop Art? Straightaway, the Who were avant garde, heavy, and they drew big at the Marquee every Tuesday night, they were major Mod heroes, and they kept throwing smoke bombs, smashing stuff and having fights. All image, they were wreckers and they replaced the Stones as number one anarchists.

More to the point, Pete Townshend had begun to write some monster songs.

He used one recurrent framework, he always has done: he cast himself as one teenage boy and this boy was the archetypal Shepherd's Bush Mod, a bit dumb, a bit aggressive, a bit baffled. His songs were about his scenes and his small hang-ups, his uncertainties, and Townshend got nothing wrong, he was imaginative and shrewd and funny, he caught everything exactly right:

> I'm a substitute for another guy,
> I look pretty tall but my heels are high.
> The simple things you see are all complicated,
> Look pretty young but I'm just backdated,
> Yeah . . .*

Often, the songs would carry quite heavy implications but they never got flabby, their surface always gleamed. No sermonizing, no crap – Townshend kept everything tight and firm, very real, and he chronicled teen lives better than anyone since Eddie Cochran.

My Generation was typical: the Mod was trying to justify himself, wanted to lash back at everyone who'd ever put him down, but he'd taken too many pills, he couldn't concentrate

*Words of *Substitute* by permission of Fabulous Music Ltd, London.

right. He only stammered. He was sick, disgusted, but he couldn't articulate, he couldn't say why. The harder he tried, the worse he stammered, the more he got confused:

> People try to put us down
> Just because we get around,
> Things they do look awful cold,
> Hope I die before I get old.*

Townshend wasn't like this Mod hero at all, of course, but Roger Daltrey was. I mean, Daltrey wasn't stupid but he was no theorizer, he was interested mostly in girls and cars, he wasn't too articulate and Townshend used him like a mouthpiece. In fact, he used all of the Who like that, he *was* the Who.

He gave them hit songs, earned them money, made them famous and, in return, they were used by him and were formed to his image. Always, they've been like one walking Pete Townshend fantasy.

Himself, he's been arrogant, generous, jumped-up, cruel, loyal, honest, complicated, always ultra-intelligent. He's kept his trowel nose but he's come to accept it. He's shot clean pinball.

Anyhow, getting back to some narrative, the Who had hits. They didn't have number ones but they kept hitting the top ten and, in due course, they became safe. They even stopped punching each other. Like any other group, they got institutionalized and lost excitement. Mod had died and, by 1967, the Who had got to be one of the truly established groups, almost like the Beatles or the Stones, almost as rocklike and ignorable as that. Simply, they'd become solid citizens.

*Words of *My Generation* by permission of Fabulous Music Ltd, London.

They finally happened in America. Admittedly, it took them three years of scuffling but they did eventually make it and then they spent a lot of time out of England, touring and getting rich.

Whenever you did catch up with them, they were disappointing – they were still going through the same old stunts and they didn't seem loud any more, they sounded stale. In the end, they tended to be boring.

It didn't matter: Townshend himself got no worse.

Myself, I think he's the best writer that British pop has produced, the most perceptive and the most original. Alone of all our major writers, he's kept close to what pop is really about, he's jumped on no post-Dylan bandwagon, he's always worked to and cared about a strictly teen public. Alone, he's written nothing phoney. And, some time, I'd back him to produce something very impressive indeed.

So far, I'd say he's never quite lived up to his real potential. In his time, he's had maybe half a dozen mindbusts (*My Generation*, *Substitute*, *Mary Anne With The Shaky Hand*, *I'm A Boy*, *Tattoo*, *I Can See For Miles*), but always he has been too pressured, too overworked to sustain right through an album.

For instance, the Who had their last album to make, *The Who Sell Out*, and Townshend thought he'd turn the whole thing into one mammoth advert, a wholesale ad fantasia, stuffed full of jingles and flashes and product-hymns, all done as fast and loud and vulgar as it could possibly be.

Obviously, it could have been great, it could even have been the first pop masterpiece. But then Townshend was touring America, he was gigging in England, he didn't get enough time to plan it out and it misfired. Half of it was brilliant and half of it was trash. It was a waste.

So I'm making no predictions. I have a few reservations about whether he'll get things completely together and bring it all back home. But, if he does, he has talent enough to dominate English pop for the next decade.

Afterword: Since I wrote this chapter, the Who have done another album and it justifies a lot of things I hoped for. Pete Townshend has finally written a full-scale pop opera, a project he's been threatening for years, and it's brilliant. In particular, two of the songs in it – *Pinball Wizard* and *We're Not Gonna Take It* – are as good as anything he's done, meaning that they're as good as anything anyone has done.

19

ENGLAND AFTER THE BEATLES: MOD

Through ten years, England had done nothing in pop, only trash, and now it had come across with the Beatles, the Rolling Stones and the Who, three heavies out of nowhere.

Also, there were the Animals, the Kinks, the Yardbirds, Manfred Mann – every time you turned around there was someone new sneaking up on you. From nothing, London had made itself almost the pop centre of the world.

Why? What was going on?

Always, there's no simple answer to any question like that. These moods just break out regardless and you can't explain them. But partly it was a product of the fat fifties, those greasy Macmillan years, when everyone was smug and thought they'd never see trouble in their lives again.

During this time, there'd seemed to be space for everything, there'd been no such word as Freeze, and you'd been free to dedicate yourself to nothing but decadence. That's why kids went into pop. That's why they became photographers or hair stylists or interior decorators or models or, like myself, gave their lives to pinball.

Of course, between the lot of them, they made only a tiny minority and most of them were huddled tight into London. Still, it never takes much, it just needs a quorum, and there were enough to make a surface sheen, to give an atmosphere of something happening.

Then, also, it was partly a matter of timing – Mick Jagger, Paul McCartney, Ray Davies, Pete Townshend and so forth, they'd all been in the first teen generation to grow up through Rock, they'd had pop pumped into them deep, they'd got it properly assimilated.

So when *Jailhouse Rock* came out, say, Cliff Richard was sixteen but Pete Townshend was only eleven. It was an important gap – Cliff was already too old to adjust himself and he always sounded like someone speaking in a foreign language, he could only ape Americans. With Townshend, though, that sense of strain didn't exist – he had pop off by heart, he thought in it instinctively. He didn't have to copy, he could just relax and he said whatever he liked.

Anyhow, it didn't matter how it happened, the pop boom was fact and, especially in London, it made teen life pretty good. All of a sudden, you could dress like a rainbow, grow your hair down your back, make noise, act most any way you felt like, and you didn't automatically get your face pushed in. Sometimes, you didn't even get called dirty names in the street.

For the first time, there was some real sense of teenage action, teen speed, teen style, and a lot of it came from the pirate radio stations operating off ships, moored just outside English territorial waters. They really mattered.

The first station to open was Radio Caroline and it was run by a young Irishman called Ronan O'Rahilly.

O'Rahilly had been around, he'd been involved in the early Animals, but this was his first big breakout and he was quite messianic about it, he did truly believe.

He had a handsome, foxy face and passionate eyes, and he didn't stop talking. And he saw Caroline as a crusade, an embryo revolution, a great uprising of the young against the massed tyrannies of authority.

184

His grandfather had fallen on the barricades of the Easter rising and so his station opened on Easter Sunday 1964. According to O'Rahilly, it was everything he wanted to get across – youth, health, energy, joy in life. In Latin, he said, Caroline meant happiness.

After all that his radio station wasn't as good as Radio London, which had none of Caroline's idealism but which was most professional, which was almost as good as an American station and American stations are great. All it did was devise good jingles, use good commercials and play good music all the time.

Why was it important? Only because it was private – you could jam that transistor way up tight against your ear and you'd hear nothing but righteous music all day long. Nobody intruded. Nothing unpop, no crap broke in on you.

Also, Radio London was marvellous for the industry itself, just because it used to play any record that was good, no matter how unknown the group was or how small the record label or how strange the sound. For the first time, you could try something experimental and still get a hit with it.

For a mixture of legal and emotional reasons, the Government hated pirate radio always and, finally, summer 1967, it outlawed the whole thing. Well, it listed reasons, but it did a dirty thing to pop, half killed it off. After three years, everything was right back where it had started – you switched your radio on and you couldn't hear pop when you wanted it, you were stuck with Tom Jones and Engelbert Humperdinck instead. You were fed by the corporation, Government-sponsored pop, the very thought, and the BBC didn't understand pop anyhow, never had done, never would.

Typically, though, even after he'd been outlawed, O'Rahilly soldiered on.

Working out of Amsterdam, he kept howling defiance at the nations and he broadcast prophetic visions of the Caroline ship floating up the Thames one day, watched by cheering crowds and honoured by the world.

All right, so he was comic but he believed it, he put his wallet right behind it. Against all the probabilities, he held out alone for almost a year. In the end, inevitably, he had to quit but he'd had a genuine heroic quality. A bit Don Quixote but heroic just the same.

One other breakthrough was *Ready Steady Go!*, which was the only genuinely teen TV show this country ever had.

At first glance, it looked like any other pop programme ever made – a resident compere, a string of groups, a few hundred teenyboppers milling round the studio and looking lost, the whole package as routine and dead as school prayers. What made *RSG!* different was, one, the quality of its music and, two, Cathy McGowan.

The good music happened because *RSG!* threw out that stock TV format of hiring anyone who'd made the charts, balladeer or comedian or ventriloquist regardless, and having them mime through their latest hit. Instead, it worked to a hardcore pop public and booked nobody that wasn't a bit hip, that didn't stand some chance of catching fire.

Naturally, there was still some dross left but there were also occasional full-scale happenings and, every so often, you'd get someone like the Stones, James Brown, Ike and Tina Turner, the Who, doing four or five songs straight off and then there'd be some kind of general freak-out.

On such nights, the teenboppers would stop milling and come alive, they'd fall about, and there'd be an atmosphere built up, speed and sweat, real action, and it would all jump out of its box at you.

Cathy McGowan was central in this. Before she made compere, she'd been one of the original Mods and she was a long gangling streak with a lot of teeth and long black hair and a fringe down in her eyes.

She was amateur. She kept stumbling on her lines, stammering and blushing, grinning pointlessly. This is a Super record, she'd say, with a Swinging beat by a Smashing artist. Holy trinity: Super, Swinging and Smashing. And when someone truly famous came on her show, John Lennon or Mick Jagger, she'd get tongue-tied and agonized, she'd flutter just like any fan.

That was the point – she was like some fan. She wasn't some fat middle-aged DJ with a toupee and a plastic smile, she was almost a teenybopper herself, and she was genuinely thrilled because she met pop stars. So young girls could watch her and they'd think, That Cathy McGowan, she's like me, I'm like her, we both want Elvis Presley's autograph. And look at her, she's on TV. That means I could be on TV myself.

In this way, she became one of the great heroines, an embryo Twiggy, and she got rich. Naturally, she wasn't quite as ingenuous as she looked, she did play her gawkiness up, but she wasn't phoney either. When she said Super, she meant exactly that.

Even after the pop boom faded and *RSG!* was taken off, she didn't starve. She put her name to a lot of fashion products, shoes and so forth, and she sat behind a big desk in a big office. So she was a tycoon but she didn't change too much. She still giggled and squeaked, she still shook her fringe out of her eyes. In the end, she became twenty-five.

Around 1964, British pop was breaking up fast into two very separate scenes, one fashionable and the other square, one In and the other Out.

In the fifties, no one had bothered with such stuff. Just so long as you had hits and got rich, that was all that counted. You were pop or you weren't. Period.

Then, after the Beatles, the concept of quality crept in and that changed things entirely. Very fast, the business revolved itself into two distinct schools, one just trying to sell records regardless and the other trying to sell records and make good music both.

Inevitably, nothing stopped there – the quality team soon found out that some among them were more quality than others, altogether more hip, and there was much frantic reshuffling done, at the end of which there emerged a definite élite, an In crowd.

Most nights, this new aristocracy used to hang out at the Ad Lib Club, getting stoned on whisky and coke, and they'd wait intently for the Beatles to show. They'd slump around in the half-dark and not move until it got light outside. After a few hours, they'd go into a stupefied dream and they'd sit there blind, not talking much, not looking and not hearing, just steadily boozing and nodding their heads. Through everything, music played incredibly loudly.

In the very end, everyone would decide who was going to bed with whom and they'd go home. Next night, they'd do the same thing again.

After a few months, the Ad Lib was all used up and they moved to somewhere new, the Scotch of St James. Later on, they turned briefly to Sybilla's, the Bag O' Nails, the Speakeasy and the Revolution. All of these places have looked different, all of them look the same.

It got to be quite addictive – groups would even cut down on gigging, flunk out on work, and all because they wanted to hang around the discotheques, get smashed and stay up past their bedtimes.

When you walked into the Scotch, you'd see the entire group world assembled there. So who was out in the dark, playing for the people? Nobody at all.

Just the same, there was a lot of talent around, whole battalions of new names – Donovan, Tom Jones, Sandie Shaw, Dusty Springfield, Lulu, Georgie Fame, the Walker Brothers, the Small Faces, the Hollies, Marianne Faithfull, Dave Berry, Petula Clark.

No doubt, if I had a proper sense of responsibility, I'd go into detailed dissertations on each and every one of them, I'd turn this chapter into one unending catalogue and bore everyone to tears. I won't, though: I'll stick to the people that interested me.

For a start, the Walker Brothers.

They were Californians and their names were Scott Engel, John Maus and Gary Leeds. All of them had hung around and been known in Hollywood. Finally, they'd noticed that things were happening here, many people were making it, and so they groomed themselves, grew their hair very long and invaded.

They could hardly miss: Engel and Maus both were beautiful, Engel could even sing. More, Engel was a natural-born heart throb.

He was a light golden colour and he had all the equipment, the tragic mouth and misted eyes and fluttery lashes, the thin hands and soft hair, and he never managed more than a small sad smile.

When he sang, his hands went up in front of his grieving face and, delicately, his body curled up like a lettuce leaf.

He looked like he needed mothering, in fact, and what more has any pop singer ever needed? In one throw, 1965, the Walker Brothers were made. They kept racking up hits, one doomed ballad after another, and they became more hysterically screamed over than anyone outside the Stones.

The only snag was, Engel was almost as unhappy as he looked. He was a bit like a new Johnnie Ray – surrounded himself with heavies, spoke to hardly anyone, and he lived in a room with all the curtains drawn, huddled tight into himself, playing romantic music very loudly, Wagner or Jacques Brel or Tony Bennett.

He didn't want to be just a pop singer, he had visions of quality. In the meantime, he toured with the Walkers but he didn't dig it, he was contemptuous of being screamed at and, also, he had very fraught relations with John Maus.

In the end, the group broke up and he went solo.

Since then, he has removed himself from straight pop, he's devoted himself entirely to flowerpots. He has a fine voice, delicate and always musical, and he's a natural for international cabaret, a throwback to the times of Sinatra, Mel Tormé and Andy Williams.

Like you might expect, he peddles some very solemn stuff, standards and Brel translations and songs of his own, atmospheric enough but top-heavy and maudlin. Everything is painted black. Never mind, he's a moody bastard, he still looks beautiful and he's a lot of image. For such things I can forgive him almost anything.

More to my own taste, though, were the Small Faces.

Originally, the Faces came out of the East End and they were ultimate Mods, small and neat and schnide, very spotty. In the first place, they were a muted echo of the Who, and they were small ravers, loud and brash and really a bit dire. Once they'd settled down, though, they turned out not to be dire at all.

Their singer and lead guitarist, Steve Marriott, had once most suitably played the Artful Dodger in *Oliver!* Now he looked like a teddy bear and showed a fine shamelessness, screaming himself purple and hurling himself at the mike as if he meant to swallow it whole. He sang well, too, wild and strangled. Bopping up and back, his knees clamped tight and his eyes screwed up, he'd be berserk and he'd be good. He'd have everything it took.

In many ways, the Faces have been the group that sums up all groups: they have that classic group gift for self-delusion. They've thought themselves artists when they've only been loons, they've talked endlessly about getting themselves together and making masterpieces but, somehow, they've wound up in discotheques instead. They've jumped aboard every arty fad possible but they've never quite got the point and, in the end, they've always made solid old-fashioned noises after all.

Finally, none of the crap has mattered: they've meant fun and they've lasted. Little and fierce and pantomime, they've come to be one of my most favourite acts.

Among the girl singers, by far the best was Sandie Shaw.

Originally, she came from Dagenham and she was skinny, short-sighted but she was sexy. She sang in her bare feet and she had a curious myopic vulnerability going for her, she made people turn very soft.

Technically, she could hardly sing at all but she had some built-in ache to her voice, a tunelessness that worked exactly right, a beautiful creak. Also, she had a song-writer, Chris Andrews, and he gave her hits every time. Between them, they turned out one of the best streaks any English act ever had: *Girl Don't Come*, *I'll Stop At Nothing*, *Message Understood*, *I've Heard About Him*.

One time, I saw her do cabaret and realized just how good she really was. Most of the time, she sat on a stool and sang too soft, bare feet dangling, bunions and all, and she was nothing but bones and angles.

Technically, she wasn't much. When she had a high note to hit, she often missed it and, when she had a low note to hit, she sometimes gave up altogether. Still, she trapped me regardless, I thought she was sexy. No question she had it going and, every mistake she made, the more I was hooked and the more I agonized for her. I got so bruised that, any time I saw a difficult bit coming up, I couldn't stand to look, I had to hide my face away.

At one point, she introduced a ballad and sang a few notes and, suddenly, she began to shed tears. Just a few, three drips and a sniff, and then she wiped her eyes, sang her song. Maybe it was fake, of course, and then maybe it wasn't. Whichever, it did me in.

191

In due course, though, having first cut *Yesterday Man* and *To Whom It Concerns*, two mother records by himself, Chris Andrews stopped writing good songs. Probably, he'd simply used himself up. At any rate, he broke his streak and Sandie Shaw was never as good again.

Still, she kept trotting out on bum TV variety shows and singing pulp. She seemed bored and you'd be disillusioned, you'd forget to feel sloppy any more. Only, every so often, you'd catch a fast flash of her bunions, just one glimpse, and you'd been caught all over again.

Through everything, she was steered and mothered by Eve Taylor, who also managed Adam Faith. Miss Taylor, a warm-hearted lady, perpetrated Sandie's name and loved her, spoiled her, suffered for her. In return, Sandie was grateful.

I only ever spoke to her twice. First time out, I asked her questions and she, having just had her first hit, didn't answer much. 'Dunno,' she kept saying.

The second time, some eighteen months later, I asked her more questions and she still didn't answer much but she had changed, she belonged to new worlds. 'Ça va,' she kept saying. 'Comme ci, comme ça.'

Marianne Faithfull epitomized everything that had changed in pop.

Her mother was a baroness, true class, and herself, she'd been to convent school. When she got out, Andrew Loog Oldham saw her at a party and employed her on the spot.

You could see his point – she was the perfect face. She had long yellow hair falling all around her and she looked incredibly virginal, incredibly sexual and she had the strangest sad smile you ever saw. When she sang, she sighed and she drooped her eyelids in poses of infinite lustful purity.

She didn't naturally belong in pop, she was high above it. In the fifties, she'd have passed it by without thinking but this was after the Beatles, pop was the most fun thing, and not only scrubbers from Wigan played the game. So she made records and, looking like she did, she got hits.

As it turned out, she was interested in sex, she talked about it most freely and she quickly became something like a resident TV pundit on it. Kid, she was frank and unashamed. And, even after she stopped having hits, she was gladly accepted as an expert and she was used by journalists everywhere as the authoritative voice of trendy, deeply switched-on and sinful female youth.

She got married to a man called John Dunbar, who ran an art gallery, and she had a child. They broke up and, later, she went out with Mick Jagger and they became the most celebrated couple, holidaying in Positano and dining in Alvaro's and arriving late at Covent Garden.

On her own, she played Chekhov at the Royal Court and made sexy films, dressed up in ballet drag and black leather suits. Beyond that, she was a personage, she was symbolic of the scene. Most of the time, she didn't do much but she was famous just the same.

Why? For the same reason as Paul Jones was famous – she was reassuring. She might be shocking but she did it in a nice accent, she wasn't vulgar with it. She could be coped with. Even in direst disgrace, she was still a lady.

She kept talking sex. For instance, she gave interviews saying that blue films should be legal and that sensitive actors would turn the sex act into something truly inspiring. What films, what actors? Umm, she said, me and Mick on a high bare rock.

Among the men singers of this time, the ones that meant most were Donovan and Tom Jones.

Donovan began as a carbon Bob Dylan. He was born in Glasgow and he was another drop-out, he'd spent a long time bumming around the nation with his friend, Gypsy Dave. He wrote songs, poems and, finally, he arrived in London.

When Dylanesque came into vogue, he was launched on *RSG!*, wearing a cap and singing in an oddly familiar retard's whine. Inevitably, everyone and me leaped at him, accused him of cynically cashing in. What's more, everyone and me was wrong.

For a start, he had none of Dylan's harshness. He was one gentle person, naïve and well-meaning, desperately sincere, and he wrote limp little nursery rhymes, all poetical and minstrelsy.

The same things that made him attractive in himself, his innocence and real sweetness, made his music unbearable. Always, he sounded angelic and folksy and fey, almost like an updating of one of those sentimental heroes in Dostoyevsky, Alyosha or Prince Myshkin, the Holy Fools. In no time, he'd become pop's best answer to Patience Strong.

After he'd first made it, he went through a bad phase, when he wasn't being promoted right and he wasn't even making records. Also, he got busted on a drug charge and badly blew his cool by leaping nude aboard a policeman's back. But then he came into the factory of Mickie Most, who is a walking hit machine, and Most brought him all the way back again.

Most is a record producer and, apart from Donovan, he's cut hits for the Animals, Herman's Hermits, Lulu, the Yardbirds and Jeff Beck. He is possibly the most successful producer in the world.

In the whole of pop, he's the only man I can think of who has unnatural powers, who really knows what will hit and what won't. He hardly misses.

In his time, he's picked some tough ones, and always he's rescued them, pulled them back from nowhere. Over the years, inevitably, he's had failures but they've been peripheral, they've never come when they've mattered. Under pressure, he wins out every time.

The strange thing is, he used to be a singer and, in those days, he had no knack whatever. Once, I saw him open the show on an Everly Brothers/Little Richard/Bo Diddley/Rolling Stones tour and he was bad, he really was. He did that whole hilarious rock routine, leaping about and falling on his knees and grovelling, but he hadn't the figure for it, he hadn't the voice either and he got laughed at.

The next thing I heard, he'd just made *The House Of The Rising Sun* with the Animals, was collecting Rolls-Royces like stamps and had bought a yacht.

Anyhow, he isn't earnest, he thinks that making records is just like making soapsuds, he never talks about Art but he's a minor miracle worker and, at times, he's even cut some good records. And he rescued Donovan and built him back into a hero and put a rock beat behind him and, between them, they made the best English folk/rock singles – *Sunshine Superman*, *Mellow Yellow* and *Hurdy Gurdy Man*.

These days, Donovan lives in a cottage and wears robes, looks beatific and preaches a return to the sun and the earth, the basic simplicities. Everyone likes him. A lot of people think he has talent and a few people even think he's a genius, a true prophet of gentleness. In America, he's huge, he's a real influence. Myself, though, I can't take him seriously at all, I think he's a writer of commercial melodies and I'm glad he survives but, as a poet, I don't think he begins.

By direct contrast, Tom Jones was true beefcake.

He was the son of a Welsh miner and he was six foot, with huge shoulders and a busted nose. By any standards, he was a virile hunk, a throwback, and small Mods detested him but their mums adored him.

What's more, he could sing. Technically, in fact, he was infinitely the best singer we'd had and he'd storm through anything you put in front of him, pop or country or standard. Also, he was already into his middle twenties by the time he made it and he was truly professional, he had range and control and command.

As soon as he'd got a couple of hits behind him, he went into film songs, country songs, big ballads, and he was hardly pop any more. Instead, he became conventional showbiz, the

Rolls and the champagne and the cigar, the whole bit, and he was incredibly successful all over the world. He was inevitable and, by 1967, he'd become the biggest-earning singer in England, one of the biggest-earning singers anywhere.

He is unfashionable. He's so butch, so square and, all right, he does make some very tedious records. But I like him, he knows what he's doing. First and last, he can sing and that, in England, makes him something.

And that's where I'm going to end this list. No doubt, I'm going to get multiple brickbats for not giving space to the other big names of this time but I really can't think of anything even marginally interesting to say on them. Dusty Springfield was a competent singer who wore too much make-up; Georgie Fame started out as high-level R&B, a cool voice backed by a compact and driving band, but then he grew pretensions as a jazz singer and wound up sounding like a poor man's Jon Hendricks; the Hollies were a flawless hit machine, they never missed, and they were very boring; Dave Berry was fun – he moved like a spider, all arms and legs, very spooky in black, and he said he was going to be reincarnated as a snake; Lulu and Petula Clark were both quite dreadful. All of them, they had hits and built up big followings and made much money but none of them had any great influence on pop in general.

Above and around all this, there was Mod and Mod got colder, tighter, more obsessive all the time.

Mods had enemies, who were called Rockers, and Rockers were updated Teds, they were in that same tradition, black leather and motorbikes and grease, and Mods dominated most of the southern cities but Rockers held the countryside.

Mods thought that Rockers were yobs, Rockers thought that Mods were ponces. They hated each other deeply. Both of them, they were fanatic sects and their fights became holy wars, each truly believing that right was might, that the gods were on their sides.

Through 1964, every bank holiday, Mods and Rockers would pick one of the southern seaside resorts, Hastings or Margate or Brighton, and they'd descend on it in their thousands, and they'd stage a three-day running battle. They'd roam along the front in packs, smashing and pillaging at random, and all the people who lived there, they'd hide indoors and peep out from behind their curtains. The police would make a few arrests and they'd change nothing.

Ecstatic weekends – seventy-two hours without sleep and all you did was run around, catcall, swallow pills and put the boot in. For the first time in your life, the only time, you were under no limitations and nobody controlled you and you caught sight of nirvana.

When it was all over, Rockers didn't change: they were solid and they went on exactly the same way they'd always done, riding their bikes and getting lushed and brawling. But Mods were edgier, more neurotic, and everything that happened now was anti-climax. Going their rounds, just making themselves beautiful and staring, they were bored and they couldn't sustain. They lost their dedication. Very soon, they began to fall apart.

Always, when you look back, you make things better than they really were. That's a cliché by now. But, with that in mind, I'd still say that Mod was fun to live through.

At any rate, I have a memory of two fat years, 1964 and 1965, when you did nothing but run loose and waste time, buy new clothes and over-eat and gab, when you thought you'd never have to work in your life again. It was futile, of course, pop has always been futile but it seemed elegant, it was easy living, and English pop was better then than it's ever been, than it's ever likely to be again.

No doubt, there'll be great records made, heftier achievements racked up – it's just that there won't be any time when you could open your *Melody Maker*, scan the clubs, walk down the street and hear so much noise for 7s. 6d.

20

P. J. PROBY

The first time I met P.J. Proby, he was at his peak. He had been in England for about a year and, immediately, he had cleaned up, he'd established himself as the most mesmeric stage act we'd seen. So he was the biggest solo star around then but he was also one long streak of trouble and he was always neck deep in hassles. He was intuitive, fast, hysterical, paranoid, generous, very funny, hugely imaginative, original, self-obsessed, self-destructive, often impossible, just about irresistible and much more besides. Truly, he was complicated.

I went to see him and he was sitting in a darkened hotel room, downing bourbon and coke by the tumblerful. He was wearing a grubby string vest, old white socks and navy-blue knickers. And he was tired, his hair hung all unkempt around his shoulders and his eyes were red, his face swollen with lost sleep. He looked quite defeated.

When I first came in, he said nothing but only handed me a scrap of paper, covered in ragged, semi-illegible handwriting. 'That's my testament,' said Proby. 'Read it.'

On inspection, it turned out to be something like a petition. Crudely paraphrased, it said that, ever since Proby had been in this country, he had been systematically hounded by enemies and fools. His name had been blackened, his life made not worth living, his career half-wrecked. Promoters, record companies and agents had conspired together to bring him down and break him. Until he had finally had enough and now he'd decided to expose them all. Near the end, in a crucial phrase, he said: 'I'm an artist and should be exempt from shit.'

All the curtains were drawn tight and the hotel room was full of people, Proby's hairdresser and assistant and publicists, his friends. Great image: Proby himself just brooded, said nothing, and everyone else watched him.

Very suddenly, Proby began to talk to me and then didn't stop for maybe two hours. He told me many things, all about his life and his soul and his many agonies, and he made everything epic, everything wild and somehow magnificent. The way he told it, his life was a composite of Jesus Christ, Judy Garland and Errol Flynn.

According to the saga, he was born in Texas, real name James Marcus Smith, and his father had been a very rich man, a much respected citizen. And his earliest years were filled with happiness, but it didn't last; he was sent away to military college, which trained and disciplined him to be a man, and then he changed his name to Jet Powers, became a singer and went west to Hollywood. He wrote songs and hustled. Waited for breaks to happen and, around this time, he got married. So he and his young bride used to sit in their window when the evening came, looking down into the street below, and they'd dream about the way it'd be when he finally made it, when his name was big in lights. That's exactly the way that Proby told it: young love, first love, filled with deep devotion.

Later, some of his songs were made into hits and he moved up. He was a Hollywood face. And Jack Good planned to stage a musical of *Othello*, Proby playing Iago to Muhammad Ali's Moor. That was really something.

But then, just as the time of his ultimate triumph was approaching, he quarrelled with his true love, and he was all capsized again. He came to England and, of course, he became a superstar but he wasn't happy, he never could be. He was hollow inside.

Picture him: a man crucified, a genius destroyed, a beautiful animal caged – he told me all of that, and, when he was finished, he lapsed into silence and stared at the floor, drank more bourbon. Finally, he raised his head, looked at me, and he flashed me his first smile. Pure malice. 'How's that?' he said. 'Did I break your fucking heart?'

(Being halfway honest for once, I have to say that there are many people around who'll tell you entirely different versions of the Proby trauma and they'll all swear blind that theirs is the only right one. Myself, I'd say that mine is as possible as any other and I stick by it.)

At any rate, I was just eighteen when Proby hit me with this and I was never so impressed by anything in my life. The darkened room, the bourbon, the knickers, the fat Texan drawl – this was true heroism and it made me shake. I never grew out of it either. At first sight, Proby was installed as my ultimate pop obsession, my real idol, and he's stayed that way ever since.

On stage, he was magnificent.

He'd stand behind a curtain and extend one toe and all his little girls screamed. Then he'd draw it back again, then he'd extend it again, then he'd draw it back again. This might continue for five full minutes, getting slightly bolder, even flashing his ankle, and then he'd suddenly bound out like some puppy St Bernard. He wore blue velvet all over, loose jerkin to hide his paunch and skintight pants, and he had his hair tied back in a bow, and he wore buckled shoes, and he was camp as hell. Simply, he was outrageous.

He'd stand quite still and then he'd turn around, he'd mince across the stage like some impossible drag-queen and then he'd stop dead again, he'd grind his groin like a really filthy burlesque stripper, and then he'd flounce across to the wings like an overweight ballet dancer, and then he'd come back all coy and demure like a small ribboned girl, and then he'd snarl, and then he'd pout, and then he'd start the whole thing over again. He'd sing a ballad and he'd agonize, he'd raise one hand, he'd let fall an invisible rose. Or he'd sing soul and he'd scream, grind, go berserk. Then he'd make a monologue and he'd explain how he was mistreated, conspired against, and how his only friends in the world were his fans, his little girls. Then he'd be camp again and he'd flaunt one hand on his hip and his lashes fluttered like fans. Well, it could all have been horribly embarrassing, it very nearly was, but he had a great voice, he owned real presence and somehow he brazened it out. The way he explained it, he'd taken all his movements, all his faces from different girls. You could well believe it. Whatever, he kept going for a full hour and he screamed himself voiceless, he sweated till he was slimy all over like a toad, till he was quite hideous, and still he piled on intensity, agony, outrage. 'Am I clean?' he'd squeal. 'Am I clean? Am I spotless? Am I pure?'

When he was done, when he'd quite destroyed himself, he'd stagger off blindly into the wings and collapse, semi-conscious, in his dressing-room. He'd just lie there for maybe twenty minutes without moving. Then Proby would rise up refreshed and he'd bound out through the stage door and into his waiting limousine, surrounded and protected at all times by his entourage, and then the whole circus would roll back to London.

Wild camp, marvellous image: P. J. Proby lay back exhausted in his cushions, the Sun King, his hair like drenched rope, his mouth full of bourbon, and everyone entertained him. No medieval warlord ever had it better.

With all this, he was talented. Specifically, he had giant range, perfect control and he was a flawless mimic, he could turn himself into anyone from Billy Eckstine to Frankie Valli, Gene Pitney to James Brown. And he was a voice. As a straight ballad singer, he entirely outclassed Sinatra or Tony Bennett or any of them, but he'd distort his action, exaggerate, melodramatize until the whole thing turned into a subtle burlesque of the original slop.

On songs like *My Prayer* or *When I Fall In Love*, he'd be so almost straight that you'd really be fooled and then, just when you'd be nicely lulled, he'd slip in something sneaky and capsize you. Always it was neatly done, never crude. So his versions of *Somewhere* and *I Apologize* and *If I Loved You* were strange little classics, almost surreal, and their great flavour was that you never knew just how you were meant to take them.

Anyhow, soon after that first time I met him, things started going very wrong indeed. *Somewhere* made number three and he landed his first headlining cinema tour, always a major milestone but, on the first night, he split his velvet trousers from knee to crotch. On the second night, he did exactly the same. On the third night, he did it one time too often, and the curtain came down and he was flung off the tour, widely banned, hammered by the press, much insulted by the industry and enthusiastically kicked in the teeth by almost everyone.

This was disaster: he did have other hits, he did hang on but he was cut off from the most crucial outlets and he got progressively cornered. More, he was never forgiven.

Even then he never walked small.

The thinking was always simple – Proby was a face, a Hollywood star, and he lived like one. He owed it, not only to himself, but to his fans and, most vital, to his image. At any rate, that's the way he figured it and, accordingly, he kept up a large house in Chelsea and supported an entourage and spent fortunes in discotheques and hired twenty-piece P. J. Proby Orchestras to back him.

He went to America for a year, tried raising horses, failed, and came back to London. This was early 1968 and, by now, he was officially bankrupt but he smiled smiles, looked angelic and said most solemnly that he was an entirely reformed character. On his first comeback gig, he was heckled. Immediately, he exploded in a rash of four-letter words and the curtain came down. And everyone was happy – nothing had changed.

Whatever else, he has proved himself resilient. His greatest gift has been that he's always been able to convince everyone around him, myself included, that he was a genius. And just so long as that gift survives, he can't ever be written off and he can't ever starve. He can always find someone to pay his bills and love him and launch him one more time.

Well, I suppose I've given him more space than he deserves and, really, I have no justifications except that I dig him so much. Along with Muhammad Ali, he is the great doomed romantic showman of our time, the Rasputin or Hearst or Jelly Roll Morton, and I'm left with two central images of him.

The first is a portrait of him (the work, he once told me, of 'an Italian old master') and it shows him all in velvet, angelic-faced, walking on the clouds.

The second is him recording his entry for a San Remo festival and the Italian composer has flown over to supervise. The Italian is a caricature composer, all twirled moustachios and rapturous eyes, and Proby, who isn't entirely sober, is a classic Proby figure, all stubble and blear. And they're standing alone in the middle of a vast studio floor and Proby is singing. He doesn't know a word of Italian, he has no idea what he's saying, and still he spreads his arms, throws his head way back and soars. He'd break your heart. Such pain, such yearning, such terrible passion – the composer has never heard anything like it and he's drooling.

At the end of the take, the Italian flings his arms full round Proby's neck and hugs him. Proby beams. 'Mr Proby,' says the composer. 'How do you do it?'

'Maestro,' says Proby. 'I don't do. I am.'

21

AMERICA AFTER THE BEATLES: ANGLOPHILIA, BACHARACH AND FOLK/ ROCK

If the Beatles meant a lot in England, they meant very much more in America.

They changed everything. They happened at a time when American pop was bossed by trash, by dance crazes and slop ballads, and they let all of that bad air out. They were foreign, they talked strange. They played harsh, unsickly, and they weren't phoney. Just as they'd done in England, they brought back reality.

Beyond that, they happened at a time when the whole of American teenage life was bogged down, when there was an urgent need for new leaders and, along with Bob Dylan, that's just what they became.

Because they weren't fake or computerized themselves, they brought it home exactly how conformist America had really become, they woke people up, they crystallized all kinds of vague discontents. They didn't sermonize, they didn't have to. Just by existing, they played a major part in turning dissent from an intellectual left-wing indulgence into something that involved maybe thirty per cent of all American teens.

Still, that's roughly what they'd done in England, too, so how come they meant much more in America? Mostly, it was a question of scale.

In England, after all, teenage rebellion had always been something quite amiable and formalized. It starts fashions, sells records, makes fun for the people but it doesn't change much, it causes no revolutions. Over the years, it moves things very gently along, but, come right down to it, England simply isn't ugly enough to make white kids feel passionate.

But in America, in the sixties, teen dissent has become something more than fashionable. On the whole, it's about real diseases, real social insanities, and it may end up making changes. And, because they're influential in all this, the Beatles have become more than they'll ever be here, they've gone beyond entertainment and they've turned into serious social influences, they matter.

At a less exalted level, when they first broke through, they stirred a hysterical cult for all things British, a fad that's only just dying down now.

This was simple: one look at the Beatles, long hair and scouse accents, big mouth and all, and America decided that something strange must be going on here, that London must be some kind of continuous space-age funfair, one endless parade of boutiques and discotheques and hip trattorias, Carnaby Streets and King's Roads.

Immediately, England became the epitome of everything elegant, enlightened, deeply switched-on, and its exports became automatic triumphs.

English pop had it fat in there and most everyone cleaned up – the Rolling Stones, the Animals, the Yardbirds, the Kinks, Manfred Mann, Donovan, Dusty Springfield. And not only pop but actors, designers, hair stylists, models – Julie Christie, Mary Quant, Vidal Sassoon, Michael Caine and, climactically, Twiggy.

Two groups, in particular, made it much bigger in the States than they'd ever done at home – the Dave Clark Five and Herman's Hermits.

Dave Clark had been a film extra and he was handsome, he had smooth skin and white teeth and a dazzling smile, he was clean-cut as hell. He played a bit of drums and he formed his own semi-professional group around Tottenham.

After a time, they made records, very crude and chaotic but quite danceable, and soon they had a number one hit, *Glad All Over*. They had no pretensions to musical class, they were only basic noise-machines and, predictably, after they'd lost their first impetus, they found the going erratic here.

When they got to America, though, Dave Clark smiled just once, flashed those perfect teeth of his, and they were made. For two years, they were hardly ever gone from the American charts and, every time they wavered, Clark only flashed his smile one time and they went right back on top again.

The odd thing was, he had no manager. He was advised by Harold Davidson, his agent, but nobody controlled him ever, nobody made his decisions for him. All on his own, he'd realized his potential and he'd pursued it, he'd grabbed everything possible. And it was really quite an impressive thing, any young boy being so sure of himself that he could set up as a million-dollar industry and not be conned, not stumble for a second. It was almost indecent.

Herman's Hermits were another strike for Mickie Most.

Herman himself was really called Peter Noone and he was a very young, very innocent-looking boy from Manchester. He had buck teeth and dimples, he looked about twelve years old, and he'd sometimes stick his finger in his mouth as he sang.

America being as matriarchal as it is, such little boy antics could hardly miss and they didn't. Mickie Most, who knows where the money is and has always concentrated on America more than anywhere, handed him one hit song after another and Herman came to be bigger even than Dave Clark.

Throughout this British invasion, the American scene stood stock still. It grew its hair long, produced a few half-hearted imitations of the Beatles, and left it at that. For one year, the English ruled unchallenged.

Outside of Berry Gordy's Tamla Motown, the only American who was thriving was Burt Bacharach.

Bacharach was a Hollywood writer/arranger, a smooth man, already in his thirties, and he was musical director for Marlene Dietrich. He'd been quietly making it for years but now, in partnership with lyricist Hal David, he began to churn out hits in clusters.

His stuff didn't vary much. Always, it was tasteful, attractive, a bit gutless. Seemingly, he could turn out hit songs almost at will, complex melody lines and cute backings, full of cellos and French horns and so forth and, taken one at a time, they were very pretty music but, when you heard them at length, they sounded limp.

His successes were endless – *Walk On By, Anyone Who Had A Heart, I Say A Little Prayer, Always Something There To Remind Me, Do You Know The Way To San Jose?* – and he won awards, wrote film themes and got called a genius by lady singers in skintight sequined dresses and men singers in toupees, by the showbiz establishment in general.

Most of his best songs went to Dionne Warwick, a lantern-jawed Negress with a fast voice and perfect control. She interpreted him just right, she was smooth and tricksy, quite flawless and quite empty. Very musical, she was, and entirely emotionless. Between them, she and Bacharach brought musak to its highest point ever.

Roughly in the same bag, a bit later, there was Herb Alpert and his Tijuana Brass, who sold more albums through the mid-sixties than anyone outside the Beatles.

Alpert himself was a very lean and beautiful-looking man, a true matinee idol, and he played trumpet pretty for the people. Mostly, his music was mock-Spanish, staccato and quite delicate, and each new record of his sounded just like the one before. In terms of content, he simply didn't exist. He was harmless, that's all, and he sold.

When the American comeback did finally happen, though, neither Bacharach nor Alpert had much to do with it. Instead, the breakthrough came with folk/rock, which was exactly what its name suggested, a grafting of serious folk lyrics on to a basic hardrock beat, and which exploded commercially early in 1965.

In immediate terms, folk/rock was fired by Bob Dylan and the Beatles but its roots reached back into the middle fifties.

At that time, the folk scene had been split into two very distinct camps. On one side, there were the ethnics and, on the other, there were the commercials and, between them, there was a seemingly unbridgeable gulf. Simply, they made no contact.

The ethnics were people like Woody Guthrie and Pete Seeger, and the material they used was part traditional, part self-composed. They were mostly middle-aged, unglamorous, strictly non-showbiz. Almost always, they were left-wing and showed it in their music and, for all these reasons, their age and their politics and their basic seriousness, they didn't have hits but they commanded a steady following and sold albums and didn't starve.

As for the commercials, they were folkniks, they were fakers and their basic routine was to take ethnic material and castrate it, swamp it in marshmallow. Beaming all over their toothpaste faces, the Kingston Trio would dig up some old warhorse like *Tom Dooley*, full of stabbings and hangings, and turn it into a Shirley Temple nursery rhyme.

Approximately, folkniks were equivalent to highschool and they didn't mean anything. Just occasionally, though, they'd look soulful and attempt something portentous, something like *Where Have All The Flowers Gone?*, bedraggled gestures at significance.

Rather surprisingly, these solemnities sold a lot of records. Simply, they had snob appeal – kids who thought themselves above Fabian or Frankie Avalon could buy folk and feel all smooth inside.

This move to seriousness hit its peak with the emergence of Peter, Paul and Mary, who bossed commercial folk right through the early sixties and had whole strings of hits with stuff that was sometimes very earnest indeed. And, all right, so they were less than anarchic – their sound was gutless, their looks antiseptic, and they were capable of *Puff The Magic Dragon*, one of the true monstrosities of pop history – but they were still a step forward from the Kingston Trio, at least they tried.

In particular, they provided a link between hardline folk and the public in general: they pushed unknown writers, used quite tough material, even peddled politics but they were always so limp that not even Ed Sullivan himself could have been offended.

In this way, they got away with stuff that would have got most people deep into trouble. For instance, they did Dylan's *Blowin' In The Wind* when Dylan himself was still very much an underground cult and no anti-war song had ever made the charts before but they so deballsed it as to make it almost meaningless and it became a hit. Musically, of course, this might have been sacrilegious but at least it gave Dylan an introduction, it got his name through to a mass pop public and, when he came out in person, people were ready for him.

At the same time that Peter, Paul and Mary were emerging in commercial folk, a whole new generation had been coming through at a more serious level. Dylan was the most crucial of these, of course, but there were others, Phil Ochs and Joan Baez and Tom Paxton, Tim Hardin and Dave Van Ronk, Buffy Sainte-Marie and Tom Rush and Judy Collins. Most of them, they were post-Beats: they wrote poems and wore blue jeans and hung around Boston or the West Village, dug Allen

Ginsberg and thought that America was sick, smoked pot. And they were passionately political, they had a raw intensity that had been missing in folk for decades and that's how they broke through, that's how they reached a teenage audience that would normally have put folk down, thinking it tired and back-dated.

So Dylan happened and, behind him, Baez and Ochs and Tim Hardin and, between them, they shut the folkniks down. At last, after ten slow years of education, the pop public was ready to take its medicine neat and fakers became obsolete. Quietly, they slid away to Las Vegas and plugged in to the middle-aged circuit, where they clapped hands and cavorted and sang fifty choruses of *If I Had A Hammer* nightly.

Meanwhile, folk proper got very big indeed – it was the perfect antidote to highschool and the manifold mindlessness that had bossed the American charts these last years, it was articulate and raw and romantic, and it made its audience feel cool just to dig it.

The way that it most affected teenage music, though, was that it made lyrics count. For the first time, words became as important as melody and groups like the Beatles or Stones, who'd started out just as sounds, quit talking in slogans and began to write real lines.

So far, the influence was all one-way: pop groups heard Dylan and were put through changes by him. But then, when groups began to write songs that meant something and smashed them out over a gutrot rock beat, the process was somewhat reversed – folk-singers, who'd always thought that rock was crapola by definition, found themselves hooked on the Beatles and they hired backing groups, stoked up a beat behind them and turned electric. So rock moved towards folk, folk moved towards rock and, where they met, what else, that got called folk/rock.

The first group to bring folk/rock through as a solid concept were the Byrds, who came from California and

210

had themselves a worldwide number one hit with Dylan's *Mr Tambourine Man*.

They had an image: they were, in fact, the first really outrageous group in America, long-haired and arrogant and mean, and their stance was classic West Coast cool, meaning that they were deadpan and remote, that they thought it was sinful to be fun.

Jim McGuinn, their lead singer, wore pince-nez and smiled strange crooked smiles over the top of them, squinting like some moth-eaten Dickensian lawyer, very devious, and the rest of the group slouched in the background, staring straight ahead, stoned and uncaring, and none of them gave off any warmth, any signs of life at all.

Musically, though, they started out strong – *Mr Tambourine Man* was brilliant and their first album was even better. They made odd insidious noises, quite soft but sneaky, sinister, and McGuinn phrased sideways like a musical crab. They weren't exciting, they weren't meant to be but their sound crept in on you and nagged you, they made you itch.

Above all, they made no concessions, they went as far beyond Peter, Paul and Mary as PP&M themselves had gone beyond the Kingston Trio, and they shaped up like something really big, they looked as if they might make the same league as the Beatles and Stones.

It didn't happen, that's all – a series of ego wars broke out inside the group, and all that good energy got wasted. Then there was a tour of England, a few singles, a rash of personnel changes, umpteen changes of policy.

At the time of writing, the Byrds are a trio and play mostly country. In six months, it's a safe bet they'll be something entirely else.*

---

*In retrospect, I haven't been quite fair to the Byrds – they did a marvellous C&W album, *Sweetheart Of The Rodeo*, that I should have spotted earlier.

Back East, very much the same thing happened to the Lovin' Spoonful, who were even better, who were quite the best group in folk/rock but who wasted themselves just as badly as the Byrds.

They were built around John Sebastian, who sang and blew mouth-harp and wrote songs, and he was people. He wore small round glasses and looked like a sleepy John Lennon, he smiled very gentle and wrote the laziest songs you ever heard. Musically, he had his roots in the country blues and Nashville C&W and the Memphis jug bands, in Fats Waller and Ramblin' Jack Elliott and any kind of good-time music he came across, and his lyrics were splendid, his melody lines curled up and purred like so many drowsy cats.

Younger Girl, *Do You Believe In Magic*, *Did You Ever Have To Make Up Your Mind?*, *Daydream*, *Summer In The City* – they were beautiful, all of them, and he wrote one line in particular that I loved: 'It's like trying to tell a stranger about rock and roll.'*

Always and always, the Spoonful was fun: Zal Yanovsky, who played guitar, lunaticked around like something from the Marx Brothers, a cross between Groucho and Harpo, and Sebastian's glasses teetered on the end of his nose and everything was mellow, everyone got stoned.

If they'd only gone on like they started, they'd have been monsters but Sebastian and Yanovsky, who'd put the group together, fell out and so pulled it all to pieces. There were a couple of bad singles, where laziness degenerated into total inertia, and then Yanovsky quit, Sebastian did nothing interesting and the Spoonful subsided.

For a long time, records were still issued and Sebastian did some lovely things – *Money*, *She's Still A Mystery* – but he didn't get big hits with them and the Spoonful, just like the Byrds, were sunk. Finally, they broke up altogether and Sebastian is now a single.

Whatever their failures, though, both the Byrds and the Spoonful were at least originals. They used a lot of influences, whether Dylan or Hank Williams, the Beatles or Gus Cannon, but they wound up with a flavour of their own, they weren't even bowdlerizers. The same thing couldn't be said of Sonny and Cher.

Sonny was Sonny Bono and he'd worked with Phil Spector, he was an established writer/producer and Cher was his wife. And the way he made it, he took the messages of Bob Dylan and cut any stuff in them about wars and ghettoes and sick Americas, any foolings with pain and waste and death. Then he picked up what remained, called it Protest and turned it into very big hit records. Him and Cher, they grew their hair long and dressed like teenybop tramps, they looked outrageous and this was meant to pass for dissent, this was the soulcry of an oppressed generation.

Commercially, it was perfect format – kids who felt rebellious but found Dylan too heavy, who wanted to smash a few windows without having to wade through all that poetry and paradox and philosophic discussion, thought that Sonny and Cher were truly peachy-keen and made them the hottest new act of 1965.

Throughout the summer, Sonny and Cher swamped the charts two or three at a time and *I Got You Babe* was a monster, all about how everyone put them down for their long hair and their clothes and their general freakishness but at least they had each other, their love was true and nothing could pull them apart. In other words, the oldest and corniest routine in showbiz. Under all the hair and hype, Sonny and Cher emerged as pop-age answers to Jeanette MacDonald and Nelson Eddy.

Predictably, they had a fat six months and then they began to die. Sonny Bono had one shrewd head, however, and he

213

came up with savers. As soon as the going got tough, he put Protest behind him and dived back fast into straight pop. Next, he put himself in the background and concentrated on Cher, who could sing and who looked good, half-Indian with great sloe eyes and wild hair hanging halfway down her back. And finally, he came through with natural hit songs, maudlin flowerpots that couldn't miss – *Bang Bang, You'd Better Sit Down Kids* and, campest of all, *Mama (When My Dollies Have Babies)*.

In the end, inevitably, the datedness of their image did them in and the hits dried up, but, by that time, they had a mansion in Bel Air, they could afford not to give a damn.

If Sonny turned protest into vaudeville, however, Lou Adler's Dunhill label built it into a full-scale industry.

Adler, as I mentioned earlier, is one smooth operator and he rode folk/rock hard. In the past, what with Johnny Rivers and Jan and Dean, he'd been less than famous as an idealist but now, with dissent suddenly selling in millions, he revealed himself as a true believer and became a one-man protest factory.

In particular, he set a song-writer called P. F. Sloan to churning out searing indictments of society at a rate of roughly one a week and, together, they were responsible for *Eve Of Destruction*, a round-ticket diatribe against everything. This was sung by Barry McGuire, an ex-New Christy Minstrel, and became a worldwide smash.

Adler's most successful folk/rock act, though, were the Mamas and the Papas, all of whom had hung around the West Village and sung in various folk groups and played bohemians.

One by one, they were John Phillips, who wrote their songs, and his wife Michelle Gilliam, who was very beautiful, and Denny Doherty, who balanced things out, and Cass Elliot, who weighed almost twenty stone and, by the time they got to Dunhill, they'd worked out a sound all their own, light and spacious, full of intricate harmonies, with the Papas singing the basic melody lines down below and the Mamas soaring away high over the top. When they were bad, they sounded like a hip Ray Conniff. When they were good, though, which was often, they'd make the most musicianly noises in the whole of pop and they'd be exhilarating.

John Phillips wrote good and witty songs for them, commercial songs, but their strongest selling-point was Mama Cass, who was maybe a gimmick, agreed, but who was also splendid, huge and tough and very funny she was, and she developed into a true heroine. She posed nude for *Cheetah* magazine. She was a big old girl, she had fun and she signalled something nice about pop, just the fact that someone that fat could now make it.

The only trouble was, the Mamas and the Papas got bored. They'd had some very big hits, *California Dreaming* and *Monday Monday* and *Dedicated To The One I Love*, but then they ran out of energy, stopped touring and they stayed home in Hollywood, they hung out and made a few records and did nothing in particular. In the end, they broke up. Mama Cass went solo and did a disastrous gig in Las Vegas cabaret. The others marked time.

The Byrds, the Lovin' Spoonful, the Mamas and the Papas – the three best and most successful of the folk/rock groups and, all of them, they blew it. The basic reason was, they weren't equipped for pop, they weren't mean or hungry enough. They enjoyed their music and they enjoyed their money but they weren't obsessive. They liked gigging in some small club on Bleecker, all high and surrounded by their friends, but when it came to ninety-day barnstormers and Greyhounds and teenybop one-nighters in Columbus, Ohio, they lost interest fast. Having got famous and fat, they'd run short on need.

The only other folk/rock figures that mattered much were Simon and Garfunkel.

215

Paul Simon was a small, serious, fuzzy-haired man who came out of a straight folk background and wrote songs about loneliness – *The Sound Of Silence*, *Richard Cory*, *Homeward Bound*, *Mrs Robinson*.

Melodically, his songs were most attractive, all tenderness and regret and gentle irony, wistful, and he sold albums by the truckload, he worked his way up steady until, by 1968, he'd become one of the heaviest sellers anywhere in pop.

What's more, there were critics who thought that he was a major talent, a roadrunner second only to Dylan. Myself, I couldn't see it but then his talents mostly fell across my blindspots, softness and tenderness, wistful ironies.

Under pressure, I liked *Fakin' It* and *Mrs Robinson* but that was just about my limit, I flagged on *At The Zoo* and bombed out entirely on *Scarborough Fair*. Still, that was most likely my fault, not Simon's.

So what, after all, about folk/rock?

On the whole, considering how much talent went into it, its results were less than sensational and its final importance probably wasn't so much in its own achievement as in its effects on pop in general.

One of these effects, obviously, was that it brought through lyrics. Another was that it canonized drugs.

Of course, in popular legend, all jazzmen had been dope-fiends for years and part of that reputation had carried over into pop but, in reality, most of the fifties rockers had much preferred alcohol and, even in the early sixties, when groups had begun to use pills and maybe a little grass on the side, nobody had got very much excited.

Folk took it more seriously. The Byrds' *Mr Tambourine Man* became the first ever drug hit, and from there on in grass grew into one of the major pop obsessions, a symbol of everything that separates hip from square. It stopped being just something that you smoked and was made mystical, was turned into a full-scale religion.

As for folk/rock itself, the style passed, as it was bound to do: it was too soft, too subtle to hold the attention of a mass teen audience for long and pop resolved back into hardrock again. But the motivation that produced folk/rock survived, the urge towards a pop that would be uncomputerized and unsweetened, that would be personal and halfway honest, and this took hold and built, and finally exploded with the Love Crowd.

22

THE MONKEES

While folk/rock was unfolding on the intellectual front, mainline American pop ran on exactly the same as always. It was almost a separate industry, mindless and changeless, eternally wrapped in a vacuum of non-singers and non-songs. Highschool lived on.

Ten years after Elvis, the charts were still filled by fantasies of heartbreak and bliss, moonlight and hearts and roses. New singers came up and sounded like the old ones. Businessmen hyped, disc jockeys spieled, pluggers plugged. Everyone had their private gimmick. Everything was always new, always old.

The only thing that had changed was that the business had become more streamlined as it went along. In the middle sixties, there was none of the knockabout farce that had brightened the fifties. Instead, pop had become safe and solid, very dull. All the time, it kept getting more computerized and everyone just methodically mopped up: earn, baby, earn.

In this move towards machine-pop, the Monkees were in a class by themselves.

What happened was that a group of Californian businessmen set up a TV series about a pop group, 1966. They didn't want to use any established group, they wanted no possible hassles, and they decided to create a phenomenon out of nowhere. Accordingly, they advertised for young men.

Several hundred youths applied. They were interviewed one by one. Gradually they were all discarded until only four remained – Davy Jones, Mike Nesmith, Peter Tork and Micky Dolenz – and these four were chosen for their faces, for their ability to project, for the balance of their personalities. They were then called the Monkees.

Straightaway, they bore a strong resemblance to the Beatles: one of them was baby-faced and motherable (Davy Jones/Paul McCartney), one was big and domineering (Micky Dolenz/John Lennon), a third was lost-looking (Peter Tork/Ringo), and the last was withdrawn, serious, the straight man (Mike Nesmith/George Harrison).

Both Davy Jones and Micky Dolenz had been child-actors and, later, had made records, not successfully. Mike Nesmith came from Texas and was married. Peter Tork had sung folk in Greenwich Village. None of them was exceptionally intelligent, exceptionally talented or even beautiful. All you could say was, they were very young.

Anyhow, they appeared in their TV series and, again, they seemed very much like the Beatles. In general, their film format was on the same lines as *Hard Day's Night* – speeded-up chase sequences, much jump-cutting, a recurrent harking-back to the Marx Brothers and silent comedy.

The major difference was only that the Monkees were aimed at a more infant public, pre-teens, six to ten. There was a lot of dressing up and falling down, a lot of bangs and face-pulling and custard pies. Everything was kept dead simple, jokes and music and characters alike. If anything needed thinking about, it was left out.

At the beginning, the Monkees didn't play on their records. It didn't matter – their sponsors hired the best writers, arrangers and producers available and the Monkees themselves were hardly relevant. No matter what, they couldn't fail: they had a weekly TV show, beamed all across America, and they had great armies of publicists, hyping and hustling them at all times. They had money behind them, talent and ambition and influence all forcing them upwards. Themselves, they only had to stand there and smile.

So they took off, they duly turned into an international industry, and they paid their investors back in full, they wound up making a big profit for them.

In the end, they played a few concerts. They even wrote songs. As it happened, they turned out to be not untalented after all.

But the point was, their talent was incidental. Even if they'd been tone deaf, they'd still have made it, they'd have worked out exactly the same. Simply, there was no way they could lose.

So the obvious question is, just how computerized can pop become? The simple answer is, very.

Always, it depends on exposure. If you have the basic equipment, meaning that you look good and you can talk and you don't pick your nose in public, if you are then hyped into something like your own TV show, you can hardly miss. If, on top of that, you're given a sustained press build-up and you don't make dumb records, you're foolproof.

(Mind you, all this only holds good in the teenybop belt. With a more sophisticated market, too much blatant hype can be fatal.

There is, for instance, the case of Moby Grape, an American group, approximately avant garde, who were given a 200,000-dollar build-up by their record company, Columbia. This involved all the standard stunts, posters and badges and brochures, blanket advertising in *Cashbox* and *Billboard*, plus no fewer than six singles issued simultaneously. And what happened? Exactly nothing: the progressive pop audience was far too hip to get bought by such crude ballyhoo and they rejected the whole package.

In any case, there's a persistent snobbery running right through the underground, a feeling that anything in the charts must automatically be a sell-out and therefore, by coming on so strong, Columbia were jumping the fastest way down the mineshaft.

The moral of this sad fable is only that, like any other sales technique, pop hype has to be applied with common-sense. It's not at all true that the underground can't possibly be steamrollered – Blue Cheer, Iron Butterfly and, as far as I'm concerned, the Doors are all good examples of bullshit at work – but it does take a certain subtlety. Where the way to break the bubblegum market is simply to shout, to be louder and flasher and more vulgar than the competition, the avant garde has to be breached by stealth, by intellectual flattery, by the suggestion that only the very finest minds could possibly understand the product offered. On that basis, though, the intelligentsia is maybe even more gullible than the kids.

Incidentally, while I'm on the subject, Moby Grape did finally make it – not big, but adequate. They went away and, a year later, came back with a music of their own, strong enough to cancel out Columbia's blag. Altogether, they've been quite an ironic saga.)

In all hype, TV is crucial. Newspaper publicity and advertising are only so much flavouring. But when you get on that box, you're at the nitty-gritty.

In any case, it's much simpler in America than it is over here. In England, pop TV and/or radio hardly exist and what there is happens to be Government-sponsored, just about incorruptible.

In the States, however, pop is run on a sensible commercial basis and payola has been properly formalized. Over there, any businessman that comes along with enough money to win himself air-space, plus the instinct to hire the right record-makers, is going to clean up. All he has to do is find a face.

That's hardly sinful, that's only what happens in any industry. At any rate, that's the direction that all commercial pop must increasingly take. Inevitably, it's going to get more standardized, more scientific and more dreary all the time. It's going to stop being so open to passionate kids with hit songs in their satchels, to Phil Spectors and Andrew Oldhams, and it's going to be bossed by a few big organizations.

These organizations will hardly be the major record companies that exist already, E.M.I. and Decca and so forth. Instead, they'll be whole new set-ups, combining management and agency and records into one huge complex. There may be half a dozen of them and, between them, they'll have everything neatly tied up.

In this way, pop will become an industry like any other. Experiments will be left to a small avant garde, way out on the left, very solemn and romantic, and the bubblegum business in general will regard this avant garde with benevolence, will steal its best ideas and talents, but will otherwise ignore it.

23

LOVE

In America, acid really mattered.

Over here, it never got much beyond being a one-shot curiosity and only a few thousand people ever used it. It was a status symbol, certainly, but it moved in very limited circles and it wasn't believed in as magic. So Paul McCartney might trip out and then announce that he'd been brought closer to God by his experiences but, when you talked to someone less eminent, some dumb post-Mod sitting on his scooter, he'd never used it. Pills and pot, he knew them well. Acid was another league, though, and everyone ran scared.

In the States, it was all different, LSD was taken almost for granted. If you went there and moved through any kind of hip circle at all, acid turned up most everywhere. You'd meet sweet little sixteen, some small drop-out, and she was already bored by the whole pitch. She scorned one-time users as amateurs.

Beyond that, it was a cause. In the home of Dr Timothy Leary, it became an organized religion and, even at less solemn levels, it was talked about as the cure of all trouble, the road to true nirvana. Users talked low and spoke of it in tones of mystic awe. They stared through the space above your head and you'd guess they were watching infinity.

Inevitably, you felt superior. After acid, you walked around bulging with your new perceptions and you thought you'd been some place nobody else had ever seen. You knew all kinds of secret answers and you were smug, you couldn't help it.

In this way, acid formed its own aristocracy and pop was part of it, pop was its mouthpiece. Not all of pop, of course. Just the underground.

The underground was anything experimental, anything outside the run of the industry, and it took in not only pop but newspapers, painting, poetry, anti-establishment expression of any kind. It was all very much in the tradition of fifties Beat (the Beatniks) but, being laced with superpop, it reached an infinitely bigger public than Beat had ever done.

Its father figure was Allen Ginsberg, the poet. Ten years back, in poems like *Howl* and *America*, he'd already been peddling what amounted to hippie philosophies and his messages still applied. Big-bearded and benevolent and exhibitionist, he was a bit of a joke but a good one and he'd influenced Dylan, he influenced most everyone.

Just as Beat had done in the late fifties, the underground came on strongest in California, where people are rich enough and time is relaxed enough and the weather is warm enough for such things to flourish. Through the early sixties, hip centres formed and grew across the state, notably in Venice, near Los Angeles, and in San Francisco's Haight Ashbury.

Always, they looked the same – streets full of sandals, cockroach apartments decorated with posters, overflowing trashcans, the smell of socks and stale hashish, cracks in the walls, beards.

Generation to generation, nothing changes in Bohemia. The heroes shift, that's all. Charlie Parker and Jack Kerouac, they gave way to Dylan and Kahlil Gibran and Muhammad Ali. Underneath, the tug of romantic squalor still stays the same.

At first, pop didn't come into this much – the staple diet was modern jazz and, later, folk. But after Dylan hired his rock 'n' roll band, pop suddenly became OK and the underground was swamped by groups, ugly bastards with beards and matted hair and intense feet, who made big dirty noises and screamed obscenities at Mister America as he passed.

Specifically underground clubs started up, the best of them being the Fillmore Auditorium in San Francisco, and they weren't like other dancehalls, the audiences didn't just drift and shuffle and be bored, they really heard the music. Very often, there'd be a genuine involvement between the crowd and the band, a sudden meshing, and straight nights would ensue. Even now, any group that played the Fillmore at its peak, 1966, will say it was the best gig they ever did.

The common denominator was acid, that was the fraternity pin, and so the term acid/rock came into use, a fairly meaningless label that got applied to any underground group whatever, no matter what its style. The other favourite word was psychedelic.

In the dictionary, psychedelic means mind-expansion but, in practice, out in California, it only meant faking up an acid trip. Instead of just standing up there and strumming, groups took to surrounding themselves with flashing lights, back-projected films, pre-recorded tapes, freak dancers, plus anything else they could think of, and the idea was that, faced by all this, you'd be hit by a total experience, a simultaneous flowering of all your senses and you'd fly.

You didn't, of course. Instead, you watched the legs of the sexy go-go dancers and wound up with a headache. It wasn't a bad idea, though – at least, it distracted from that fixed boredom of staring at a group staring back at you.

Usually, the acid/rock groups didn't come up with monster singles but they sold a lot of albums and they earned good gig fees. Who were they? Jefferson Airplane, Love, the Doors, Captain Beefheart and his Magic Band, Moby Grape, the Grateful Dead. Better, Country Joe and the Fish. Even better still, Janis Joplin with Big Brother and the Holding Company. And then, not only in California but back in the East as well, the Fugs and Andy Warhol's Velvet Underground, quite a lot of music.

Commercially, the biggest of all these are the Doors, out of Los Angeles, who turn around Jim Morrison, the wildest white American act since Elvis itself.

He is tall and smooth and lean, quite innocent-looking, and he doesn't smile. Staring at his photograph, you'd think he was gentle, a bit melancholy. A nice man.

Then he comes out on stage and he's not a nice man, after all; he's a phantom. He has black leather pants so tight that his machine shows through and he's tortured, he looks as if his mind had gone away to lunch. He writhes, reels, staggers. He gropes for the mike like some blind man and his face dissolves into rage and fear. Exactly, he looks like a man on a bad trip, driven insane by nightmares, by things he can't understand. First he pleads and then he's obscene and then he collapses and then he pleads again. He stammers, stumbles, can find no words. In turn, he is sadist and masochist. He blurs, his face turns into jelly. In the end, he's a psychopath: 'Father? Yes, son? I want to kill you. Mother, I want to . . . Aaaaaaauuuugghh.'

You guessed it, he's an exhibitionist. Offstage, he is surrounded by myths and legends, the heroic acts of Jim Morrison, all about how he's a superman and how he acts tough with the groupies that hang around. So his stage is no uncontrollable fit – it's all theatrical, rehearsed, perfectly calculated, and it has become a ritual, the bit when he suddenly collapses, jack-knifes as if he's been kicked in the balls, the bit when he, umm, accidentally falls off the stage. Nothing's wrong with that, of course, it's all showbiz anyhow, and he burns you just the same.

Musically, though, he's no great singer and the Doors are no great group – they've made a couple of strong hardrock singles, they used some potent riffs, they're strictly competent but, when you get inside their album, their range is minimal and some of Morrison's more poetical songs are dire.

Really, they're another case of a solid rock band, sexy but unclever, being ruined by their own compulsion to get into Art and much more to the point has been Janis Joplin, who started out with Big Brother and the Holding Company but later went solo and is potentially the most exhilarating white girl singer in the world, not profound at all.

She's something, she really is, a big tough woman from Port Arthur, Texas, and she'd eat you live for breakfast. On stage, she stomps and pounds and grinds, she bosses, and she has a truly brutal voice, a killer. She's no lady. She picks her songs up and annihilates them. Leaves them crippled ever after. Her face all twisted and scornful, she's fierce and she's sweet, a good old girl like they don't make any more, and you could love her easy, it wouldn't take you much at all. Just to hear her roar, watch her shake her stuff, that's enough.

Of all the underground groups, by far the most anarchic have been Frank Zappa and his Mothers of Invention.

Zappa was an adman and he came through in 1966, a skinny man with a long nose, crow's-nest hair, a droopy moustache and a small dagger beard. By any standards, he was quite outstandingly ugly but the Mothers, his group, left him looking like Robert Goulet. Bearded and gross and filthy, entirely obscene, they looked the stock *New Yorker* cartoon of beatniks brought to life.

They were freaks. They were meant to be. They were playing the same old game again, *épater le bourgeoisie*, but this time around it wasn't called Dada or Existentialism or Beat, it was Freak-Out.

'On a personal level,' wrote Zappa in what should have been a put-on but wasn't, 'freaking out is a process whereby an individual casts off outmoded and restricting standards of thinking, dress and social etiquette in order to express CREATIVELY his relationship to his immediate environment and the social structure as a whole.'

To this end, he assembled his Mother freaks and loosed them. On their first album, cutting a track called *The Return Of The Son Of Monster Magnet*, he went into the studio with a small army of auxiliaries and the whole lot of them banged, strummed, pounded and thrashed any musical instrument they could lay hands on, the total effect being a bit like a small army banging, strumming, pounding and thrashing any musical instrument they could lay hands on. It worked, what's more. It made you wish you'd been in there yourself, banging and thrashing with the rest of them, and so it carried a sense of real release, exorcism.

Still, there was more to Zappa than knockabout – his albums were extended post-Dada montages, visions of adman insanity and, under all the pantomime, they were really very ambitious.

In them, he'd take the direst clichés of vaudeville, showbiz and highschool, he'd link them with small declamatory non-tunes of his own and he'd weld the whole thing into a series of satiric pop operettas, surreal American nightmares. Probably, it was the most self-conscious and articulate use that pop had ever been put to and sometimes he missed his target completely, sometimes he was only verbose and self-indulgent but sometimes he was funny, sharp, true.

In one album, he'd be smug and imaginative and flabby, pretentious and infuriating and hilarious. Mostly, he was a bore but, every so often, when he forgot to be solemn, he'd pull out something good and he was never quite dismissable. If he was draggy, that was almost the point.

Of the other West Coast groups, my own favourites were Jefferson Airplane and Country Joe and the Fish.

Jefferson Airplane had a pretty girl singer called Grace Slick with a foghorn voice and she wrote some potent, vengeful-sounding songs, *White Rabbit* and *Two Heads*. *White Rabbit*, in fact, a dope-oriented version of *Alice In Wonderland*, was a small classic and it remains by far the best thing they've done. For the rest, when Grace Slick steps back and the rest of the group take over, they're musical but they're cluttered and self-conscious, badly short of punch. They sell a lot of records. They aren't enjoyed by me.

As for the Fish, Country Joe McDonald is a roughneck with a bashed-in face and, at times, he's comical. Stuff like *I'm Fixing To Die Rag* and his James Brown riff, they're the only true belly laughs in the whole of contemporary rock and, as such, are to be treasured. The only trouble is, Country Joe isn't all laughs, he has his poetical side as well and that's not so hot, that's downright dire. With all of these groups, it's the same endless hang-up: when they stomp, they're fine and, when they turn profound, they're a pain in the arse.

Beyond all these, there have been other good groups, Al Kooper's Blood, Sweat and Tears, for instance, and Bob Dylan's one-time backing group, The Band. Still and all, the American bands as a whole have been disappointing – there's been far too little excitement and it's all been taken with absurd intensity, it has almost stopped being fun. The new breed of American fans, post-Beatles and post-Dylan, weaned on folk and social consciousness, they sit and get stoned with the lights off, they write treatises and split pedantics, just like jazz fans and, mostly, they hardly remember Fats Domino's name, they think him trivial, and any suggestion that rock is a joke is greeted in shocked silence.

Anyhow, going back to the story, the underground kept expanding, its followers kept increasing and, somewhere along the line, they got called hippies and the name stuck.

In Haight Ashbury, 1966, when the word was still new, they formed a real community, they forgot possessions and shared most everything they had. The way they saw it, they were in at the birth of a whole new society, a format to save the world, and the word they used was Love.

The rules were, you had to love everyone and everything. You had to turn your back on the bitch goddess, on

229

materialism and war and all that stuff, and you had to get way back to the roots again, you had to rediscover the basic simplicities.

This was nothing new in itself, of course, it was the oldest chestnut imaginable. What was a bit different, though, was that something actually got done. This time, it wasn't just some poet preaching away in the woods, it was people, several thousands of them.

What's more it caught, it sparked similar communities all across the country. Hashbury got famous, was much glorified. Journalists moved in and started to publicize it. So highschool kids heard about it then, the way that its streets were paved with pot, and they came down from suburbia for their vacations. And tourists came with cameras to watch the weirdies. Within a few months, the whole thing had become a circus. The original hippies had all escaped and what remained was an acidburger nightmare. The streets were filled with beggars and pushers and pubertal panhandlers. Everything was filthy, decaying, rat-infested. Instant freaks sat on the sidewalks, munching hash sandwich, and the tourists took hippie-snaps.

Scott McKenzie, a folksinger straight out of a toothpaste ad, sang a song called *San Francisco (Wear Some Flowers In Your Hair)* and it was a worldwide smash. In England, the Flowerpot Men did *Let's Go To San Francisco*. Everyone loved everyone else, everyone got rich. George Harrison visited Hashbury itself. Eric Burdon blessed us all.

And what remained of the original concept, the first flush of innocence? Hardly anything.

All over the world, kids walked around in rainbow robes and wore beads, bells, flowers in their hair, but it was all down to play-acting now, it was only a new toy, something on the level of Mods and Rockers.

It wasn't just confined to kids either, the game spread through to young white liberals everywhere, even to academics and journalists and hip admen. So all right, they didn't stretch to robes but they smoked pot and bought *Sergeant Pepper* and used words like groovy, they filled their houses with joss sticks. They were flirting with bohemia, that's all. So much for the new society – it was summer and everyone had fun.

The high point of the whole junket was the Monterey International Pop Festival, June 1967, which ran right through a weekend and show-cased almost the entire range of progressive pop. Eric Burdon and Janis Joplin and Jimi Hendrix, the Who, the Mamas and the Papas, Simon and Garfunkel, and even people like Otis Redding and Ravi Shankar.

Maybe seventy thousand people went to it, the entire hippie population of California, and they descended on Monterey like some obscene plague. The city was scared out of its wits, of course, but it didn't have to be, the love crowd was perfect. It slept in the open and sang songs and got itself high. It broke no windows, caused no riots. Everyone loved everyone. The groups played for free, the music was endless and sometimes marvellous. Everyone was flying, half on pot and half on sheer idealism, and even the people who'd come to put it down, pressmen and such, were caught and began to believe. By the end of three days, the police themselves wore flowers.

Inevitably, as soon as it was over and everyone had gone home again, Hippie began to decline. Monterey had been wonderful, yes, but then the people went back to their jobs and their lives, their sadder realities, and everything seemed anti-climactic. Other attempts to catch the same excitement never quite worked. Always, the first time is the only time. And when autumn came and the sun went in, the whole thing fell apart. In retrospect, Monterey had been the beginning and the end at once.

After this, the next step was transcendental meditation, which I covered in my chapter on the Beatles, a craze that blossomed one day after the Beatles took it up and dropped dead exactly one day after they abandoned it again.

While it lasted, though, it was big: meditation centres sprang up all over America and any rock musician that didn't practise it got branded as bubblegum. The climax came when the Beach Boys did a concert tour with the Maharishi Mahesh Yogi, an act of faith that was both the high point and the destruction of meditation as a cult, because most of the gigs were half-empty and even the people who turned up walked out in droves as soon as the Maharishi appeared. It was soon after this that the Beatles recanted, much to the general relief, and everyone went back to getting happily stoned again.

In any case, the whole meditation bit had been very much a legacy from the LSD period – pop had stuffed itself so full of acid that it addled its mind, it went light-headed and got itself mixed up in mysticisms and whimsicalities that it would normally have dismissed with a few fast farts. After a few months, when the effect of acid wore thin, sanity returned and everyone went back to the discotheques.

So the question remains, what next? Astrology? Roman Catholicism? Alcohol? The answer is, all of them and none of them – the fashions change maybe three times a year and they're hardly relevant, they're all jokes anyway. Only the underlying restlessness remains and is real.

And it was this restlessness, this basic hunger for solutions, that gave rise to acid-rock, love-rock and meditation, and that's going to give rise to the next move. And whatever that next move may be, it's going to be expressed through rock, because pop is the new American religion, it's the major rallying-cry and nothing is too hefty or too dumb to be put aboard it.

Just possibly, in fact, rock is going to be a real political factor in America over these next years. After all maybe one in three American young do passionately believe in tolerance, gentleness and peace and, for almost all of them, pop is their platform. It won't last, of course: within a decade, the intensity will have gone and this generation will sink into the same uneasy apathy as any other. In the meantime, though, rock may count.

24

ENGLAND 1966

By this time, America was back in control, California was the
new pop centre. England just took the signals as they were
given and followed the best it could.

Simply, London had run out of steam. It had used itself up.
It had produced a lot of heavy talent in one flurry and now it
had nothing left in the bag. So when an established act turned
boring, nobody new came up instead to replace it. Everything
slowed down, everything petrified.

Neither the Beatles nor the Stones played concerts any
more, groups spent more time in discotheques than they did
on the road, and you were left with a nucleus of maybe ten
acts, coming round time after time, the same faces and the
same tired songs. Running through everything, there was a
persistent sense that something had ended.

The atmosphere had changed. The economic crisis and the
freeze, these things didn't actually change people's standard
of living much but they shifted the mood. When you went
abroad and came back again, you noticed something like
defeat in the air, a growing drabness and depression. Really,
it was only a return to sanity, to responsibility. And sanity, of
course, is purest poison to everything pop.

As I said in my opening chapter, entertainment always
turns soft when times turn tough. Accordingly there was a

massive swing back to old-fashioned balladeering. Even at the height of the pop boom, there'd been occasional freak ballad hits but now the charts were completely swamped in the stuff. Ken Dodd, Harry Secombe, Frankie Vaughan – all the old comedians, they cleaned up. Tom Jones was never out of the hit parade.

After Jones the biggest success of all was Engelbert Humperdinck. He was really a danceband singer called Gerry Dorsey, and he'd been around for a full decade, scrabbing and halfway starving. Finally, in 1966, he became managed by Gordon Mills, who also handled Tom Jones, and Mills changed his name for him.

Engelbert Humperdinck – it was good back-dated gag publicity and, immediately, he was joke fodder for every bad comedian in the country ('Has Engelbert got the hump?'). Then he came on TV and he was a matinee idol from way back, hollowed cheeks and big mournful eyes, Regency suits and moody sideboards. He looked exactly like some hero in Georgette Heyer, the man who has known sadness, and he mooched around in poses of graceful melancholy, one hand stirring small gestures of resignation. Mostly, he reminded me of a King Charles spaniel.

With all that riding for him, how could he miss? Early in 1967, he made a record called *Release Me*, an archetypal big ballad from any time in the last forty years, and it went to number one. A bit later, he made something else called *The Last Waltz* and that did even better, it sold a million without even being a hit in America and that hardly ever happens. Delicate and droopy, he stared back at you every time you turned your telly on. And by the beginning of 1968, he was the hottest thing in England.

All this time, he lived in a council flat in Hammersmith. He was into his thirties and he was married, he even had children. He was a throwback, an afterthought on the Sinatra line, and he didn't get screamed at much, he was more swooned for.

He posed with his fans and they were women of all ages. On stage, he'd look mournful, be gorgeous, stretch out one hand and let it fall. Out of the dark, everyone sighed.

While the monster ballad was taking over, pop itself was splitting into two distinct approaches, just as it had done in the States.

On one side, there were the straight noise-machines, angled at a mass teen public and at sub-teens, ages six to twelve. These were just old auto-pop from any time in the last ten years: simple songs, one-line lyrics, gimmicks, big smiles and a dash of good clean filth for flavouring. It's a format that's changed only fractionally with time and some new groups did very well with it – the Troggs, the Tremeloes, the Love Affair and Dave Dee, Dozy, Beaky, Mick and Titch – but there's nothing I could possibly say on any of them except that they had hits.

On the other side, there were specialists: soul bands, blues bands, folksingers, freaks and just people who wanted to make good music. In the middle of this, there was a small avant garde, musical experimenters. Most of them, they took their bearings from the Beatles and they were hip to everything that came out of America, they tagged along with California. Between them, they formed something approaching an Underground, flabby and untogether but going in one direction, trying to make pop expand and progress.

Around the end of 1966, they climbed aboard Psychedelphia.

This was the first fashion that England had stolen from the States in years, the first time that London had had to look outside itself for novelty, and the result was only a bowdlerization of the American original. Nothing fresh was added – British mind-expansion meant not much more than a few flashing lights, a bit of back-projection, a handful of discords and some smoke bombs thrown in for luck. In any case, nobody was too sure what psychedelic actually meant.

By far the most earnest attempt at local psychedelphia were the Pink Floyd. Mostly, they played instrumentals, twenty-five-minute scream-ups, formless and tuneless and colourless but always incredibly loud. And they were into electronics, free form and all sorts: very solemn, they were, most artistic and, for me, boring almost beyond belief.

As it happened, buried under all the crap, there was a good lead singer/writer called Syd Barrett and he came up with one fine single, *Arnold Layne*. After a time, he quit and, from then on, the proceedings were all dire.

Much more to the point was the Jimi Hendrix Experience.

Hendrix was an American Negro, born in Seattle, 1946, and he'd spent most of his late teens touring the States near the bottom of mammoth package shows, picking them up at one town and quitting them at another. Then he had a spell in Greenwich Village, playing blues guitar and singing a bit, and finally, 1966, he was brought to England by Chas Chandler, who'd played bass with the Animals and who now became his manager.

As blues guitarists go, he was hardly mainstream. He had none of that repose, that inevitability that you get from people like B. B. King or John Lee Hooker. Instead, he squealed and squittered all over the place. He played guitar behind his back and above his head and between his legs, he played it with his teeth, he rubbed it against his amps. A lot of the time, he used it as crude sex, his clean machine.

He was all image. Hendrix, he had long tight-napped hair that stuck up all around his head like some grotesque fuzzy halo, and he was most cool, he had one slow schnide smile and he talked very drawled. Superspade, he knew exactly what he was doing.

He was an outrageous ham showman, of course, he camped it up like mad. Still, he was good. He had presence. Under the gimmickry, he had it all going. And he did play fine guitar after all, he carried real exhilaration. He was mesmeric. He was ferocious and sexy. He was an ugly man and he had endless charm.

Also, he wrote strong songs. He stormed so hard on them that he half-obscured his own quality but they worked, they were an odd cross between the old tough blues and post-Dylan imagery, and he sang them in a non-voice, wry and one-note, strangely effective. So he was a showman, a black regardless and he was real excitement.

Among the home-grown groups, the best was Cream.

Cream was Eric Clapton, who'd played guitar with the Yardbirds and the fine blues band of John Mayall; Ginger Baker, who'd drummed with the Graham Bond Organization, the toughest, most evil jazz/blues noise that we ever had; and Jack Bruce, who sang, played bass and had worked with almost everyone.

Within the business, each was generally regarded as the best man going on his particular instrument. Themselves, they agreed with this and that's why they used the name Cream.

Basically, they were an updated blues band but they borrowed from anything that caught their minds, rock 'n' roll or jazz or Dylan. Always, they stormed. Always, they crunched and burned and sweated.

Ginger Baker had long red hair hanging lankily all down his face and a matted red beard and the most agonized face you'd ever see, his cheeks all cavernous and his teeth rotted and his eyes quite cancelled. He was the final drummer, head lolling and mouth open and schizo eyes staring out into nothing, but he was no phoney, he laid down one brutal churning beat, all looped and doubled back on itself, the deepest pulse imaginable. Sunken and suffering, he was epic.

Around him, Jack Bruce pumped out nothing but goose-grease bass and, way over the top, Clapton played the best guitar in Europe. Probably, he was musically stronger than Hendrix but he had none of that flash. Instead, he hunched in tight and watched nothing but his guitar. He concentrated so hard, he worked so much that you'd get hooked by his own obsession, you'd start to ride on him. Held by him, you'd listen very hard, you'd be stretched. When you walked out at the end, you'd be exhausted.

On stage, they'd be magnificent and, both in Britain and the States, they were huge. But on record, they never quite came off. They weren't strong writers and, canned, they lost most of their impact, they didn't get you fully involved.

In two years, they cut one great single, *I Feel Fine*, and that's the only time they worked out their fullest potential. Finally, they disbanded.

Hendrix and Cream, they've both had mass followings, they've both sold albums by the ton but they've never had number one hits. At the best, they've made the ten – that's the way that pop has drifted, that's how much ballads hold control, and even the best, the most successful progressives, are only allowed the leavings. More and more, their stronghold has become the album charts.

The Move came from Birmingham and they took over from the Stones and the Who as rabble-rousers in chief.

They were managed by Tony Secunda, a King's Road hustler from the early sixties, and Secunda was one fast stroke-puller. Any bandwagon that passed, he'd be up on top of it so fast you couldn't blink. And he was clever with it, what's more, he had bursts of true inventiveness. At the least, he was entertainment.

In 1966, he launched the Move from the Marquee and they were impressive. They stood in a straight line, four-part harmony, and they were natural rockers, they wore Capone gangster suits and they looked mean as hell. Eternal Brummers, dour and monosyllabic. And Carl Wayne, their lead singer, did a nice line in mike-throwing and Ace Kefford, a guitarist, was the singing skull itself, his face set rigid in infinite boredom. So they were the nastiest-looking bunch you could hope to meet and they sang well, they made a big bad noise.

When Psychedelphia came in, Secunda made his first jump – he set them to smashing TV sets on stage, assaulting them with an axe, and destroying images of Hitler, Ian Smith and so such. This, if you hadn't guessed, was a comment on the society in which we live and, meshed with a few flashing lights, it spelled mind-expansion. It was all poor man's Who, and it got them publicity, it freaked them into their first hits.

In the summer, 1967, psychedelic was replaced by Flower Power and Secunda jumped again – the Move forgot their gangster suits, their axes and their snarls, and they took to frolicking in cornfields, all robed and garlanded. Ace Kefford, Singing Skull, cast as a daisy chain – it wasn't a likely concept but, once more, it worked.

They made a record called *Flowers In The Rain* and, to publicize it, Secunda circularized what amounted to a dirty postcard of Harold Wilson. Inevitably, Wilson sued and they had to give all their royalties to charity. Still, it had been their biggest bonanza yet and it finally got them established.

By the winter, Flower Power had duly faded and there were signs of a rock 'n' roll revival. So, you knew it, the Move suddenly had their snarls back and they cut *Fire Brigade*, complete with Duane Eddy twang guitar. As it happened, this was their best record yet and they were right back where they began, hardcore rockers again. That's what they'd always been good at, anyhow.

At a less exalted level, there were the Bee Gees, Traffic and Procol Harum, all of them competent enough but none of them so wild that I have to go into any great detail on them.

The Bee Gees were Australian, built around the three Gibb Brothers, who wrote a lot of melodic, catchy and maudlin ballads, heavily influenced by mid-period Beatles. More to the point, Barry Gibb was pretty.

Traffic was formed by Stevie Winwood, who was probably the closest to a soul singer that England had ever had and who had already racked up two number ones with the

Spencer Davis group. On paper, Traffic were all musical and should have been formidable but somehow they never made it, they only functioned in spasms and their first hit, *Paper Sun*, remained easily the best single they made.

As for Procol Harum, they made one classic record, *A Whiter Shade Of Pale*, and then kept reviving it in different names and disguises, until everyone got sick to death of it.

A Whiter Shade Of Pale, incidentally, was produced by Denny Cordell, the most successful new English producer since Mickie Most. Beyond Procol Harum, he handled the Move, the Moody Blues, Georgie Fame and had hits with all of them. Ironically, though, his two best cuts of all – *Hush* by Jackie Edwards and the epic *Marjorine* by Joe Cocker – failed to make it.

Most of the progressive groups had their fattest periods during the Flower Power boom in the summer of 1967, which I already mentioned when I was talking about the Move.

As fads go, Flower Power was less than impressive. Just as it had with Psychedelphia, London was content mostly to ape California. Everyone wore kaftans and beads and bells. Everyone spoke in hushed tones of San Francisco and Monterey, of acid and Love and the Maharishi. Nobody threw fists any more. The whole city was cloaked in incense and the smoke of joss sticks. Every last groupie had turned prophet.

The centre of the local hippie movement was UFO, a basement club in Tottenham Court Road, and its Saturday all-nighters turned into major weekly happenings. It was a nice atmosphere down there, very lazy, and the music was fun. Most everyone laid about and, if there was ostentation in it, if there was a lot of flash love-making and out-freaking, there were some mellow times had.

After some months, though, UFO's lease ran out and nothing so fresh happened again. There were other hippie clubs, of course, but they became stale, ritualistic. There

240

was no fever in it any more. Instead, everyone stood and gawked and listlessly shook their beads. They were bored again.

Throughout the Flower Power fairy-tale, the role of bad witch was played by the drug squad.

By their very nature, all teen movements need something to be paranoid about and, this time out, the fuzz asked for all the hate they got because, from the beginning of 1967, they got into the habit of raiding clubs and stopping kids in the street, searching them for drugs and pushing them around at random, bullying them and making them strip and lumbering them down to the station. Small stuff by American standards, of course, but fascist just the same.

I was stopped a couple of times myself and I didn't get hit but there was a lot of shoving and grunting, a lot of unprovoked aggression flying about. Always, there was this basic resentment that I was young and wore tight pants, bright shirts. Before I opened my mouth, I was hated.

In the summer, there was the Jagger/Richards trial and that hardly helped things. By this time, both sides were hysterical – smokers saw pot as some magic cure-all, the police saw it as a deadly plague. I mean, either way, marijuana is something so trivial, but it had become almost a national obsession, a professional bore.

Anyways, it was a warm summer and people believed in Love. But then autumn came and it turned cold and suddenly people didn't believe in love, after all.

In any case, Flower Power had always been very much a London thing – kids everywhere else had gone on butting each other regardless, schnide and moody as ever. The summer's music, rarefied and mimsy, all full of transcendental meditation, had meant less than nothing in the dancehalls and teenagers had been left with nothing they could understand or relate to. Trapped between Engelbert Humperdinck's

241

flowerpots on one side and George Harrison's curry powder on the other, they'd completely lost out.

Accordingly, in the winter, there was a swing back to basic pop, instant noise, and there was even a small revival in rock 'n' roll. Bill Haley, Jerry Lee Lewis, Buddy Holly and Eddie Cochran, they all had their old hits reissued and did quite well with them. Nothing sensational but they sold.

More to the point, present-day groups climbed down off their clouds a bit and went back to work. *Lady Madonna* by the Beatles, *I Can See For Miles* by the Who, *Fire Brigade* by the Move, *Jumpin' Jack Flash* by the Rolling Stones – it was renewed aggression, an intelligent mixing of basics and progression.

These were only a few singles, though, and everything else looked pretty grim.

For a start, the pirate stations had been outlawed and they'd been replaced by the BBC's Radio 1, which was dire. Under the new regime, you got thin slices of pop wedged in between great sobs of children's requests, recipes, Joe Loss, mighty Wurlitzers and Jimmy Young chatting with housewives. No flair, no speed, no flash. No hard plugging, either, and that meant that any weird sounds, any experiments were doomed before they even started. Everyone was forced to play safe, nothing moved forward. By spring, 1968, the entire industry had ground to a standstill.

The only DJ peddling anything at all was the Emperor Rosko, an American working out of Paris. His real name was Mike Pasternak (he was the son of Joe Pasternak, the Hollywood producer) and he was a greyhound spieler, one slippery mouth. He knew pop from the beginning, he played amazing noise. Always and always, he was fast.

On French Radio Luxembourg, he had a daily hour-long show and an epic three-hour freak-out every Saturday night, a veritable mind-snapper. On Radio 1, he got exactly one hour a week. Precisely, that was what had happened in English pop.

Since mid-1967, only one new group has emerged with really heavy potential and that has been the Crazy World of Arthur Brown.

Arthur Brown used to be a philosophy student at Reading University and he was one long gangling skinny streak, complete with haystack black hair and great staring eyes and an elephant's nose. And when he came on stage, he was wearing Sun God robes, a science fiction mask, the Bug-Eyed Thing, and his head was on fire.

He wore a blazing crown and it threw flames up high towards the ceiling. When the fire burned low, he'd go into a wild sideways-leaping dance, his head flickering, his robes flapping like a shroud, and he screamed, he howled, he snarled. Then he tore off his mask and his face was painted with woad, he looked like something neanderthal, half man and half beast. His eyes burned up in the dark and his head kept thrashing.

When he sang, he told you stories about black magic, about death and destruction, about fire and the way it cleanses, the way it heals. Mister witchdoctor, he made spells and all the time he'd be dancing, whirling, his head kept spinning. So he was scary and he was comic, he was a monstrous ham but he had these sad eyes and this big nose, he looked tragic and the major fantasy he conjured up was King Kong, big doomed animal.

Beyond all this, he could really sing – he had a freak voice that ranged all the way from a Boris Karloff rumble through Tom Jones and Mario Lanza right through to a James Brown scream, a hysterical screech that he'd keep up for whole choruses at a stretch, a killer.

During the same period, there also emerged Julie Driscoll and Joe Cocker and the Incredible String Band.

Julie Driscoll is a skinny girl from east London and she toured the circuits for years without getting anywhere in particular, until, autumn 1967, she suddenly got herself a Jimi Hendrix hairstyle and called herself Jools and was launched as a new ultimate in London dollydom, deadpan and strange, very freaked.

She was a vegetarian and lived off carrot juice. She dressed up in improbable antiques bought in junk shops, all feathers and mangy furs. And she made up her eyes to look huge and she moved her shoulders like a cobra nodding, she hardly ever smiled, she froze.

With all of this going for her, she came in for fast publicity and, in 1968, she had her first hit, Bob Dylan's *This Wheel's On Fire*, and she was voted Britain's top girl singer. What's more, many people thought she was a good singer and many people thought she was sexy. Myself, I thought she was the best and sexiest thing in Europe but that's no kind of competition and, truthfully, I thought she was mannered and monotonous, and I detected no trace of feeling in her singing at all.

Joe Cocker was a fat ex-plumber from Sheffield and I liked him very much. On stage, he was greasy and he sang white soul, very sweaty, and he waved his arms like some demented windmill, he was hilarious and he sang quite splendidly. His first record, *Marjorine*, was a small classic and bombed. His second, Lennon/McCartney's *With A Little Help From My Friends*, was less good and made number one.

Finally, purely in my role as chronicler, I should note the existence of the Incredible String Band, a folk duo whom several English critics described as the best song-writers since the Beatles. This mention made, I will make no further comment.

At any rate, the good thing that Cocker and Jools and Arthur Brown all shared was that they worked hard, that they raved and rampaged some and this alone made them exceptional. In this time, most English performers have gotten entirely lazy.

So I'd say this was the worst phase that English pop has been through since before the Beatles and it's not easy to see how things are going to get better again. Basically, as I said at the beginning, this isn't a pop age, it's much too insecure and careful. Get down to it, there simply aren't any heavy new talents coming up and there's nothing anyone can do about it.

At a less bedrock level, though, there are changes that could be made. Two changes in particular. First, the Government has to bring in commercial radio and let pop work as it wants. And second, the musicians themselves have to stop playing games, have to stop winking at each other's cleverness and they have to get right back down in the alley, go back on the road and start reaching their audience all over again.

25

ENDING

Probably, it's not been a bad time to write this book: pop is at its most important junction yet, it's the gap between two major phases, and this has been quite a clean moment to make some interval notes on it.

What I've written about has been the rise and fall of Superpop, the noise machine, and the image, hype and beautiful flash of rock 'n' roll music. Elvis riding on his golden Cadillac, James Brown throwing off his robes in a fit, Pete Townshend slaughtering his audience with his machine-gun guitar, Mick Jagger hanging off his mike like Tarzan Weissmuller in the jungle, P. J. Proby – all the heroic acts of pulp.

Superpop? It hasn't been much, it's been simple always, silly and vulgar and fake, and it has been a noise, that's all. In the end, specific records and singers have hardly mattered. Instead, it's been pop itself, just the existence of it, the drone of it running through everything.

Myself, I was ten when it started, I'm twenty-two now, and it has bossed my life. It has surrounded me always, cut me off, and it has given me my heroes, it has made my myths. Almost, it has done my living for me. Six hours of trash every day, and it's meant more to me than anything else.

Superpop, it's been like a continuing Western, it's had that same classic simplicity, the same power to turn cliché into myth. It's had no mind of its own. All it's ever done has been to catch currents, moods, teen obsessions, and freeze them in images. It has made giant caricatures of lust, violence, romance and revolt, and they've been the most powerful, most accurate fictions of this time.

And then, beyond the heroes, beyond anything, there's been the noise, the endless and perfect and changeless beat. Noise has been everything.

Anyhow, it's finished now, the first mindless explosion, and the second stage has begun. Pop has gotten complicated. That was inevitable, everything ends, nothing remains simple. Pop has split itself into factions and turned sophisticated. Part of it has a mind now, makes fine music. The other part is purely industrial, a bored and boring business like any other. Either way, there are no more heroes and no more Superpop. It has all been reduced to human beings.

What's left? In England, the industry is split roughly eighty per cent ugly and twenty per cent idealist.

The ugly eighty are mainline pop, computerized, and they hit a largely teenybop or pre-teen market, ages six to sixteen, plus a big pocket of middle-aged parents. They have a function and they sell records. They make money. When I've said that, I've said everything.

The blue-eyed twenty are hardly even pop stars any more. With very few exceptions, notably the Beatles and the Stones, they don't sell records and, after all, what's pop about unpopularity? In ten years, they'll probably be called by another name entirely, electric music or something, and they'll relate to pop the way that art movies relate to Hollywood.

How good could they be? Logically, there's no limit – amplified music is an obvious art form for this century and there's no reason whatever why it shouldn't produce major works.

Very soon, you'll have pop composers writing formal works for pop choirs, pop orchestras; you'll have pop concerts held in halls and the audience all sat in rows, no screaming or stamping but applauding politely with their hands; you'll have sounds and visuals combined, records that are played on something like a gramophone and TV set knocked into one, the music creating pictures and patterns; you'll have cleverness of every kind imaginable.

Myself, though, I'm not interested. Not that I have anything much against masterworks in principle but I'm hooked on image, on heroics. It's like films – the best in art movies have no doubt been most sensitive, brilliant and meaningful works of art, and where have I been? In the back row of the Roxy, of course, gawking at Hollywood. The art movie carries the quality and Hollywood carries the myth.

Superpop is mass media, it is teen music always, it has to hit. Ideally, it has to do what Bogart and Brando and Monroe have done in films, Gable and Fred Astaire – it has to be intelligent and simple both, it has to carry its implications lightly and it has to be fast, funny, sexy, obsessive, a bit epic.

The words of Little Richard still apply. They summed up what pop was about in 1956. They sum it up now and always:

AWOPBOPALOOBOP ALOPBAMBOOM.

AFTERTHOUGHTS

It's about 18 months since I finished the hardback version of this book and, in that time, there have been so many changes that some kind of updating seems called for.

Specifically, there has been the resurgence of Elvis Presley. As he approaches 35, he has come out of his mansion and he's begun to do live shows again. He has lost weight, he has grown his hair, he has dressed himself in black leather. He has rediscovered his hips and brought the rasp back into his voice. He has leered and squirmed and strutted, plundered and burned and, on stage, he has become again what he used to be, total sex and total speed, total energy – the beginning and end of rock 'n' roll.

Elvis apart, the other major revival has come from the Rolling Stones. Now that Brian Jones is dead, they've lost any sense of group identity and have become merely Mick Jagger, plus backing. Emphatically, Jagger has risen to the challenge: he's more unisex, more satanic, more mesmeric, more everything and, if there is a Youth revolution, which I doubt, he's going to lead it.

Musically, too, both Elvis and the Stones have brought it back home – Presley's *From Elvis In Memphis* and the Stones' *Beggars Banquet* and *Let It Bleed* have been easily their best ever.

Still, if Elvis and Jagger have returned, they've been balanced by a bumper crop of failures. Jimi Hendrix has repeated himself *ad nauseam*; Janis Joplin, who was once the real thing, has sunk into abject self-caricature, screeching and caterwauling at random; the Beach Boys have done nothing; Arthur Brown has taken himself seriously; the Mamas and the Papas, Traffic, the Small Faces and Manfred Mann have broken up; and most of the new groups – Led Zeppelin, Iron Butterfly, King Crimson, Blood, Sweat and Tears – have been merely embarrassing.

Against all this, only three good groups have emerged: Delaney & Bonnie & Friends, probably the best fake-black band yet; The Band, Bob Dylan's back-up group, who work somewhere between Country and Rock; and the Flying Burrito Brothers, who work roughly the same territory but even better and are the most impressive new band since the Who.

Essentially, though, the situation is unchanged. America is frantic but third-rate. England is entirely vacuous. Either way, I've found it easy to remain a reactionary.

Looking back through this book, in fact, my major regrets have been about the things I've missed out. I wish, for instance, that I'd given more worship to the Everly Brothers; that I'd been less ashamed of my love for highschool; and that I'd been very much more vitriolic about the new Rock, the Pepsi generation.

However, these are only details. And in my overall view, I remain completely unrepentant.

penguin.co.uk/vintage